Utilizing the 3Ms of Process Improvement in Healthcare

A Roadmap to High Reliability Using Lean, Six Sigma, and Change Leadership

Utilizing the 3Ms of Process Improvement in Healthcare

A Roadmap to High Reliability Using Lean, Six Sigma, and Change Leadership

Richard Morrow, MBA

Foreword by Erin DuPree, MD

CRC Press
Taylor & Francis Group
Boca Raton   London   New York

CRC Press is an imprint of the
Taylor & Francis Group, an **informa** business

A PRODUCTIVITY PRESS BOOK

CRC Press
Taylor & Francis Group
6000 Broken Sound Parkway NW, Suite 300
Boca Raton, FL 33487-2742

Version Date: 20120127

International Standard Book Number: 978-1-4398-9535-1 (Paperback)

Library of Congress Cataloging-in-Publication Data

Morrow, Richard, 1956-
    Utilizing the 3Ms of process improvement in healthcare / Richard Morrow.
        p. ; cm.
    Utilizing the three Ms of process improvement in healthcare
    Includes bibliographical references and index.
    ISBN 978-1-4398-9535-1 (alk. paper)
    I. Title. II. Title: Utilizing the three Ms of process improvement in healthcare.
    [DNLM: 1. Process Assessment (Health Care) 2. Organizational Case Studies. 3. Organizational Innovation. W 84.41]

610.73--dc23   2011048977

Visit the Taylor & Francis Web site at
http://www.taylorandfrancis.com

and the CRC Press Web site at
http://www.crcpress.com

This book is dedicated to my wife, Jan, and my children, Adam and Janelle. I could not be more proud of you all. I love you and thank you for allowing me to follow my passions, which often took me away from being there for you in person.

Contents

Foreword

High reliability is the aim of any complex industry. In 2011, healthcare qualifies as a complex industry with myriad drugs, devices, computer systems, and personnel that are part of every patient encounter. Whether it is preventing the next readmission or decreasing the cost of the devices used in complex surgery, the challenges in healthcare are endless. The 3Ms provide a platform for high reliability.

With 247 people dying each day in U.S. hospitals as a result of healthcare-associated infections, high reliability is a term that is not often applied to healthcare. Understanding the roadmap to high reliability is critical for anyone who is part of the healthcare industry today. As an obstetrician-gynecologist, I cannot allow for any compromise in the care that my patients receive. As a hospital administrator, it is my job to create a culture of learning and continuous improvement for all of those who work at our institution. On my quest to engage healthcare professionals in process improvement, I had the great privilege to work with Rick.

Rick has worked to transform other industries by applying the lessons of process improvement. He led improvements globally in manufacturing, communication, and transportation industries. His expertise translated easily to healthcare where every patient encounter is loaded with processes and opportunities to improve. His work to reduce the risk of wrong-site surgery, improve hand hygiene, and improve communication has contributed to better care for patients around the world.

As Rick points out in this book, reliability is a factor of measuring the key variables that affect the outcomes and cost of patient care. Measuring these attributes before a patient has experienced harm is fundamental to our success in achieving high reliability. Measurement is the key to all of our successes. How many times have we witnessed a sentinel event only to find that no one had been paying attention to the warning signs that something was starting to go wrong? We were probably not measuring or didn't have the appropriate management technique in place to appreciate the measurements.

Utilizing the 3Ms is absolutely vital to change that lasts. Measurement was, and still is, a requirement of each effort. The stories that Rick shares in this book, I think, everyone can relate to. His ability to translate difficult lessons into easy, memorable stories will engage even the most skeptical readers.

The answer might be simple if your organization has simply avoided the 3Ms in improvement efforts. For other organizations, getting people to appreciate the importance of the 3Ms might be the issue. This book includes a step-by-step approach to change that begins with proven techniques. Rick includes templates that guide teams in driving change and utilization of the 3Ms for process improvement.

This book is a great place to start your journey in process improvement. The key to longevity and success in process improvement is the utilization of the 3Ms. I can't imagine succeeding without the concepts shared in this book.

Erin DuPree, MD
Deputy Chief Medical Officer
Vice President Patient Safety
The Mount Sinai Medical Center
New York, NY

Acknowledgments

Acknowledging the many who have contributed to my understanding of leading change is most difficult. Please let me begin with these dear friends and colleagues and my promise to acknowledge you who write to me how the 3Ms have contributed to your success.

Alan Houser, my classmate, friend, colleague, boss, and provider of performance excellence extraordinaire from Carroll Catholic Grade School through our executive master's of business administration at the University of Illinois and thirty years of applying process improvement.

Claes Rehmberg, my boss and coach at SKF, a Sweden-based leader in reliability engineering, who not only taught me what high reliability really takes but also how not to be an "ugly American" on the world stage.

Dr. Dave Munch, my friend and boss who teaches and coaches me and is always there for me when I have crazy thoughts and ideas on health-care improvement.

Dr. Terry O'Malley, Mass General, my teacher of healthcare issues and friend.

Charles Hagood, president, HPP, Healthcare Performance Partners, a MedAssets company, who allows me to help healthcare every day and to give back to society.

My colleagues at Healthcare Performance Partners, who are the nicest people to work with.

Sarah Cook, David Buki, Ernie Perez, and Carrie Mayer, my most prized colleagues who exemplify utilizing the 3Ms for process improvement and applying the golden rules in change leadership.

Don McCann and William Kelly, who gave me my first chance and had faith in me that I could maybe solve some issues.

Tom Johnstone, chief executive officer at SKF, who saw how Lean Six Sigma can make a high-reliability organization even better.

George Dettloff, former president at SKF, who met Al and me and gave us a chance to apply Lean and Six Sigma globally for SKF.

Bill Spaniol, my dear departed friend who was a catalyst for so many actions including going for the Exec MBA and downhill skiing. I miss you dearly.

My mom, Patricia, who loves me no matter what I mess up and gave me the confidence to do what I love, whether it was piano, changing to a real musical instrument (the drums), or solving issues like how to get two glasses of water to the same place more easily.

My dad, who also loved me and taught me how to do just about anything when you do not have the money to pay someone to do it.

Adam, my son, who shared his talents creating the illustrations.

Janelle, my daughter, who reminds me why life is to be enjoyed; this book is a way of giving back.

My "band of brothers," Mark and Mike, who are always there for me when I need them. Mark is the rock of the family who we know will always be there to protect us. Mike is the roll, who teaches me how not to get too stuck working all the time to enjoy family and Florida.

Kris Mednansky, senior editor for CRC Press, who has had the patience to help me share with you how to improve processes.

My clients over the thirty years who allowed me to learn from them, experiment, and then share with others how to utilize the 3Ms, their successes, and lessons learned.

Preface

Why is it that some improvement efforts succeed and many fail despite the analytical skills, leadership cheerleading, change management programs, and sometimes a "do-or-die" pressure to improve? Quite simply, there are three elements that come in a "package" that differentiate improvement efforts that succeed from those that fail. To make it easier for you to remember them, I call them the 3Ms (Measure, Manage to the measure, Make it easier). Absolutely every improvement that has succeeded and sustained had the complete package. This is a "how-to" book to improve processes in healthcare using these three elements "packaged" for you in a step-by-step fashion.

I weave in stories throughout the book of role models who have succeeded. Failed improvement efforts, I think, also are powerful learning experiences, and those also are shared. The specific element that was missing or defective teaches us a lot about how the three elements work together.

This book is for you whether you are your community hospital's chief executive officer preparing for a major change in reimbursement that could bankrupt your organization and leave your community without healthcare, a nurse manager dreading the resistance your nurses will vehemently evoke when yet another new technology hits your unit from the chief information officer, or one of the millions of people in healthcare worldwide who is asked to change when you simply want to care for your patients and want the change to help you help them. Or, are you interested in how Ben Franklin discovered that lightning was a source of electricity or Dr. Livingstone's (I presume you have heard of him) demonstration of how to improve have lessons for us in leading great changes?

I believe we learn best by doing. Leading by example, I want you to "do" one of our first process improvement tasks. I want you to Measure how well this book meets your expectations. To make Measure simpler for you, I include an easy-to-use template (Table P.0.1) for you to list your expectations from this book. Now is a great time to list your expectations. Go ahead; you

Table P.0.1 My Expectations from Utilizing the 3Ms of Process Improvement in Healthcare

My Expectations of This Book Are	How I Will Measure Success in This Expectation Is	I Want to Achieve This Expectation by (Date)	How Did I Do? Lessons Learned?
Example: I want tips on how to reduce resistance and get changes implemented right the first time.	Fewer false starts from changes Higher satisfaction from those impacted by changes	The initiative starting September 21 with improvements implemented by December 30	My team used the Stakeholder Analysis template in the book and the 3Ms. Five of six changes worked the first time with satisfaction higher than any other change. The Net Promoter Score* was 80%!

will be glad you did. Please fill in the Table P.0.1 with at least one expectation from this book, *Utilizing the 3Ms of Process Improvement in Healthcare*.

Please consider referring to your expectations frequently as you explore *Utilizing the 3Ms of Process Improvement in Healthcare*. If you prefer simply to read and enjoy, that is fine, of course. Perhaps measuring your enjoyment of the stories of real change in healthcare for patient safety, the leaders who were involved, and how change leadership truly works is enough of a measure. Meeting your expectations is my measure. I hope I hear from you by your sharing your table of expectations and success with me at my Web site www.rpmexec.com.* You can download all of the templates I describe

---

* Net Promoter Score is from Frederick F. Reichheld's article, "One number you need to grow." *Harvard Business Review*, 2003.

in this book, such as the Stakeholder Analysis, Charter, and charts from this site. Please feel free to upload your work to share with others on this site.

Best wishes and thank you for your time learning how to improve processes to achieve performance excellence utilizing the 3Ms. I hope you also enjoy reading this book and sharing your successes. The 3Ms worked for Ben Franklin, Abraham Lincoln, Dr. Livingstone, and my teams across the globe. I am sure the 3Ms will work for you. And, I know what surely does not work.

Rick

About the Author

 Rick Morrow is a consultant with more than 25 years of senior leadership experience in healthcare, aviation, construction, automotive, and high tech. Morrow leads the automotive industry Healthcare Performance Partners' Quality, Safety, and High Reliability unit, a MedAssets company. He has authored Lean Six Sigma performance excellence courses and taught and deployed programs internationally for Eaton Corporation, SKF, Motorola, United Airlines, The Joint Commission, and Healthcare Performance Partners.

Morrow is the author and leader of HPP's Six Sigma consulting and wrote and leads the Belmont University Lean Healthcare Certification Program for Supply Chain Professionals, which is a blend of The Toyota Production System, Six Sigma, and Change Leadership. Morrow also wrote and taught The University of Penn's Penn Medicine Leadership and Performance Improvement courses. He authored the Lean Six Sigma Program at The Joint Commission and led its Center for Transforming Healthcare, where he and his team led collaborations improving patient care and safety with major academic medical centers including Cedars-Sinai, Johns Hopkins, Mayo Clinic, Intermountain Healthcare, North Shore Long Island Jewish, and Stanford University.

Morrow earned his MBA from the University of Illinois' Executive Program and has a B.S. in business from Illinois State University. His certifications include Motorola Master Black Belt and Lean Enterprise from the University of Tennessee. He is an international speaker on Lean Six Sigma, Quality, and Safety at conferences including NPSF, ASC, and ASQ.

Morrow is also the author of the companion book, *Utilizing the 3Ms in Process Improvement*, and is a contributing editor on performance improvement, quality, and safety publications.

He is as proud of his work coaching his son and daughter in baseball and soccer as he is of leading as president of the Holy Family Commission of Education.

Chapter 1

Overview of Process Improvement and the 3Ms

Outcomes Are the Result of Processes

If better outcomes are desired, improve the processes. Sounds simple, so why do we sometimes struggle achieving better outcomes? This is a "how-to book." You will discover how to improve processes and how to achieve better outcomes. In addition, I share how to sustain the gains, the "Achilles heel," in performance improvement for many organizations.

An outcome in healthcare we want to improve is a patient's response to treatment. Treating a patient is a process, often a complex set of processes, one that often involves more than one person and more than one discipline. The discharge process often fails and fails in multiple ways. Patients are often readmitted to a hospital because processes inside and outside the hospital fail. An example is the need to maintain a proper diet in the control of congestive heart failure or chronic pulmonary obstruction disease. The discharge process explains the diet needed to continue the recovery process, but the process may result in confusion for the patient. Adding to this failure may be the process outside the hospital to maintain the diet, such as how to buy healthy food in neighborhoods without such stores. Currently, healthcare is learning how to improve the process of care throughout the "value stream" of healthcare. A value stream is a stream of energy flowing among entities resulting in a service or product. "Accountable Care Organizations" and similar value stream approaches are being considered to unite the entities in the value stream to coordinate care, resulting in improved outcomes.

Personally, enjoying our family is an outcome. Sharing time together on trips, helping our children or spouse with homework, and attending social events are processes that lead to enjoying our family. What would happen if we never improved the trips we took as the children grew? Would the same trip to the park, playing explorer with make-believe forts, bring the joyous outcomes when our children became teenagers? What if bloodletting, extracting blood from a patient to cure or prevent disease, which was promoted for two thousand years until the mid-1800s, was still the primary treatment by surgeons?[1] What can we learn about process improvement from what must have been a terrific amount of change—a change from a practice performed from antiquity? But life is not about process improvement, at least it is not for me. Is process improvement what you get up for in the morning?

Performance Excellence

So, why does the title of this book include process improvement? Why didn't I name it *Performance Excellence*? Isn't that why we improve processes? Better yet, why do we strive for performance excellence? Maybe we improve processes to achieve higher performance that leads to better outcomes for our patients. Why didn't I include in the title "Excellent Outcomes" or what some companies consider their mission, "Contribute to Society"? I wanted this book to work for those who want to apply it in their home life as well as their work life, so how about reaching beyond the workplace to engage our entire selves with *How to Get to Heaven* if that is our ultimate goal in lives? I wrote this book to help you and your organization achieve better outcomes and, in fact, excellence in performance. Process improvement is the way to get there.

3Ms for Process Improvement

1. *M*easure
2. *M*anage to the measure
3. *M*ake it easier to do the right thing

Measure

I can **Measure** processes that lead to the outcome. Simply measuring the outcome does not directly change the outcome. It does not improve the outcome. If I measure the process that gets me the outcome and improve the process, I can get a better outcome.

Getting to work in the morning is an example of how measuring contributes to process improvement. Measuring the time it takes me to get to work provides an answer that is nice to know, but if I want to get to work faster, this measure does nothing for me. However, if I measure the process in getting to work, including the time it takes for alternate routes, I might be able to improve the process of getting to work, my desired outcome. If I could measure occurrences and severity of accidents relative to traffic congestion before and during my trip, I might be able to adjust my process of getting to work and achieve a higher performance—getting to work on time.

If I and my family members could measure the amount of gas left in the tanks when we return each other's vehicles, which of course we can, we could work together to improve the return process. Wasted time in getting to work is caused by having to stop to refill the gas tank after someone borrows my truck. Measuring is the first M, but measuring without doing anything is not going to get to a better outcome. Simply telling each other the gas level is low does not put gas in the tank.

This entire issue is caused by my owning a truck, which is a highly valued vehicle when it comes to hauling lots of friends or stuff. You know what is even better than owning a truck? Having a dad who owns a truck, I think. My kids borrow my truck frequently and I find myself driving my son's or daughter's little Mustangs to the airport instead of my nice, comfortable four-wheel drive truck. What we decided to do is to *Measure* the gas level in each vehicle before returning and holding the keys hostage.

Manage to the Measure

With measuring emphasized, we now needed to **Manage** to the measure to improve the process. Holding the keys to each other's car managed to change the process to ensure that we return the vehicles with at least enough gas to get to work, but it was not always easy to replenish the gasoline late at night. Gas stations in our area are not open late, so it is difficult to bring the vehicles back with gas in them after a long day on the road. We needed an easier way to do this. For every will, there's a way, and so it is for every father, son, and daughter (Adam and Janelle are ours).

Make It Easier

Adam, our son, also borrows my lawnmower and its gas can. One morning, I had an early flight and found my truck's tank too empty to make it to the airport. In a hurry, and not wanting to look for a gas station on the way, I reached for the gas can in my garage and fueled my truck. Voila! We now have improved the process to make it easier to return a vehicle with some gas in it. Keeping that container in my garage **Makes** it easier for all of us to return vehicles with that spare gallon or two in the container for those really late nights or horrible weather we might have. There you have it, utilizing the 3Ms for process improvement. Measure the amount of gas, manage to get it filled, and make it easier to replenish.

Any time I can **Measure**, **Manage**, and **Make** it easier to do the right thing, I progress toward performance excellence. It is that simple, yet so many organizations fail to do one or more of the Ms. I bet that is often the cause of the failures you see in achieving your desired outcomes.

We Need All Three Ms to Sustain the Improvements

Here is an example of what happens when just one M is weak or missing. We have all been measured by others and probably have failed to achieve the improvement or outcome desired. In this story, the surgical services team was struggling to have everything needed in surgery when they needed it. There are often braces used in orthopedic surgery to support the patient's limbs. Using the correct attachments for supporting a patient's leg for orthopedic surgeries facilitates the surgical team in performing the procedure. A hospital found it often did not have the correct brace near the operating room (OR). The frequency of times the correct brace was available was measured, the first M. It was surprising how many times braces were missing.

Managing to the measure started occurring when the director of the OR brought up the issue in daily huddles with the OR staff. They would review the chart showing the number of occurrences from the preceding day. The staff knew how important it was to get the surgeons the correct brace. When the director of OR asked the team how it was going, she wanted to hear that the measure of occurrences had improved. She was definitely showing an interest in improving the measure by asking daily. The OR team also wanted the measure to show improvement. After a few days, the director and staff decided to observe the next case needing such a brace to find out why the improvements had not occurred. However, the measure did not seem to improve. The same number of cases was missing the correct brace. Which M was missing? Making it easier to get the correct brace is my answer. Simply measuring and managing to the measure is cruel if the change is too difficult. The next section will share how to make it easier, the third M.

The Science of Process Improvement

Process improvement best occurs using a scientific methodology. What I cannot do in this one book is show you all the tools in the process improvement tool chest. However, utilizing the 3Ms and using a few tools I teach in this book will improve most of the issues organizations face today. Dr. Ishikawa, professor of engineering at the University of Tokyo and leader of the Japanese Union of Scientists and Engineers, promoted team problem solving and developed much of the training given to problem solvers today. He is also considered the "father" of Quality Circles (teams trained in continuous improvement) and inventor of the Cause and Effect Diagram, also known as the Ishikawa Diagram or "Fishbone" chart used in root cause analysis.[2] He was also a promoter of mistake-proofing methods. Dr. Ishikawa believed that just seven to ten tools will solve 95% of the quality issues and should be taught to all employees. They are discussed next.

Quality Foundational Process Improvement Tools

- Chartering: defining the problem
- Stakeholder resistance analysis
- Brainstorming
- Data collection techniques (check sheets, concentration diagrams, etc.)
- Cause-and-effect analysis and "Five Whys"
- Pareto analysis
- Histograms and scatter diagrams
- Control charts
- Stratification

I also include in this list tools for productivity issues not caused by quality issues. These include tools to reduce the wasted time from disorganized areas, excessive motion looking for supplies, and excessive resources, including inventory. Toyota and others have developed these, and they are discussed next.

Productivity Process Improvement Tools

- Eight wastes
- 5S (sort, store, shine, standardize, sustain)
- Standard work
- Value stream mapping
- Just-In-Time inventory methods of pull replenishment, including kanban
- Continuous flow

As you can see from his list of preferred tools and the list of productivity process improvement tools, Dr. Ishikawa and leaders in quality and performance like Toyota are firm believers and teachers in measuring, managing to the measure, and making it easier for people to do the right thing.[3]

You probably have already used most of these tools, but I find many people are not confident about how to get started or which tool to use and when. To thank you for reading my book and utilizing the 3Ms, I include an example of each tool in the appendices with my Roadmap for Performance Excellence™ (see Appendix 1). This roadmap guides the process improvement team in asking the right questions at the right time and suggests the tool that best answers the question. All of the foundational tools can be found on the Roadmap and in Appendix 2, which shows them graphically or in figures for easier understanding. I teach more advanced performance improvement methods for more complex issues and speedier process improvement, but I always rely on these fundamental tools first.

Change Leadership

To improve is to change. To be perfect is to change often.

Winston Churchill

Learning and applying Change Leadership is as important as utilizing the 3Ms and dependence on the 3Ms at the same time. I cover Change Leadership in its own chapter because it is that important to process improvement. Leading change is a skill everyone can learn and one that cannot be overemphasized.[4] All the science in the world and all the tools in the tool chest are worthless if one leading a team cannot lead the team through change. I share stories of great Change Leaders and share their methods in leading others in change and process improvement. I also share sad stories of failed changes because of a lack of Change Leadership. I think we learn best by learning the good and the bad.

Case Study in Process Improvement

In the instance discussed previously, a team was formed to discover why the correct brace was not available when surgery started. The team was trained in how to improve a process using scientific methodology. Scientific methodology is a standard way to define the issue clearly, calculate the current state of performance, analyze for contributing factors or root causes to the issue, develop countermeasures to improve the issue, and last, to control the process to sustain the gains. I share with you the scientific method with a unique "roadmap" included in Appendix 1 that helps you navigate even the most complex of issues.

The director of the OR also knew science alone would not improve a process. Even in the simplest of issues, there can be many people affected in process improvement. She engaged the people in the process, asked them to apply their process improvement skills, and enabled them by allowing them time to work on the issue. Not engaging them and trying to solve it herself might work, but how much can one person do alone?

Utilizing the 3Ms for Process Improvement

The team members introduced themselves, reviewed the issue, and began the process. They soon discovered the technicians were aware of the measure of occurrences and aware that their manager wanted them to ensure the correct brace was in the OR in plenty of time. It did not take long to find out what was going wrong.

Actually, two root causes were found. The first root cause was an insufficient number of braces on days when two of their highest-volume orthopedic surgeons were performing surgeries. The second issue was somewhat related to the first. The cases that were missing the brace most often were in another part of the hospital. There were not enough ORs in the primary suite used for orthopedic cases to handle the demand. The cases that most often were missing the braces were in the other building. These ORs were at least a five-minute walk from where the braces were stored in the primary building.

The first two Ms were in place. Measure was happening and adding value by highlighting the issue of missing braces. Managing to the measure, the second M, also was occurring, as evidenced by the director and staff watching the measure and creating a dialog among staff on how to get the measure moving in the right direction. Because the measure was not moving simply from awareness, the team knew process improvement was needed. The director managed to the measure more fervently by engaging and enabling a team to work on the issue. The team informed the orthopedic surgeons about the issue and suggested they work together to smooth the demand between the high-volume surgeons as much as possible. The team also discovered a couple of braces that were off in a corner, needing repair.

The team got the okay to expedite the repairs, thus increasing the number of braces. And, when the number of cases still exceeded what the primary ORs could handle, a team from the primary OR staff for these procedures "chipped in" by walking the braces over to the remote building. By bringing the two staff teams together, another benefit ensued. The primary orthopedic team often stayed and helped set up for the first case of the day. The OR staff in the remote building remarked how appreciative they were of this extra teamwork. The teamwork and extra braces **Made** it easier to get the correct braces. The **Measure** of cases without braces improved as well as staff satisfaction. And the team continues to **Manage** to the measure to continuously improve.

The director of the OR showed signs of a person who can achieve change. Change is difficult enough for most of us, especially when we are not the instigators of the change. I often do not know at the beginning of process improvement efforts what changes are necessary to get to performance excellence. I sure do not profess to know at the beginning how to obtain the desired ultimate outcomes, especially in complex organizations like those involved in healthcare. What I do know is that process improvement leads to higher performance, which in turn leads to better outcomes.

3Ms, Scientific Methodology, Change Leadership

This book is about how to utilize the 3Ms to improve processes to achieve performance excellence. It is as much about the science of process improvement as it is about how to lead process improvement utilizing the 3Ms. Without both the scientific methodology of process improvement and how to lead others in change, we will fail. We also know it starts with an effective Change Leader. It takes a Change Leader to instill the need for the science of process improvement. I share with you how to utilize the 3Ms in process improvement and lead change that sustains the gains. The 3Ms work every time, and I have never seen sustained improvement without the 3Ms. It is truly this simple.

I believe it helps to practice, so throughout the book, there are exercises to practice. I hope you try them all because practicing will build your confidence. I sincerely hope you enjoy our time together utilizing the 3Ms for process improvement and introduced with stories of some of the greatest Change Leaders of all time.

Key Points

- A better outcome is the end in mind. Performance excellence achieves better outcomes. Process improvement leads to performance excellence.
- The 3Ms are
    - *Measure* what is important.
    - *Manage* to the measure.
    - *Make* it easier to do the right thing. Make it happen, Make it work, Make it better, Make it worthwhile.
- A scientific methodology and change leadership combine to enable teams to improve processes.
- It does not take advanced tools to improve most process issues. Seven to ten tools will solve 95% of most quality issues.
- Change Leadership is vital to process improvement and is as important as utilizing the 3Ms.

Notes

1. K. Shigehisa, Interpreting the history of bloodletting, *The Journal of the History of Medicine and Allied Sciences*, 50 (1995), 11–46.

2. Don Dewar, *The Quality Circle Handbook*, Quality Circle Institute, Chico, CA, 1980, pp. F2-4, F9-13-14.
3. Yasuhiro Monden, *Toyota Production System, an Integrated Approach to Just-in-Time*, 2nd edition, Industrial Engineering and Management Press, Norcross, GA, 1993, p. 237.
4. Peter F. Drucker, *Management Challenges for the 21st Century*, Jossey-Bass, San Francisco, 1999, pp. 73–93.

Chapter 2

Change Leadership

Change Leadership —as necessary as the science in healthcare's greatest discoveries in improving processes.

What Is Change Leadership? Change Management? How Do They Differ?

Leadership is the key word that differentiates the two terms *Change Leadership* and *Change Management*. You have probably heard of Change Management and may have heard of Change Leadership and thought the terms were synonymous. They are not. Change requires someone to lead. If we wanted only to manage, we would not have change. Have you experienced a change gone wrong in your organization?

The Need for Leadership in Change: A Case Study in Healthcare

The healthcare improvement champion for a health system and I were called in to help a hospital's chief executive officer (CEO), chief nursing officer (CNO), and chief financial officer (CFO) find why a change to help nurses spend more time with patients and less time in charting failed. Who would argue that such a change made sense? The change was to buy computers on wheels so nurses could roll the cart into the patient's room and do the required charting while spending time with the patient. In the past, the nurses would leave the patient's room, walk to the nurses' station, and enter the data on computers at the desk. What we found was a complete failure to achieve any additional time with patients.

It is no wonder. When we first walked to the floors, we found the computers on wheels outside the patient rooms, not inside any room. We observed nurses still doing their charting at the nurses' station or at one of the computers on wheels parked near the nurses' stations. In addition, 50% of these expensive tablet computers, which cost far more than a desktop computer found at the nurses' station, were inoperative, having been unplugged and their batteries drained. They were now taking up vital space in the corridors or stashed away in a storage area.

What went wrong with this change? It is not that the computers did not work as well as the desktop computers. In fact, they had features such as biometric scanning that made signing on as easy as swiping a thumb over the sensor. But not one nurse was using this feature, and many nurses complained about the many keystrokes needed just to sign in. They had touch screen capability and a strap to allow one hand to hold the tablet while the other hand was free to enter patient data. So why did we see large desktop-size keyboards added to these handheld computers and hear that nurses found the touch screen frustrating? Worse, why were the "COWs" (the not-so-kind nickname for the computers on wheels) never, ever, taken into the patient's room to achieve the primary objective of nurses charting in real time and spending more time with patients?

The computers worked, technically. What did not work was leading the changes. The nurses told us they had little input into the change. No one could remember anyone from the supplier coming to observe how a nurse from these units performed the tasks. No one spoke to them and asked them their ideas. Most nurses had not been trained in the unique features of the tablet computer. None even knew what the biometric sensor on the front of the tablet was. Even more surprising, more than one nurse did not realize the computer had a strap on the back so it could be taken from the mount and held in one hand.

After the computers arrived, not one nurse could remember the tablet maker or distributor coming to demonstrate the computer or to address their complaints. Managers were as frustrated as the nurses about the new computers and the lack of support by the instigators of the change.

We reported our findings and recommendations to the hospital executives and the corporate CFO and CIO (chief information officer). The CFO was told originally that the changes would improve patient and nurse satisfaction. We shared how 100% of the investment was wasted. The CFO promptly canceled the program. He then addressed the hospital's CNO and promised he would support whatever she and her staff decided they needed for charting that increased time with patients, improved charting for better patient care and information, and made the nurses' work life better.

Too Many Examples of Not Leading Change Well

We see similar changes that have failed throughout healthcare. We see managers as frustrated as the staff. We also see changes that have made a significant impact, such as improved cultures in the operating room (OR). One organization changed the culture in the OR so that surgeons, circulating nurses, surgical techs, and anesthesia providers work as a team and respect each other's opinions. This culture has led to an improvement in safety, as evidenced by a control chart posted every day measuring a statistically significant reduction in slips, lapses, and mistakes. What we find different between the changes that fail and the changes that succeed is not so much the management but how change is led.

Management and Leadership: "Scientific Management"

Frederick Taylor (1856–1915), the father of "Scientific Management," is considered the first consultant to management. In Scientific Management, tasks and behaviors are measured against outcomes. He pioneered the differences in management and leadership by working with an organization's leadership, management, and the workers. He worked in both industry and healthcare; the workers involved, for example, could be caring for the patient or shoveling coal.

Leaders, Taylor believed, were responsible for developing managers who developed workers. Measurement was key to knowing how well work was being done. Taylor found that measuring a task allowed management to know what was needed and how much work could be done by each person. This measurement allowed managers to predict the number of workers needed and to respond. Scientific Management starts with leadership's vision of a more productive workplace with better outcomes.

Perfect Example of Scientific Management

In 1912, Frederick Taylor testified before Congress that the perfect example of Scientific Management was found at the Mayo Clinic. Perhaps he judged it based on the Mayo Clinic as the world's first private integrated group practice and stressed a teamwork approach.[1] By being cured, patients discovered the advantages of doctors pooling knowledge.

The late Peter Drucker, arguably one of the foremost experts on management and leadership, suggests there have been seven assumptions close enough to reality until the early 1980s to be operational. He writes,[2] "They are now so far removed from actual reality that they are becoming obstacles to the Theory and even more serious obstacles to the Practice of management." One of these assumptions is that, "There is, or must be, ONE right way to manage people." He postulates that, "One does not 'manage' people. The task is to lead people. And the goal is to make productive the specific strengths and knowledge of each individual."

Drucker honors Taylor's work in developing management theory and practice. However, he suggests these assumptions are no longer valid, or maybe we misunderstood Taylor. Even Taylor recognized that the importance to management is outcome. Patients at the Mayo Clinic recognized value was how the doctors performed, not how they managed their workers. Drucker writes that, "Maybe we will have to redefine the task (of management) altogether. It may not be managing the work of people. The starting point both in theory and in practice may have to be 'managing for performance.'" Measuring performance seems like the thing to do. Managing to the measure to get performance is the logical next step. How do we get started? Do we manage ourselves into starting or will it take a leader?

Definition of Manager and Leader

The Small Business Administration differentiates managers and leaders. *Managers* are defined as those who adopt impersonal, almost passive, attitudes toward goals.[3] Managers choose goals based on necessity instead of desire and are therefore deeply tied to their organization's culture, and they tend to be reactive since they focus on current information. Management is planning, organizing, staffing, directing, and controlling.

Leaders, however, tend to be active since they envision and promote their ideas instead of reacting to current situations. Leaders shape ideas instead of responding to them, have a personal orientation toward goals, and provide a vision that alters the way people think about what is desirable, possible, and necessary.

Leaders are to change what inventors are to innovation. We do not get innovation without inventors, and we do not get change without leaders who create a vision and motivate others in changing.

What Happens When There Is No Leader?

Ballroom dancing requires a leader. The leader takes an active role in creating a vision of the routine in movements and timing. Both dancers will manage the routine to achieve the vision, but the leader initiates change from one location to another, in one direction to another, from one move to another. The aggressiveness and pace of the dance comes from the leader. The maintenance of rhythm and sequence may come from either partner as they manage the routine. The leader's intensity during the routine will change based on the management of the routine and performance quality. The leader may intervene during the routine to adjust the dance if the vision is to win a competition or to create a sensual experience between two lovers waltzing romantically as one across the dance floor.

What happens if the leader's vision is not the same as his or her partner's vision? Are you envisioning what I am? It is not a pretty picture. We have all seen video of the falls in the popular ballroom dancing shows or in pairs figure skating competition when one partner is not in synch with the other. When the leader and partner are working together, it can provide a beautiful scene and story. Leading change is beautiful, but like ballroom dancing, it takes practice. Getting good at Change Leadership can result in quite a few bumps and bruises. It is worth it when one looks back on changes that seemed so impossible to have occurred.

Think back to changes you have been a part of that succeeded beyond expectations. Who was the leader? What was different about the leadership of those successes versus changes that failed? Maybe you were the leader. How did you feel at the beginning of the change, midway through, and at the end? Has the change sustained? If change has not sustained, why not? We explore successes and failures in leading change and help you with techniques that work to achieve and sustain changes in healthcare.

Change Leadership becomes more successful and easier once one achieves success and momentum. This comes with practice. Great Change Leaders analyze their successes and failures and improve their skills continuously.

Leadership Principles

In this chapter, you will learn that process improvement should start with a vision, engage others, and include methods to sustain the improvements. Further chapters detail how to create vision statements and how to engage others with methods to sustain changes. You will learn step by step with templates whenever possible, and I include examples from healthcare. You will learn how to communicate the vision and to whom it is necessary to communicate. Most important, I share the pitfalls to avoid. You will learn more on leading change. Unless the one leading the change has the skills we are covering in this chapter, managers will not know what change to plan for, how to organize, staff, direct, and last of all, control. Leading change differentiates this book from others that talk about managing change.

Abraham Lincoln on Leading Change

Abraham Lincoln was one of the greatest leaders of all time. A Change Leader could learn many lessons from "Honest Abe." Honesty is perhaps the first and greatest lesson of a Change Leader, if you want to achieve more than one change with the same organization.

> You can fool some of the people all of the time, and all of the people some of the time, but you cannot fool all of the people all of the time.

> **Abraham Lincoln**

Just about anyone can get one change through, especially if the person has organizational authority. But, revolutions and death have come to some who force change dishonestly and against the interest of the people. A Change Leader's skills go well beyond being honest, but a Change Leader could do well starting out with being honest about changes coming, and observing Abe's principles of leadership he consistently used to govern managerial conduct and change.

Abraham Lincoln's Principles of Leadership

- Advocate a *vision* and continually reaffirm it.
- *Circulate* among followers consistently.
- Build strong *alliances.*
- Search for *intelligent* assistants.
- Encourage *innovation.*
- *Persuade* rather than coerce.
- Influence people through *stories.*
- Be *results* oriented.[4]

You will learn how to practice each of Abe's principles with exercises along the way. Let us start with the end in mind. A Change Leader gets results, and Change Leaders often achieve results beyond expectations. How do they accomplish so much? How have others failed so we can learn what not to do? To learn Change Leadership, I share lessons learned from those who failed to achieve results as well as those who have succeeded. We start with one who led one of the most significant changes for humanity.

Leading Change to a Slave-Free America

Lincoln was a Change Leader who envisioned a slave-free America and engaged the North and the South in one of America's most significant changes. He was also a Change Manager during the war because he planned, organized, staffed, directed, and controlled the North's war effort.

Lincoln's leadership to abolish slavery started with advocating a vision of abolishing slavery. His means to that end, however, was to stop its growth, believing it would eventually die out. His intention was not to act immediately to abolish it, believing this change to be too great for the nation. At the time, civil war itself was not beyond comprehension. One certainly does not want to manage a nation into war with itself. Manage a war effort, yes, once the change started, but leading includes having a vision of change and not reacting to a change. A Change Leader knows well how much change can be managed at any one time and place.

We know Lincoln and America were successful in the change to a slave-free land. We also know change is difficult at times, and Change Leaders may pay the ultimate price. We all benefit today from Lincoln's Change Leadership, and we use Lincoln's story to become better Change Leaders, leading to better process improvement.

Healthcare's Change Leaders

Healthcare has had its share of Change Leaders. Dr. Brent James, a physician at Intermountain Healthcare in Salt Lake City, Utah,[5] is identified as one who could reform healthcare. I had the pleasure of working with a team improving handoff communications at Intermountain and seeing firsthand the methods that lead to change. Dr. James and his students reduce change by reducing variation in practices that are proven to improve care. They rely on measuring to know if changes make an impact on care. He uses statistical run charts highlighting differences between methods, such as which method is better at reducing mortality.

Intermountain had worked on heart failure and discovered that a beta-blocker could make a difference in the outcome. This beta-blocker treatment was not discovered by Dr. James, but by measuring its use and the outcome, Intermountain was able to validate improvements. Physicians are schooled in evidence-based medicine and appreciate having such measures of processes and outcomes. Dr. James manages to those measures at Intermountain and expects the same of others in this environment of evidence-based care. Sharing the measures in real time and acting on them are key to success. Dr. James focuses on the charts instead of arguing. He lets the charts prove the theory. This is his leadership philosophy.

In my work inside Intermountain and with staff and physicians, it is clear that Dr. James believes in measuring and managing to the measure. He, like all good leaders, teaches his methods of using data and charts, and he does this in a well-orchestrated training program. He also offers this training to others outside Intermountain.[5]

Walking the Talk

Techniques that Change Leaders like Dr. James use are taught in this book. Process improvement leaders, like Change Leaders, use measurement instead of merely debate or arguments about philosophy. The book *Lincoln on Leadership* indicates how Abraham Lincoln would personally walk to the war department's telegraph office to know as soon as possible the "score" of the battles being fought.[6] What message did his desire to measure progress constantly and quickly send to the generals in the field who knew about this practice? They knew their measure, and they knew Abe would manage to that measure. Lincoln managed to change general-in-chief four times in the course of the Civil War, finally finding the general who could achieve the measure: winning the war. We see measurement as a differentiator, but it takes more than measuring. Process improvement leaders measure, then they manage to the measure. Lincoln simply did not measure progress. He wrote letters to the generals sharing thoughts, coaching them, and asking for their ideas. We also see that making change easier is what Change Leaders do better than those who fail. The 3Ms (measure, manage to the measure, make it easier) must all be in place, and when they are, they can change a nation. They are helping improve processes in healthcare today.

Definition of Common Terms across Methodologies

"Go to the Gemba" seems to be what Abe Lincoln was suggesting. This is a Japanese and English term that means go to where the work is and the people are. The reverse is not to go yet still make decisions and promote change without ever being in the process. *Genchi Genbutsu* is yet another term for this same concept. *Takt time* is used by Toyota, and it means the rate at which the process should flow. *Takt* is a German word that means "beat."

Alas, we would all be "Leaner" if we simply minimized the number of recipes, tools, and terms in process improvement. Some terms are simply the same word but in different languages. This book, I hope in whatever language it is translated into, avoids words that are not self-evident. Do not get me wrong; I explore and attempt to learn the language of the country where I am working. However, my purpose is to be able to learn and share in the leanest, most effective fashion. To use another language to share a Change Leadership term only then to have to explain it seems like waste. Worse, this use of an unknown term often hinders change because we may be perceived as demeaning and arrogant. Arrogance is not an attribute label I believe process improvement people should have.

Key Points

- Change requires someone to lead. If we want only to manage, we would not have change.
- Changes that succeed are not so much the work of management as they are the leader's work. Changes that sustain are very much those of the manager.

■ Measuring a task allows management to know what is needed and how much work can be done. This is Scientific Management.

■ Management is planning, organizing, staffing, directing, and controlling. Managers react to change.

■ Leaders shape ideas instead of responding to them. We do not get change without leaders who create a vision and motivate others in changing.

■ Abe Lincoln's Principles of Leadership:
  – Advocate a vision and continually reaffirm it.
  – Circulate among followers consistently.
  – Build strong alliances.
  – Search for intelligent assistants.
  – Encourage innovation.
  – Persuade rather than coerce.
  – Influence people through stories.
  – Be results oriented.

■ A Change Leader knows well how much change can be managed at any one time and place.

■ Sharing the measures in real time and acting on them is key to success.

■ Use the 3Ms to know the best treatment and reduce the debating and arguing.

Notes

1. Mayo Clinic, Mayo Clinic history. http://www.mayoclinic.org/history/.
2. Peter F. Drucker, *Management Challenges for the 21st Century*, Jossey-Bass, San Francisco, 1999. Copyright © 1999 by Peter F. Drucker. Reprinted by permission of HarperCollins Publishers.
3. Small Business Administration, Leading vs. managing—they're two different animals. http://sba.gov/leadvmanage.
4. Donald T. Philips, *Lincoln on Leadership, Executive Strategies for Tough Times*, Warner Books, Hubbard, OH, 1992. From Lincoln on Leadership by Donald T. Phillips. Copyright © 1992 by Donald T. Phillips. By permission of Grand Central Publishing. All rights reserved.
5. Intermountain's Institute for Health Care Delivery Research home page. http://intermountainhealthcare.org/qualityandresearch/institute/courses/Pages/home.aspx.
6. Philips, *Lincoln on Leadership*.

Chapter 3

Resistance to Change and Process Improvement

Everybody has accepted by now that change is unavoidable. But that still implies that change is like death and taxes—it should be postponed as long as possible and no change would be vastly preferable. But in a period of upheaval, such as the one we are living in, change is the norm.[1]

Peter Drucker

Forces against Change: Resistance, Time, Natural Laws

One of the most valued skills in our work in leading change is how to reduce resistance. Resistance is the greatest force acting against change. I will teach you how to reduce resistance. There are other forces that a Change Leader needs to recognize and address. Time, whether it is too much time or a lack of time, can also be a force against change. Procrastination may occur when people are given too much time for a change.

And, of course, too little time for people to change also does not allow process improvement. Trying a change that defies the laws of nature is a waste of time. A Change Leader cannot change time itself nor the laws of nature. A Change Leader has to address other variables, and I show how to indirectly reduce the effect of these two forces on change. A Change Leader can, however, directly reduce resistance. The force of resistance is often the most common force.

A Quick Win against Resistance

If you have any expectation about how to reduce resistance, as most do, perhaps we can get a quick win in our very first chapters. Let us start with a question. Do people resist change? I have asked this question of hundreds of people in hospitals, surgical centers, clinics, physician offices, emergency department (ED) waiting rooms, and countless other healthcare environments. I get the same answer. Yes, of course people resist change. One afternoon after delivering a speech on leading an organization in performance improvement, another speaker came up to ask me if people resist change. After initially being perplexed that such a wise person would ask such a question, I answered with a yes. I will never forget his next question, "Or do people resist being changed?" Peter Senge has been credited with this interplay.[2]

The resistance of people to change is a phenomenon that has stuck with me ever since. I have learned to use it to my advantage every time I lead change. I had to try it out, of course, to prove it to myself. I tried helping people be a part of the change next time, instead of directly trying to change them or their process. Instead of promoting what I thought the change should be, I engaged the team and guided them in discovering the issues that convinced me a change was needed. Lo and behold, once they understood what was causing the issue, they chose and implemented the same changes. Try it. Let me know how it works for you. Just trying what we share in this book should make you better at leading change because practice builds confidence to become better at process improvement.

Do you want another quick win that saves lives? Check how many alcohol-based hand-cleaning stations are empty or broken in an area that concerns you about healthcare-acquired infections. Find a person working in the area and ask how one knows it is getting low or broken. Next, find out who is supposed to refill it. Last, find where the stock is located. I thought I was finished with this chapter until today. We found four of six dispensers in the operating room hallway empty. We looked at the dispenser, and there was a little window in the cover of the dispenser, but none of us could figure out if the window would indicate the cleaner was getting low. When we asked the people in the process who can refill the dispenser, they said it was housekeeping's job. We asked if they could refill it, and one said they could, but they did not know where the refills are kept. Asking why again, this time with housekeeping's manager, she said that there was a problem ordering. Each day, 247 people die in U.S. hospitals from healthcare-acquired infections, which often are passed on by healthcare professionals' hands. Make it easier, folks, and wonderful things happen to your measure.

Role of the Change Leader

The role of the Change Leader is the first discussed among roles in process improvement. What separates those who initiate the change from those who are targets of the change? Is the answer simply the organizational hierarchy in healthcare? In organizations with top-down decision making, this may be the case. Can the amount of change healthcare needs be done in this manner? Peter Drucker states, "Unless it is seen as the task of the organization to lead change, the organization—whether business, university, hospital and so on—will not survive. In a period of rapid structural change, the only ones who survive are the Change Leaders."[3]

A Policy of Change and Continuous Improvement

Drucker believes there are four requirements for change leadership, beginning with making policy to make the future. Simply stated, the organization must make change a policy. Measuring an annual rate of change is living it. Abandonment is a policy of change leaders and means to have a process to prune old products and services. The second requirement of the organization is to drive continuous improvement for continuous improvement starts the chain of events that leads to fundamental change. This chain goes like this: Continuous improvement leads to product innovation, which leads to service innovation, which leads to new processes, then new businesses, and finally fundamental change. Steve Jobs and Steven Wozniak improved the computer, which started a chain of events that created new businesses and fundamentally changed the way we buy music, read books, and work. This is transformation, and it all starts with continuous improvement.

Piloting Changes

Drucker's third requirement is to pilot on a small scale. "Neither studies nor computer modeling are a substitute for the test of reality," according to Drucker.[4] He recommends the right way to introduce change is through piloting of new or improved systems. This is why the more successful improvement programs have piloting built in. A Roadmap to Performance Excellence is introduced further in this book. I have never introduced change perfectly despite some valuable methods to get it right the first time. Continuous improvement works best when we start small and test our changes. It can really reduce the anxiety and make change easier; this is a fundamental skill of Change Leaders. Piloting is a requirement and comes before full implementation.

What Can Happen if Change Is Not Piloted First

In October 2011, the U.K. National Health System (NHS) announced scrapping the biggest civilian information technology (IT) project ever initiated. After wasting ten years and over £12 billion, the NHS decided that smaller local solutions are better able to provide the electronic aids healthcare needs. Maybe piloting the concepts locally on a much smaller scale would have exposed the issues that eventually convinced one of the largest health systems in the world that fundamental change comes from continuous improvement.

Focusing on opportunities is more important than focusing on problems. The Change Leader should measure the opportunities and obtain them from a budget immune to economic cycles. Time spent is time lost. The "opportunity cost" of having knowledge workers working on the past versus building for the future can kill a company.

Balancing Change and Continuity

This opportunity cost leads us to Drucker's fourth requirement, the need to balance change and continuity. The organization needs to engage its partners. Partners include its knowledge workers and all workers as well as its suppliers, customers, and community. Dr. Deming's name for balancing change and continuity is "constancy of purpose." Change is difficult for many, especially in an organization in which change is not yet the norm. Stability in the mission, strategy, and rewards provide a balance to changes. Strong relationships will be seen in this book as fundamental to making change the norm. Information sharing is vital between partners, and reinforcements to sharing and learning and who gets new challenges all provide constancy of purpose. What will crush change and result in losing the knowledge workers is an organization that does not promote those who deliver continuous improvement. After all, the knowledge worker is the worker of the twenty-first century, according to Drucker. To lose the knowledge worker is to lose a change leader who will lead many others to performance excellence.

The Emancipation Proclamation

Abraham Lincoln practiced all four of Drucker's requirements. Lincoln's policy included writing the Emancipation Proclamation, which prohibited the expansion of slavery to states, "That on the first day of January, in the year of our Lord one thousand eight hundred and sixty-three, all persons held as slaves within any State or designated part of a State, the people whereof shall then be in rebellion against the United States, shall be then, thenceforward, and forever free." See Appendix 3.

He attempted in this historic document to look for and anticipate change and resistance to freeing slaves by writing, "will recognize and maintain the freedom of such persons, and will do no act or acts to repress such persons, or any of them, in any efforts they may make for their actual freedom."

Now, the third policy, the right way to introduce change within and outside the organization, was argued by the South. However, the Emancipation Proclamation was not Lincoln's first attempt to introduce a change to freeing the slaves. In fact, the Emancipation Proclamation came a year and a half after the first shots of the Civil War were fired by cadets from the South at Fort Sumter on April 12, 1861. Lincoln had tried engaging the South in dialog well before the start of the Civil War, to no avail.

Evidence that Lincoln also practiced what Drucker would describe as a Change Leader's fourth and last policy—to balance change and continuity—is found in Lincoln's words that the freed slaves should continue to labor faithfully for reasonable wages after receiving their freedom versus impose an imbalance of change among U.S. citizens: "And I hereby enjoin upon the people so declared to be free to abstain from all violence, unless in necessary self-defence; and I recommend to them that, in all cases when allowed, they labor faithfully for reasonable wages."[5]

Lincoln continues with, "And I further declare and make known, that such persons of suitable condition, will be received into the armed service of the United States to garrison forts, positions, stations, and other places, and to man vessels of all sorts in said service."

Lincoln ends with a statement of balance and continuity, "And upon this act, sincerely believed to be an act of justice, warranted by the Constitution, upon military necessity, I invoke the considerate judgment of mankind, and the gracious favor of Almighty God."

Count the recent changes in your organization. How many were initiated by the people doing the work versus the manager? How does leading change work in a top-down organization when changes are initiated by the front line? I promised we would learn from those who excelled.

Another good way to learn is from those who failed.

What Happens When One or More of the Ms Is Missing?

The answer to the question of what happens when one or more of the Ms is missing can be answered with a story from healthcare, a story about a Hungarian physician, Dr. Ignaz Semmelweis. Dr. Semmelweis practiced medicine in the middle of the nineteenth century. He is best known for a discovery that saved many mothers' lives during his work at the Vienna Clinic and countless lives since the time of his discovery. However, his story is also one of failure in process improvement due to a failure in Change Leadership. His story is also a lesson on how missing one of the three Ms can devastate a change that could have saved many more lives. This is our first lesson on how change can fail.

He had a vision of a safer hospital for mothers so they might live. He used a scientific method to test his hypothesis of how to save lives. He also engaged his colleagues and superiors and instructed them in a safer practice. Before we hear his story of change, an overview of the force against change is provided so we can appreciate Dr. Semmelweis's story even more.

Dr. Semmelweis and Washing Hands: The Right Change, but ...

The time is the 1840s. Dr. Semmelweis discovered the benefits of physicians washing their hands to prevent mothers from dying after childbirth of puerperal fever. He practiced at the Vienna Clinic in Austria. These clinics could be any clinic or hospital in any country. Mothers were dying after giving birth assisted by physicians in hospitals. One may ask, "Aren't these unfortunate practices and deaths the reason most births today are not in the homes,

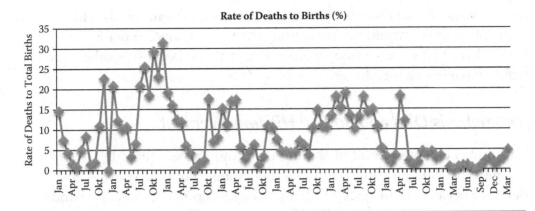

Figure 3.1   Rate of deaths to births.

but in hospitals?" The cause of mothers dying was correlated with where and with whom mothers gave birth. However, these horribly unfortunate and devastating fatalities may not have been occurring where you would think. Mothers who were perfectly healthy who had chosen to give birth in hospitals with a physician attending were dying at a significantly higher rate than the mothers who gave birth with assistance from midwives.

Dr. Semmelweis found a correlation with physicians assisting in births after leaving surgery or autopsies and deaths of those mothers giving birth. Beyond any doubt, a mother giving birth in a hospital in these circumstances had a higher rate of infection and death than one who gave birth outside the hospital or even within the same hospital with a midwife's assistance. An Oscar-winning short film, *That Mothers Might Live*,[6] shares Semmelweis's story.

His technical skills in performance improvement resulted in one of the most significant discoveries in healthcare, if not in the history of humankind. He reduced the mortality rate from a mean of 10.5% to 2.5%, as shown in Figure 3.1. Researchers believe even these numbers are conservative because mothers who left the clinic and died may not have been counted in these data.

Why Is Change Needed in Healthcare?

Each day, 247 people die from healthcare-acquired infections in the United States according to the World Health Organization (WHO).[7] In the Vienna Clinic in Austria where Semmelweis practiced, if Semmelweis's changes would have been implemented in 1841 when the mortality data started, 1,532 mothers who died might have survived.

Beyond the number of mothers who would have died, how many other patients, doctors, and hospital staff would have died if it were not for Dr.

Semmelweis? Weren't we told by our parents to wash our hands? How many of us today would not be reading this story if it were not for Dr. Semmelweis? How many people are not here today because mothers died before having a chance for another baby?

Semmelweis Dies and So Did His Improvement

This brings us to the point of sharing Dr. Semmelweis's story. Dr. Semmelweis died an early death in a mental institution, depressed and destitute because of his lack of Change Leadership skills. Washing hands, a simple proven solution, was itself not enough to create sustained change. Change Leadership is as important as the science in healthcare's discoveries.

What went wrong in his process improvement? His own colleagues resisted the change to washing hands. His superior resisted even the thought that he, Semmelweis, and the very surgeons who had achieved the highest respect of any profession, could be the cause of death. Who could think that the same surgeons who had saved so many from so many illnesses were actually causing death? Despite the evidence so clearly showing a correlation between their actions and mothers dying, they resisted scientific evidence. Did they resist because of poor Change Leadership skills, despite knowing washing hands was effective?

The resistance against Semmelweis was clear. In the film, an early scene showed a man carrying instruments in the hospital. He drops several on the floor and picks them back up as he continues his journey. This same man is shown later in the film resisting Semmelweis as he demands that this behavior change. Dr. Semmelweis's colleagues also openly resisted. A passive-aggressive colleague is shown mimicking washing instead of actually cleansing. Semmelweis catches him and berates him in front of his colleagues. Even Dr. Semmelweis's superior resisted.

Forcing Does Not Always Work

Semmelweis tried to police his peers and staff with stern warnings, and resistance only grew stronger. There is no evidence that Semmelweis maintained the chart and posted it for all to see after his initial tests. So strong, in fact, was the resistance, he was dismissed from the clinics. Having failed at leading the change within his hospital and actually being dispelled, he reached out to the community and wrote letters to other doctors and institutions; he still failed to lead the change. The simple change of washing one's hands was resisted.

Those in healthcare know this resistance continues. In fact, studies by WHO and the Centers for Disease Control and Prevention, my own work with the Joint Commission's Center for Transforming Healthcare, and information from hospitals worldwide prove many healthcare professionals still do not wash their hands. WHO identifies Five Moments when hand washing is important and provides charts to remind us when to wash. These charts can be found in most hospitals. Can anyone reading this book honestly say that he or she has not heard about the importance of washing hands before and after certain "moments"? Yet, have we resisted washing at times? The very reasons we resist washing hands vary as they did in Semmelweis's time. However, the point of the story is not that we resist washing. The point is his colleagues resisted the doctor more than his ideas. The best changes can be lost due to poor Change Leadership.

The Force of Resistance

Change Leadership can be learned using the principles of electricity, especially in understanding the force of resistance against change. Do not worry if electricity, or reading a book about it, scares you. I mix in some little-known facts and entertain you a bit. No, I do not recommend shock therapy or cattle prods if that is what you think I have in mind in getting people to change.

Ben Franklin, Electricity, and Change Leadership

Ben Franklin was a great Change Leader, wouldn't you say? Who was more important to America's change to independence? Yes, he also knew a bit about electricity. I hope you enjoy his story as we learn how the principles of electricity help us believe in, and understand, Change Leadership and its power.

Electricity flowing to power devices to make our lives better is analogous to change flowing to make our lives and those of our stakeholders better. What prevents electricity from flowing is resistance. If this is not enough to convince you, let me explain. We will stay close to healthcare as we learn Change Leadership through Ben's leadership stories and his discoveries linking lightning and electricity.

We have all experienced an electrical shock, whether the minimally risky static shock delivered when shaking hands or while kissing our loved ones, to the more painful household electric shock. Electrical resistance is a barrier to the free flow of electricity. Components in your computer, television, and hair dryer manage the flow of electricity by using components named, not surprisingly, resistors. Resistors! We will learn more about these stakeholders. For now, do you know some of these folks who might be scheming to prevent the change you are looking for in your organization?

Principles of Electricity Explain Resistance to Change

How electricity works for us and against us also explains how Change Leadership works. Let me start with a lesson learned early in my career in electrical safety products, "What you can't see that can kill you, don't touch it." We learned better ways to handle the energy than ignoring it and proceeding. Being aware, such as in an analysis of who the stakeholders are, is a way of "seeing" the potential danger before "touching" the process and stakeholders with changes. Channeling that energy also is what we do in Change Leadership. To prevent lightning from damaging your house and worse, starting a fire, we install lightning rods to channel the energy to the ground, where resistance works for our safety, earthworms excluded (see Figure 3.2).

Change leadership and electricity also have in common a method to actually benefit from the energy. What if we can channel that energy and resistance to do good?

What You Cannot See Can Hurt You

Ben Franklin's experiment showed that what you cannot see can hurt you. His actual experiment involved flying a kite into clouds to prove if lightning

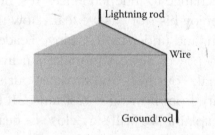

Figure 3.2 Lightning rod and resistance.

Figure 3.3   Ben and his kite.

is electricity (Figure 3.3). All we knew in 1752 was that lightning looked like an arc of electricity. In those days, arcs could only be produced that were an inch long—nothing like a miles-long lightning bolt.

Ben and his son theorized that if they could get the kite in the clouds, the invisible electricity could be captured by channeling electricity down the kite string to a jar with a key in it. Lightning did not actually strike the kite, we understand, but enough negative charges in the clouds transferred down the kite string to the key in the special jar that stores electricity. Ben "proved" that lightning was electricity, which was actually not proven yet. When Ben touched the key, he received a shock because the positive charges in his body were strongly attracted to the negative charges in the metal key. Ben now knew how to channel the energy from lightning to a safer level of resistance. Again, what you cannot see that can kill you, do not touch it. If you cannot see resistance, do not touch it. What Change Leaders do is eliminate the resistance or reduce it safely to achieve the changes desired. Learn to see it even if it is invisible to the naked eye (where did that term come from?) and channel it. Electric meters were invented to see electricity. Stakeholder analysis is to see resistance—the energy that can work against your team's efforts to improve healthcare.

Figure 3.4   An electronic resistor component.

Figure 3.5   What a resistor might look like in your organization.

Using Resistance to Help Lead Change

The next lesson in dealing with high energy is to use resistance in our favor to help lead change. To manage electricity, we actually use a component aptly named a resistor. One is pictured in Figure 3.4.

If there is too much energy for what is needed, or what a device can handle, a designer inserts a resistor to restrict the flow of electric current. An example is to place a resistor in a circuit to lower the flow to light a call light at the nurses' station. If we want to increase the flow, we reduce the resistance (Figure 3.5). The same is true in leading change: Reduce the resistance to get the changes flowing.

Electricity and Forcing Change Can Be Dangerous

The next lesson is really helpful. Electricity is dangerous. You are probably reading this book because you fear change or perhaps you fear leading the next change. Even if you have all the confidence in the world, you are reading this book because you know change can be dangerous to you and your company if not done well, and you want to improve your Change Leadership skills. Leading major changes can be career limiting if you are not careful "what you touch."

Getting Change to Flow

Let us go back to Ben's experiment. We also know others have died from shock trying the same experiment Ben did on that stormy day. Change is like electricity. We want change to flow. Therefore, the best way to increase changes is to reduce resistance. Shock occurs when our body's resistance is low enough that the current through the body allows the high voltage to flow. The voltage required for electrocution depends on the current through the body, which depends on the resistance of our body to the voltage wanting to flow to a state of equilibrium. There is actually a law about this, Ohm's law. For those who learn better through math, it is $I = V/R$, where I is the current passing through your body, V is the voltage, and R is resistance. When R goes down, I goes up. This is what we want in Change Leadership. So, our goal is to flow change by reducing R.

The Resistance to Change Can Vary within the Same Person

There is more to be learned from electricity in leading change. As in leading change, the same person at different times of the day can be more resistant to change. The body's resistance to electricity varies as the moisture in the skin varies through the day. Hmmm, is this another quick win (an improvement that does not need a lot of analysis)? What if we announced the next change at a swimming pool party because wet skin is less resistant? Better yet, also wet the insides of everyone with some enticing drinks? My attorney wanted to scratch this little humor, but I left it in anyway with a statement that you should not attempt this yourself. This should only be tried by a professional on a closed course.

As in Ben's key and Ben himself, the greater the differential is, the greater the shock will be. Therefore, engage stakeholders early and often to reduce the differential of knowledge and potential for shock between what you know and what they know. If we both know what each other knows, then we will feel like each other feels, and we will do as we each would do.

Resistance between Two Bodies

Change has the same properties. We have a differential between two bodies, the Change Leader and a Stakeholder. The phrase "there is electricity between these two people" is appropriate. Remember that, like electricity, there is energy in each party and a desire to reach equilibrium. The two bodies with different potential energy coming in close contact result in the shock and a new state of equilibrium. Remember the negative charges in the metal key and Ben's positively charged body. After the shock, both the key and Ben were again in a state of equilibrium. Wow, who would have thought kissing your loved one on a dry winter day on carpet is part of the science in Change Leadership? In addition, we see that two bodies do not have to be in direct contact. Think of when that person identified on the Stakeholder Analysis walks into your team's meeting with his arms folded (Figure 3.5).

Electricity also teaches us that the higher the differential between two bodies, the greater the shock will be when they come near each other. If there is not much differential between two bodies, then the shock will be minimal or nonexistent.

Resistance at Home

Think of when you and your loved one are picking a color for the kitchen. If you and your spouse both want to change the kitchen to blue, there is no shock or resistance here and off you go to the paint store. My wife, Jan, is good at Change Leadership. As proof, let me share with you how she leads change that makes for a great marriage inside and outside our home. Jan loves green. Blue is by far the color for me. There is something about blue that makes it the right color for just about any wall. Come to think of it, blue is the right color for anything. Anyway, we have been married for over thirty years, so whenever we are picking colors for a room, the differential is just how green it will be. Here is how Jan's mastery of reducing resistance from me inside our home works. Although our house is usually a palette of green, we often have a blue car in our garage. Compromise is a wonderful thing and is a great tool in reducing resistance. By the way, did I tell you we still have the '65 Mustang with blue and white seats we drove when we were sixteen? And, she sold her green Cougar before we married. Jan and I have a nice marriage with compromises inside and outside our home. This is a lesson for Change Leaders.

Key Points

- Change Leadership is as important as the change itself. The greatest scientific discoveries may fail if leaders do not lead others to benefit from the science.
- Change Leaders envision a change, engage stakeholders, and start the change. Change management plans, organizes, staffs, directs, and controls the change process.
- Healthcare has many great examples of change, including physicians and staff today who are eliminating infections, improving care, and reducing mistakes. What is common is that changes are led, not just managed.

Practicing Change Leadership

1. In the foreword, we asked you to list your expectations of this book. Take time now to review your expectations and update any expectation that has begun to be met.
2. Read more about your favorite leader to see if what we share in this chapter is also true with your favorite leader of change.
3. We are ready for an experiment for you in your healthcare organization. Apply the rules of electricity in a small and, I think, fun exercise. Pick an object that you think is better located elsewhere, maybe the mail trays for your office, a picture hanging in your unit or lobby, or supplies in the storeroom or on a common desk. Practice your Change Leadership in where the item is better located. Reflect on what you did and who resisted the idea. How could you have led change better?

Notes

1. Peter F. Drucker, *Management Challenges for the 21st Century*, Jossey-Bass, San Francisco, 1999.
2. Peter Senge, *The Fifth Discipline: The Art and Practice of the Learning Organization*, Doubleday/Currency, New York, 1990.
3. Drucker, *Management Challenges*.
4. Ibid.
5. Donald T. Philips, *Lincoln on Leadership, Executive Strategies for Tough Times*, Warner Books, Hubbard, OH, 1992.
6. *That Mothers Might Live*, Warner Brothers Home Entertainment, Broadway Melody of 1938, Special Features. Director Fred Zinnemann.
7. World Alliance for Patient Safety, *World Healthcare Organization Guidelines on Hand Hygiene in Healthcare*, World Health Organization, April 2006.

Chapter 4

Process Improvement Methodologies

We don't need any more recipes. We need cooks to change groceries into meals. That is adding value.

Overview of the Most Popular Methodologies

Plan-do-study-act (PDSA); plan-do-check-act (PDCA); Lean; Six Sigma; and other scientific performance improvement methodologies adorn the walls in many different industries. It is recipe madness. I wish I had a nickel for each time I heard debates about one methodology being better than the other, about which one should be started first, and how complex one is compared to another. Most problem-solving or process improvement methodologies are described using the steps and sequence in the methodology.

An example is Dr. Shewhart's plan-do-study-act. The acronym PDSA is applied and is useful to remember the four steps. Dr. W. Edwards Deming modified Dr. Shewhart's PDSA to plan-do-check-act (PDCA). Drs. Shewhart and Deming were on friendly terms, and in the effort to continuously improve, Dr. Deming added his recipe.

In Six Sigma, Bill Smith and Mikel Harry originally described the Six Sigma methodology as MAIC: measure, analyze, improve, and control. They and others using Six Sigma found that issues needed better definition, so the term *Define* was added, thus giving DMAIC.

The Toyota Production System (TPS) is Toyota's methodology to improve a production system. TPS is used widely in virtually all industries now. We use it often to reduce inventory in healthcare organizations, to improve the flow of patients through a hospital and ambulatory surgical center, to improve surgical safety, and to get people to wash their hands to improve hand hygiene.

Lean is another methodology, and it is not an acronym. Lean includes TPS and is a popular performance improvement methodology in healthcare and many industries. Lean is a term coined by a group at the Massachusetts Institute of Technology (MIT) who studied the auto industry. In the book *The Machine that Changed the World*,[1] James Womack and Daniel Jones shared the origins of the term. Lean describes the Toyota processes compared to Ford, GM, and Chrysler processes. The amount of time and resources to do similar tasks at Toyota were much less than at Ford, GM, and Chrysler.

We could list many more methodologies and acronyms, but this book is about making process improvement simpler for you and your organization. Therefore, I walk the talk here and purposely be "Lean" by sharing the vital few and most popular "recipes."

You Need at Least One Recipe and Do Not Forget a "Heaping Tablespoon" of Change Leadership

The key point I want you to leave this chapter with is that these methodologies are all you need, and you need them all with Change Leadership. I could point to elements of Six Sigma, Lean, PDSA, and Change Leadership in each of these methodologies. Reducing waste is often associated with lean, and statistical process control (SPC) is considered Six Sigma by some.

Which Recipe Delivers the Culture and Change Leadership Skills?

Some consultants have hijacked culture change and leadership development, claiming that only their Lean or their Six Sigma delivers skills beyond the tools of a methodology. This is untrue. Certainly, some "Lean Purists" have hijacked culture change to be delivered only through Lean. And, I have heard some Six

Sigma purists claim that Lean-trained people do not use data or other quality tools. Many Six Sigma consultants[2,3] have helped organizations change their cultures in much the same way as those consultants who describe themselves as primarily Lean. This is a shame and a waste of time to even debate.

Work with Toyota and for Motorola

I have worked with Toyota, taught its former employees Lean and Six Sigma, and toured its sites. I am one of the few who has also worked for Motorola. The two most popular methodologies were developed by these two leading organizations. At Motorola, I coached and trained process improvement teams while in Motorola's Corporate Initiatives Group. I also led performance excellence in Motorola's automotive business unit. However, Motorola did not sell to Toyota, so my experience with Toyota comes from time with SKF, a global manufacturer based in Sweden, as SKF's vice president of Total Quality and Lean Six Sigma.

Motorola and Toyota Use Lean and Six Sigma Tools and Concepts

I know firsthand that Toyota and Motorola use the same tools some want to categorize as Lean or Six Sigma. Jeffrey Liker states in his book *The Toyota Way* that the tools that some associate with Six Sigma are used in Toyota.[4] Although Liker makes a statement that quality specialists and team members use only four key tools, I can assure you that Toyota teaches its team members many of the same tools that are taught in Six Sigma courses, such as fishbone charts, control charts, and data collection methods. Toyota also values and uses histograms, SPC charts, data analysis, and failure mode and effects analysis, and Toyota often demands the same from its suppliers, as Liker states. The key is to teach what adds value. It is also true that there are tools taught in both Six Sigma and Lean courses that may never be needed.

I may never forget a former Toyota employee's "aha" moment at a United Airlines (UAL) process improvement course my staff was teaching. She had joined UAL after many years on the shop floor at a Toyota vehicle assembly plant. She stood up during a module on SPC, histograms, and how to test if there are statistical differences between two methods, exclaiming, "Oh, now

I understand why quality was so good at Toyota." Not every employee is taught all the tools that make Toyota quality a benchmark.

PDSA and PDCA Compared to Six Sigma

Experimentation is the essence of PDSA and PDCA. Drs. Shewhart and Deming were scientists and experienced at experimentation; they believed in cycling through PDCA until success is achieved. The PDCA cycle refers to the practice of continuous improvement through repeated successive experimentation. PDCA describes experimental design we were all taught in primary school. Fortunately, the Institute for Healthcare Improvement (IHI) in its improvement model recognized that not all of us are so skilled in setting up an experiment, so they added three questions before the PDSA cycle.[5] These three questions, not surprisingly, make PDSA and PDCA as complete as DMAIC:

- What are we trying to accomplish?
- How will we know a change is an improvement?
- What changes can we make that will result in an improvement?

Question 1 closely mirrors the Define phase of Six Sigma; the team brings consensus to the issue, customer-centric metrics, goals, scope, and impact.

Question 2 refers to measuring the current state to know when change has occurred. Too many times, people show a line chart with a few points going in the favorable direction without a representative baseline period. This baseline period should be measured to validate change has really occurred. Another tool often associated with Six Sigma is SPC in the chapter about Measure. For now, consider that all of these methodologies reinforce measuring the current state early in the process to know if change has really occurred.

Question 3 is the weaker connection to Six Sigma's Analyze Phase. Let us start with what the Analyze Phase entails and then relate it to the third question.

All Good Methods Analyze for Root Causes before Solutions

Analyzing for contributing factors and root causes is what the Six Sigma team discovers in the Analyze phase. PDSA, PDCA, Lean, and Six Sigma all focus on analyzing root causes before implementing countermeasures. In PDCA, Shewhart and Deming promote analyzing before the plan step. Otherwise, they would have wasted doing, checking, and acting on every single possible variable. One must remember that both of these people were well versed in experimentation that starts with defining the issue, stating a hypothesis, and then planning an experiment. If one knows the root causes, improvements are often self-evident.

Case Study of Sterilized Instrument Processing

I was working with a hospital that needed to reduce the time to process sterilized instruments. Sterilizing instruments is not something that you want to shortcut. Many departments struggle to keep up with demand, especially coming from surgeons with patients on the table in the operating room (OR). Several of the team members came into the project believing the solution was to hire more staff. The support of the executive team at this hospital was tremendous, and the team might have requested and gotten more staff if it were not for the manager and team members knowing they should analyze for the causes first.

Do not get me wrong here about the leadership. The leaders would have asked about the root causes because they were trained as champions (leaders trained how to support teams) and were aware of the Define, Measure, and Analyze Phases. They might have assumed the team validated a shortage of staff for the work to be done. Visible measures of the current state are required in the Measure Phase. Depending on the consequences if wrong on the root causes, Six Sigma team leaders trained in measuring capability can achieve this validation statistically. The leaders may have supported the request for more staff with confidence the team validated root causes, perhaps by measuring the amount of work required and the number of persons required.

The team came into the project with a clear definition of the work to be done, measured the current state, and then used the tools in the Analyze Phase to find the contributing factors to the issue. What they found using value stream mapping and spaghetti diagramming (see Figure 4.1) was a lot of wasted effort in the process, starting from the surgical rooms through sterilization. One spaghetti diagram showed the amount of walking required of the people who were to move dirty surgical instruments from the back hallway of the ORs to the sterilization department. Some of the measures showing the waste were

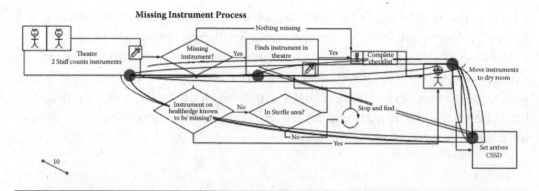

Figure 4.1   Spaghetti diagram of instrument flow. CCSD stands for the central sterilization services department.

100 meters walking around looking × 20 times each day × 300 working days annually = 600,000 meters annually

Time used = 140 seconds each trip = 14,000 minutes = 233 hours

233 hours × $32 an hour = $7,500 annually

A "Milk Run"

Like many multidepartmental projects, the team met their internal supplier or customer, walked through each other's processes, and discovered the wastes. Simply adding a regularly scheduled "milk run" solved most of the wasted walk time. A milk run is a TPS term for when employees make a circuit frequently enough to service customers along the route with supplies. This is a simple and effective method, just like that used by the milkman of earlier times, at least in my neighborhood. It is interesting how some services in this so-called service economy have diminished while the home delivery of groceries ordered via the Internet has replaced less-valued services.

Cross Reference of PDSA, Six Sigma, Lean, Change Leadership

Figure 4.2 may help cross reference PDSA, PDCA, Six Sigma, and Lean process improvement methodologies. I also include a band describing the change leadership methodology. The Roadmap for Performance Excellence™ also

Process Improvement Principles				Act / Plan / Study (Check) / Do	
PDSA Cycle with leading questions*	What are we trying to accomplish?	How will we know a change is an improvement?	What changes can we make that will result in an improvement?	What are the possible solutions and how do we implement the best solution?	How do we maintain the gains we have achieved and standardize?
Six Sigma	Define the work to be done	Measure the current state	Analyze for root causes	Improve and Design	Control to sustain the gains
Lean Principles	Specify what customers value	Identify all steps and inputs in the value stream	Eliminate waste and variation at the root cause	Stabilize, reduce variation and defects to create flow letting customers pull	Standardize, level flow sustain and continuously improve
Change Leadership	Prepare for Change -Train, Envision, Engage, Enable and Empower	Explore Together	Explain	Experiment, Explore, Build Consensus	Train, Enable, Empower, Hold Accountable, Celebrate

Figure 4.2 Process improvement principles. What are we trying to accomplish? How will we know a change is an improvement? What changes can we make that will result in an improvement?

has this information with more details on the tools. We share this roadmap in Appendix 1.

Human Factors and Ergonomics in Process Improvement

Human factors is a term describing how humans perceive a situation and react. Human Factors work often is cited regarding the airline industry, which has been studied often due to catastrophic accidents.

Ergonomics is closely related to Human Factors. Ergonomics is sometimes relegated to the physical and mental stress associated with work. Let us relate Change Leadership and Human Factors and Ergonomics with a story.

Case Study: Human Factors Added to Lean Six Sigma?

A nurse black belt trained in Six Sigma joined a collaboration I led with other hospitals to improve hand hygiene. She asked early in our first collaborations if we intended to use human factors in our work to improve hand hygiene. I quickly answered yes to her question and thought how odd to ask what seemed obvious. We know performance improvement in human-controlled activities versus automated processes always had to factor in the human element and our variation we add to a process. To others in the group trained by certain Six Sigma consultants, the question seemed reasonable and needed. We discovered that each other's definitions of Six Sigma or Lean or whatever recipe the other experts came in knowing varied regarding the degree of Human Factors in Change Leadership we learned and applied in performance improvement.

Hand Hygiene Change Leadership Issue

The 3Ms (measure, manage to the measure, make it easier) have not only worked in reducing the resistance to hand washing but also are vital to leading change when humans are key in the process. Here is why. Dr. W. Edwards Deming said:

> If I had to reduce my message for management to just a few words, I'd say it all had to do with reducing variation.

The best technical solution may fail due to variation in how people have different interpretations of the same issue. Understanding by all parties of the change leads to more effective change.

> If people know what each other knows, they may feel like each other feels, and they may do as each other does.

Dr. Semmelweis understood the issue of unclean hands but could not teach others the issue to understand the impact. Self-preservation is innate and still not enough of a motivation to understand the value of hand washing. There is something different about pediatric units. We often see hand hygiene practiced better on entering these units than entries into adult units. Maybe those entering have done a stakeholder analysis of those impacted?

Could it be that the chart that Dr. Semmelweis had showing clear correlation was not shared with all? Could it be it was a one-time presentation and was hidden by those who feared that this chart in the hands of others would result in humiliation of the surgeons with the hospital staff? There is no evidence that this measure was shared in the hospital.

We need to understand measures used in research and measures used in processes. They are similar but have important differences in purpose and use. This is covered in the chapter on managing to the measure.

Dr. Semmelweis's discovery is also considered a catalyst for Dr. Pasteur discovering the process of pasteurization, which itself has saved millions of lives worldwide. His discovery is linked with the microscope for discovery of what could not be seen that was killing mothers.

Failure to Engage Others with the Measure

Performance improvement needs change leadership. The 3Ms are the binding force that is necessary to achieve significant and sustained change. How will we know if improvement occurred without a measure? We do not know with whom Dr. Semmelweis and his superior and colleagues actually shared the measure. There is nothing in the film *That Mothers Might Live*[6] showing that he shared the measure with anyone. The film suggests he tried sharing the measure, but many failed even to open his correspondence. Sharing a measure is often not enough to change behaviors and improve a process. We must manage to the measures for the measures to have their impact with those who resist the measure. Regardless if managing to the measure failed in Dr. Semmelweis's work, we see winners managing to the measures every day.

Baseball and Managing to the Measure

Baseball is often regarded as one of the most measured sports. I had a young college intern join my staff one summer. His goal was to become a statistician because he loved the statistics in baseball. He loved the statistics so much he had entered thousands of statistics for fun and became very skilled in statistics for one so young. He had studied the pitch count and if there was a correlation with the pitch count and performance of the pitcher. Coaches and players count the number of pitches thrown, and this statistic is considered a key measure to manage changing to another pitcher.

The manager of the team will manage pitching changes when the pitch count is high and other factors suggest a pitcher may start varying. Note that here is that variation concern again. Some managers will make a change on pitch count alone. Loss of control may be felt a hazard with a pitcher nearing his or her pitch count threshold. Pitch count is especially important with young boys and girls to avoid potential injury.

As we see in baseball, measuring pitch count is one thing. However, managing to the measure is what is critical. Did Dr. Semmelweis and his superior manage to the measure? They had the measure, so what went wrong? Was it a one-time study, or did Semmelweis measure and display to the surgeons frequently? Was it all data from the past that he then "sprung" on his boss and colleagues, who may not have understood what the measure was telling Semmelweis? We do not know. What we all have experienced are people resisting our changes, saying things like, "Well, that is just one sample." "How do we know if tomorrow will show different results?" "You haven't proved anything."

Measures for Research Purposes

Data and measures for research result in statistics that describe a period in time. It is a "batch" versus flow of data. Measurement in research is often to test if there are differences between two or more groups. There is usually a probabilistic determination in research that requires knowing the sample size to estimate the confidence in the decision. Research is nothing about real-time analysis and early knowledge if a process is changing.

Measures for Process Improvement Purposes

Process improvement is about knowing if the process is in control and helping us make decisions about the process as it runs. Think of research data as a batch and process control data as a flow of data. Process control data continue to be gathered; thus process control sample size tends to be infinite.

Cedars-Sinai Using Measure and Manage to the Measure

Sharing data with people in the process is also necessary in process control, as is sharing as the process runs. A 20% increased improvement in one unit at Cedars-Sinai Hospital was achieved with the help of measuring and managing to the measure.[7] Make change easier with measuring and managing to the measure, and we can achieve amazing changes. Just one outcome is 95%

hand hygiene compliance that makes healthcare organizations safer, causes fewer healthcare-acquired infections or conditions (HAIs or HACs, respectively), and saves lives.

Key Points

■ Scientific methodologies include PDSA, PDCA, Six Sigma, Lean, and others.
■ Acronyms often shorten the steps describing the methodologies and help us remember the steps.
■ Change Leadership is critical in addition to the methodologies.
■ A step-by-step process improvement approach provides higher-quality improvements in less time.

Notes

1. James Womack, Daniel Jones, *The Machine that Changed the World*, HarperPerennial, 1991.
2. Ronald D. Snee and Roger W. Hoerl, *Leading Six Sigma*, Prentice Hall, Upper Saddle River, NJ, 2003, pp. 184–186.
3. Michael L. George, *Lean Six Sigma*, McGraw-Hill, New York, 2002, pp. xii, 127.
4. Jeffrey Liker, *The Toyota Way. 14 Management Principles from the World's Greatest Manufacturer*, McGraw-Hill, New York, 2004, pp. 135, 252–253.
5. IHI improvement model. http://www.ihi.org/knowledge/Pages/ HowtoImprove/ScienceofImprovementTestingChanges.aspx.
6. *That Mothers Might Live*, Warner Brothers Home Entertainment, Broadway Melody of 1938, Special Features.Directed by Fred Zinnemann.
7. With permission of Cedars–Sinai.

Chapter 5

Roadmap for Process Improvement

Introduction

The 3Ms (measure, manage to the measure, make it easier) are for everyone. Process improvement should be taught to everyone. Keeping it all straight, such as the steps in PDSA (plan-do-study-act), can be difficult, though. People who are part-time process improvement practitioners find it more difficult to remember the steps in process improvement because they do not get the repetition that a person who works full time in performance improvement gets. The third M is to make change easier. The best way I have found to make process improvement easier is to give a step-by-step plan. The Roadmap to Performance Excellence™ is a step-by-step plan. It is called a roadmap because it is much like a highway map. Its purpose is to make it easier to navigate to your destination—successful improvement and celebration with the team. We use the Roadmap for the balance of the book to keep you on the right path for process improvement. I also hope it prevents you from getting lost. See Figure 5.1 for the Roadmap. You can also see the roadmap on my Web site, http://www.rpmexec.com.

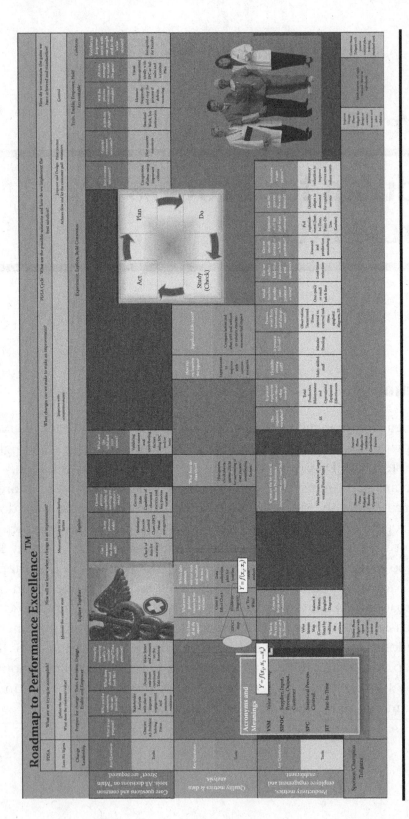

Figure 5.1   Roadmap to Performance Excellence.™

Start the Journey on Main Street

We start in the upper left corner of the Roadmap and follow the Change Leadership path in this book (see Figure 5.2). Notice that I have included the Lean Six Sigma path above the Change Leadership path. I also include the PDSA path with its leading questions. These are high-level paths that guide many teams well enough in process improvement. These are the steps to process improvement discussed previously, and one can see how the methodologies are similar and follow the same flow. For the purpose of this book, the upper paths provide enough granularity to know how to utilize the 3Ms for process improvement. I teach and use the more detailed areas in the lower part of the Roadmap for advanced skills. For those who need to know how the lower Roadmap paths work, I share a brief "how-to." This brief lesson will satisfy most of you who want to know how to use the Roadmap in its entirety.

	PDSA	What are we trying to accomplish?			
	Lean Six Sigma	Define the issue What does the customer value?			
	Change Leadership	Prepare for change - Train, Envision, Engage, Enable, and Empower			
Core questions and common tools. All decisions on "Main Street" are required.	Key Questions:	What is our purpose?	Who are the customers, who are involved?	What does demand look like?	Primarily improving quality or productivity? Data analysis potential
	Tools:	Charter/ A3 Problem-Solving Form	Stakeholder Analysis with plan to improve engagement and minimize resistance	Demand rate from customers. Takt time.	Main Street and Avenues on the Roadmap

Figure 5.2 Paths and streets.

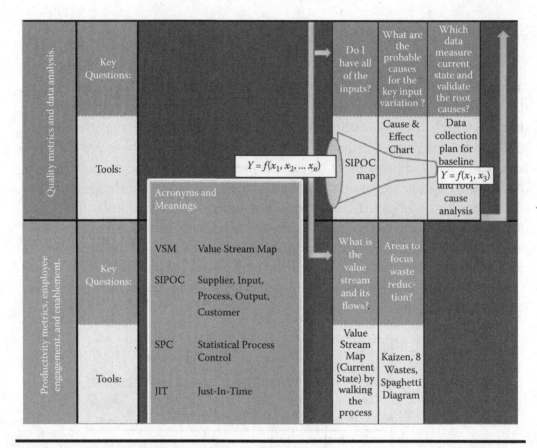

Figure 5.3 Quality and productivity streets.

Below the Change Leadership path is the more detailed part of the Roadmap that guides the team by posing questions to consider in process improvement. The Roadmap has three "streets," including Main Street, which holds the questions that are core to any process improvement and design effort. Depending on the measure and the issue, there are two other streets. The middle street holds the questions and tools for reliability, quality, and safety issues. The lower path adds value by guiding the team in possible questions that are important to answer to improve productivity and reduce waste and time (see Figure 5.3).

Let Us Start on Our Journey

We start with the Change Leadership path above Main Street. Every project should start with the step, "Prepare for change." Note, we purposely do not write "Preparing for *the* change." Process improvement leaders do not

Roadmap to Performance Excellence™

PDSA	What are we trying to accomplish?	How will we know when a change is an improvement?	PDSA Cycle - What are the possible solutions and how do we implement the best solution?	How do we maintain the gains we have achieved and standardize?
Lean Six Sigma	Define the issue What does the customer value?	Measure the current state	Measure /Analyze for	Improve and Design Achieve flow and let the customer pull	Control
Change Leadership	Prepare for change - Train, Envision, Engage, Enable, and Empower	Explore Together Explain	Experiment, Explore, Build Consensus	Train, Enable, Empower, Hold Accountable Celebrate

Figure 5.4   Change Leadership steps.

presume they know the change well enough at the beginning of the plan. Change Leaders know a change is needed and stay flexible to stakeholders, helping create the specific change needed. The 3Ms work in healthcare as in every other organization that uses them. See Figure 5.4 for the steps in Change Leadership.

At the top of the Roadmap, look for the Change Leadership Plan. By the way, the Roadmap is also an integrated training system to learn process improvement, and it is a management tool to support teams. This Roadmap is everything you need to navigate to performance excellence. We take each element in order. If you have heard that process improvement is not linear and thus more complicated than we think it is, keep an open mind. Like the best scientists, work to disprove your theory, versus working to reinforce it. I think you will find it quite linear.

Possible Shortcut

If you consider yourself a novice or want to take the full route so you do not "get lost" on the Roadmap, you might want to stay with me here. If you consider yourself fairly well trained in process improvement and change leadership with a well-trained executive team joining you in leading change, or if you are acting independently for now and have confidence in your skills, then consider taking the shortcut to the engage section. The shortcuts are shared as we progress. I know your time is valuable. See Figure 5.5 on preparing for change.

Prepare for Change

- Train the change leadership team
- Envision the desired future state
- Engage the stakeholders now, not later

Roadmap to Perform

	PDSA	What are we trying to accomplish?			
	Lean Six Sigma	Define the issue What does the customer value?			
	Change Leadership	Prepare for change - Train, Envision, Engage, Enable, and Empower			
Core questions and common tools. All decisions on "Main Street" are required.	Key Questions:	What is our purpose?	Who are the customers, who are involved?	What does demand look like?	Primarily improving quality or productivity? Data analysis potential
	Tools:	Charter/ A3 Problem-Solving Form	Stakeholder Analysis with plan to improve engagement and minimize resistance	Demand rate from customers. Takt time.	Main Street and Avenues on the Roadmap

Figure 5.5   Prepare for change.

- Enable the stakeholders and the change leadership team to contribute using the Roadmap to change, including coleading and even debating assumptions
- Empower the workforce, truly empower

Train

The training in this path refers to training the process improvement team in process improvement. Train is seen as a principle again on the Roadmap referring to training in the new changes. This training refers to training the people in the process in the changes and new ways. Just like change leadership benefits from a vision of the future, leading change benefits from knowing the vision of change leadership's elements. It is much more effective to have your performance improvement (PI) team trained in change leadership before you set out on the Roadmap.

Envision

Change Leaders and process improvement leaders create and share a vision of the future. Note we do not say a brighter future, for not all change promises that. In our tremendously ever-changing world, we have had, and will have, changes that set us back. Vision should be a powerful graphic that can move nations to a new state. What comes to mind right now for you? President Kennedy's speech in 1961 to Congress and the world that, "I believe that this nation should commit itself to achieving the goal, before this decade is out, of landing a man on the moon, and returning him safely to Earth."[1]

Many chief executive officers (CEOs) love to talk about vision. Maybe your CEO's recent letter posted in the break room reads something like, "Our hospital will be in the top percentile in patient satisfaction by the end of the year." How about your vision as a worker? How does a vision of a better future strike you? What about envisioning that dream traveling through Europe?

Articulating a Vision

You, the leader, see a current state that does not meet your expectations. I am sorry for the lack of bravado here. One might be expecting a grandiose statement to launch this lesson in articulating a vision. My reason to stay somewhat scientific is to share that creating a vision can be as much science as art and bravado. In fact, starting your vision statement with unbiased eyes will help you lead others to the change. Most likely, the majority of the targets of the change, those your vision will surely affect, may not initially share your view and emotion for the need to change. Taking a more scientific approach now will allow your words with emotion to be created for the ears of the targets and the emotions to build to a crescendo at the right time. The best vision shared before the targets are ready to accept your "vision" will be wasted.

Therefore, develop your vision statement to speak to your stakeholders at their current level of understanding, not yours. In fact, a vision statement should be in the present versus the future, as seen in the elements discussed next.

Elements in a Vision Statement

- Positivity: Safety versus risk; health instead of sickness; satisfied instead of complaining.
- Present tense: "Our patients are ... ," "Employees experience ... ," "Stakeholders receive ... ."

■ Succinctness: "Our patients receive safe and affordable care."
■ Challenge: "Our patients receive the safest care free for life."
■ Relevance to stakeholders: "Our patients receive the safest care free for life through achieving the most reliable value stream of care."[2]

What is the probability of achieving the vision? First, the vision may be years away from realization. Progress is therefore important. In *The Progress Principle*,[3] the authors state that people in your organization need to see progress to have any chance of staying engaged and committed. There is nothing like collecting some data to estimate the probability of your success. Note that my questions to you come in order. It is much easier to collect data on a change with a well-crafted vision statement. Try your vision statement with stakeholders.

Include stakeholders who will be important to engage and stakeholders who are targets of the change. Try it with those who will most resist, although "spilling the beans" can backfire at this stage in your Change Leadership, so choose these representative voices carefully. Confidentiality is nice to ask for, but keeping secrets is often not an attribute of others, especially if your change is considered highly desired or you expect heavy resistance. Many will desire to share your vision and what may be coming. This early communication to others makes managing the change process difficult.

Try Out Your Vision Statement

Once you had selected your sample to try your vision, what did you find? Did they offer feedback indicating and understanding of your vision? Alternatively, did your vision statement confuse them? If confusing, what words created the confusion? A good trick to check their understanding is to ask them to paraphrase. You might find using their words may improve your vision statement. This is another benefit of trying out your vision statement early in process improvement.

How did they react to your vision? Did those you expected to welcome the change glow and vow to commit with you in reaching the vision? Were they even more positive than you hoped? Alternatively, did it fail to ignite any emotion or commitment? This will be a hard vision to achieve and makes for a difficult change process.

Did those you expected to resist, resist less? More? The same technique of asking them to paraphrase often identifies confusion, which may fortunately be the major contributor to resistance. Remember, if others know what I know, they may feel the way I feel and will do as I do.

If their resistance comes not from misunderstanding of your vision but from other reasons, the two most likely reasons are fear and political resistance. Change leaders have techniques to address both types of resistance. Do not worry at this point. Use these early data to know the reasons for resistance, and we will address tactics to minimize resistance.

How Does One Communicate the Vision?

Assuming that the small sample that you tried the vision statement on has not completely communicated the change, now we discuss tips on how to share. The first rule is to share the vision in person versus remotely. Unless we are the world's best vision statement writers, most of us do not get it perfect the first time. Our ability to read audiences tells us how our vision is being understood, and we adjust accordingly. We get feedback and fine-tune our communications, improving understanding and perhaps actually adjusting our vision with new knowledge from our stakeholders.

Campaigns are vital to communications. The management portion of change now bears fruit. As we confirm our vision's value, we begin to develop others' ability to share the vision. Planning, organizing, staffing, directing, and controlling these "disciples" allow us to communicate the vision exponentially and engage stakeholders. Yes, that is what is meant by sharing a vision and engaging.

Abraham Lincoln's Vision

Abraham Lincoln's principles included having a vision. Lincoln would consistently govern by his vision statement. Vision statements were to be taken seriously and not just a media relations tactic. His principle is to advocate a vision and continually reaffirm it.

Advocate a Vision and Continually Reaffirm It

Let us share a true story of a great change leader and how he envisioned a better future, his actual vision statement, and how he communicated the vision and engaged his organization and other stakeholders.

Preserving the Union was Lincoln's vision and mission. Abolishing slavery was also Lincoln's vision but preserving the Union was most important. Although abolishing slavery was not his entire platform as he ran for the U.S. presidency, it was what differentiated his 1860 campaign. Lincoln's vision was more precisely first to abolish slavery's expansion. He thought that trying to get the nation to change to a slave-free America in one step would meet with too much resistance. His vision is found in the Emancipation Proclamation. This historic speech and document were shared later in his presidency after a series of events and time. See Appendix 3.

A few weeks before signing the proclamation, he wrote a letter in response to an editorial by Horace Greeley of the *New York Tribune*, who had urged complete abolition.[4] Lincoln writes:

> My paramount object in this struggle is to save the Union, and is not either to save or to destroy slavery. If I could save the Union without freeing any slave I would do it, and if I could save it by freeing all the slaves I would do it; and if I could save it by freeing some and leaving others alone I would also do that. What I do about slavery, and the colored race, I do because I believe it helps to save the Union; and what I forbear, I forbear because I do not believe it would help to save the Union. I shall do less whenever I shall believe what I am doing hurts the cause, and I shall do more whenever I shall believe doing more will help the cause. I shall try to correct errors when shown to be errors; and I shall adopt new views so fast as they shall appear to be true views.

For Whom the Bell Tolls

What are the pitfalls to sharing a vision and people starting to "march" to the vision? Ernest Hemingway's book *For Whom the Bell Tolls* shares a vision of a military leader taking a bridge in battle.[5] It remains unclear if all the effort to destroy the bridge made an impact on the final outcome of the Spanish Civil War. Many lives were lost, and many resources were expended. How do we ensure the vision is worthwhile? How do we know this vision is for a positive change? I suggest we all spend time creating our vision because many changes affect many people. Make sure that the vision is understood.

What will help you achieve your vision and that of your company? What differentiates achieving the vision from those other visions that never were achieved? Were there milestones along the way that were well laid out and achieved? Did you support achieving your vision with some measure if you reached it? Maybe you had goals with dates to achieve? Did you actually measure progress along the way? Did you have early warning that you needed assistance when the measures showed risk of achieving the milestones?

For the first time, perhaps, you now have a scientific approach to leading change by starting with the vision statement. The next step is to engage others.

Engage

Envisioning a better future while not engaging the entire organization, its patients, suppliers, and community is destined to fail. An Accountable Care Organization (ACO) in healthcare is a concept to improve care and reduce costs. It is essentially to reinforce healthcare organizations to work together to improve the process of care. For example, readmissions to a hospital may occur for reasons outside the hospital. The patient may be transferred back to a Skilled Nursing Facility after a hospital stay only to become sick again because the facility is unaware of special dietary needs. An ACO is intended to engage stakeholders in a way seldom seen in the history of healthcare.

Engaging stakeholders in the vision is part of the envision step. Despite recent press that the U.S. president killed Public Enemy number 1, it took a team of people joining in this vision to remove this menace. President Kennedy's vision of getting a man on the moon before the decade was out is one of the more famous visions. The nation also achieved it. Change Leaders also receive plenty of help if they are wise. Do not be so tough on yourself. Kennedy had NASA and thousands of others. Process improvement and creating a vision statement are not meant to be tried alone the first time. Coaches should be provided. This is a part of enable, the next step.

Enable

Providing resources to the team to proceed in process improvement is the next step. Have you ever been given an assignment without the tools or resources to carry it out? Once the team has been engaged, it is critical to give them time to work on the improvement process, to explore, to train others in new ways, and to control the process for long-term gain. It is cruel not to enable team members. Why would anyone train people in process improvement but give them no time to actually work together to improve a process?

Quality Circles

In 1980, Quality Circles were gaining popularity in America after a successful start in Japan.[6] The one thing most companies got correct was to give them an hour a week, or so, to train and apply the learning. I cannot count the number of times I hear from organizations both at the leadership level and at the frontline level that their programs are struggling. They train, they have projects to work on, and they get nowhere. Well, enabling them to work is a good start. I know that the pressures are tremendous, and margins are low to nonexistent. I share a story of one of my first managers and what he did in the same, if not more difficult, situation.

Enabling during the Recession of the Early 1980s

I was a first-line supervisor in one of the largest plants in the company. I was also the least-senior management person in this site of over 600 people. The recession hurt our business deeply, and people were being laid off in droves. The plant manager came up one day and said he had an idea. He started with what I expected him to say, "Rick, we are shutting down your department for lack of work." Oh no, I thought. Just out of school and now out of work. However, his vision of the future was different from mine. He envisioned a much leaner and higher-quality facility when the economy recovered. His idea was to train me and a few other supervisors in process improvement. They also had no one to supervise. Although I was hired to improve processes, I was never trained specifically in process improvement.

The next week started with learning industrial engineering that enabled us to spend our time working on the biggest issues. The plant manager's strategy paid off. When the economy returned, the teamwork, solutions, and improvements paid off handsomely. None if this would have occurred without being enabled.

Quality Circle training also taught employees how to work together in teams. It is not natural for many to engage others in process improvement. I have too often seen people with great pride in their training also feel that it is their responsibility to improve processes alone. After all, they are the ones trained by the university. In getting these people trained in team process improvement, we found we also needed to train them how to enable others to find truth and allow debate. We needed to enable team members to participate knowing that assumptions and decisions are part of the process.

Assumptions and Decisions

Debating assumptions is what good teams do, not debating decisions. This is a good time to train your team in

- Assumptions
- Truth
- Consensus
- Decisions

Assumptions facilitate getting us to truth. Another term for assumptions could be hypotheses not tested. Assuming is what we do when we do not know. Assuming is a short-term condition that must be respected for what it does for us in change leadership and what it does not do. Assuming looming danger walking down a dark street in an unknown area may be the reason you are here today reading this book. So often, we have to assume because we cannot be sure of everything and devote the time to validate. In process improvement, we make assumptions and then explore those assumptions to find truth or different assumptions. Truth is what we have validated to occur. For Descartes followers who want to debate the truth that we even really exist, please relax those mind muscles or go off to another book. Change leadership is not for you, yet.

Consensus is what we achieve after making assumptions and before decisions. We work to turn assumptions into truth and then all commit to the findings. Consensus is critical in change leadership because it is the glue that holds the change process together and ultimately sustains the change. It may be easier to define consensus by what it is not. It is not everyone in agreement. One may still have different assumptions from the team and question if the assumption or decision is the best, but for the sake of progress, everyone commits to the decision and actions. Think of this situation as team members agreeing to move forward together in the same direction, never in different directions. A good technique in gaining consensus when there are team members in disagreement with an assumption is to promise to continue listening. Use the exploration with the countering assumptions in mind. Setting up formal reviews periodically shows respect for everyone's opinions and assumptions.

A decision is the choice of direction when multiple choices exist. Direction is based on assumptions proven either to be truth or still to be determined with consensus reached. Decisions are progress. The Progress Principle described in HBR's May issue supports that change is facilitated by teams achieving progress frequently. The breakthroughs are nice to have, but a small amount of progress keeps the change progress alive.

Empower

Empowerment entrusts decision making with others and includes sharing of responsibilities with those being empowered. Peter Garber, in his book *Managing by Remote Control,*[2] shares that empowerment enables everyone to make greater contributions to the organization and to reach his or her highest potential. Empowerment also includes the one who empowers others to set boundaries. These boundaries make it safer for both parties and clarifies the empowerment.

The boundaries can expand as you and the team mature. If you are not a good communicator and confuse your team, you may very well be concerned about some of the team's decisions as they near what you perceive to be the limits of their skills and your uncommunicated boundary. It takes skill and trust to set boundaries but set them and communicate them clearly. Soon, relaxing boundaries will be a sign of your maturity and your team's success. Everyone wins, but start with boundaries. We have completed the first step in the Change Leadership path. Next, we will drop down to Main Street for the mandatory questions to answer in process design or process improvement.

Key Points

- The Roadmap makes process improvement easier by giving us a step-by-step route.
- The paths in the upper area of the Roadmap may be all that are needed to guide the team. More details are in the lower section of the map.
- Preparing for change is the first step on our route to process improvement.
- This step includes Train, Envision, Engage, Enable, and Empower.

Notes

1. Adapted from sources including Dream Achievers Academy, www.dream-achieversacademy.com/five-elements/
2. Peter Garber, *Managing by Remote Control. How to More Effectively Manage People and Resources When You Can't Always Be There*, CRC Press, Boca Raton, FL, 1999. history.nasa.gov/sp–350/ch–2–1.html
3. Teresa M. Amabile and Steven J. Kramer, *The Progress Principle: Using Small Wins to Ignite Joy, Engagement, and Creativity at Work*, Harvard Business Press, Cambridge, MA, August 9, 2011.
4. Donald T. Phillips, *Lincoln on Leadership. Executive Strategies for Tough Times*, Hachette Book Group, New York, 2009.
5. Ernest Hemingway, *For Whom the Bell Tolls*, Scribner, 1950.
6. Don Dewar, *The Quality Circle Handbook*, Quality Circle Institute, Chico, CA, 1980.

Chapter 6

Chartering the Process Improvement Work

The Charter

The first question in process improvement is, What is our purpose? In PDSA (plan-do-study-act), the question is the same, What are we trying to accomplish? The tool now presented answers the questions best and avoids the danger of missing any key element. Chartering work is actually the most important skill in process improvement and design. Chartering is the act of defining the work to be done. I walk you through the chartering process using a charter template provided to you in Appendix 4. Again, I want to make process improvement as easy for you as possible and provide several templates that I have used in launching Performance Excellence initiatives for global companies.

Feel free to think of an issue now that you would like to lead a change to improve. This will make chartering easier to understand. After the instruction, I also include an exercise with a completed charter.

> There have been many authorities who have asserted that the basis of science lies in counting or measuring, i.e. in the use of mathematics. Neither counting nor measuring can however be the most fundamental processes in our study of the material universe—before you can do either to any purpose you must first select what you propose to count or measure, which presupposes a classification. (Roy Albert Crowson)[1]

What to measure is often difficult to determine. I spent a winter in the middle of nowhere Wisconsin because what I thought was being measured is not what my client thought was being measured. This also taught me a lesson on managing to the measure and specifically managing to the measure in real time. If I had shared what I was measuring more frequently with the sponsor, I would have been able to move on to a much more interesting assignment—Puerto Rico, turning a failing site around, with a beachfront cottage at my disposal. Because I did not have consensus on what to measure, I had to stick around in snow and cold, staying at a Holiday Inn Express off a noisy two-lane highway. Process improvement teams—I hope you learn from my mistakes.

As I learned in Wisconsin, sometimes what to measure is a decision of multiple stakeholders who are not necessarily in agreement. Resistance to change was more than our company could handle due to confusion regarding what should be measured. Hindsight being 20-20, I should have not gone until I had the measurement in writing and signed off by the sponsors. It is clear our team did not have the measurement right for the person who turned out to be the key stakeholder.

Be assured that if you followed the steps in this book, the story that follows would have had a happier ending. This is a story of what can happen when people do not follow the process improvement steps—in order.

No Charter? Big Problem

A long time ago, I received a call from our headquarters asking if I could do a perioperative assessment for my fellow project executives. Right away, warning bells should have gone off in my head. There were three leaders? Usually, we have one person in charge.

Two project executives called my colleague and me. The purpose of the call was to share the purpose of our work at the client. The third project executive was not available at our first meetings, until the meeting right before our visit. As it turns out, I did not know everything that happened before my involvement. The measurements shared by our colleagues were common to assessments, and this was a relatively simple project. We were to observe procedures and record the reasons and times when surgical staff had to leave the operating room (OR), paying special attention to events when the case was delayed. We agreed that the deliverables would be

- The count of occurrences when the staff had to leave the OR once the procedure was started
- The time away
- The reason for needing to leave
- The amount of time the case was delayed

The scope was to include only the time during the actual case. The time between cases was not in the scope. We can do this type of assessment plus observe other activities, which the project executives thought would be useful, but we were to stick to the intraoperative time only. This concerned me because typically the clients need to understand what happens between cases that might give a clue regarding why someone would have to leave the room. There are failures that can occur between cases that will increase the occurrences of staff needing to leave the OR. I asked our team to confirm this study was to include only the time between the patient arriving at the OR and the patient leaving the OR. We come back to this in the following paragraphs.

If the turnaround and setup of the OR for the next case are not done well, retrieving forgotten supplies can create a revolving door to the OR during a case. Besides wasting time and delaying the case, possibly there is evidence that improper entries and exits may contribute to surgical site infections. Therefore, I suggested we stay between cases to observe any variation and deficiency in the turnaround. My colleagues agreed but stated the client wanted us only to observe intraoperatively.

We thought we had a good definition of the issue, measurements, and scope. We knew there was some risk because we never spoke directly with the client. We had nothing from the client confirming the measurements, and we had multiple project executives on this assessment. My strategy is always to meet with the sponsors on arrival, especially when we have no signed charter with metrics.

The two sponsors were the director of the OR and a surgeon. These sponsors were not available by phone prior to the visit, but we were told and did receive an e-mail from the director stating that he would arrange for us to be greeted by his scheduling manager.

We also did not get a stakeholder analysis (SHA). I teach you this important tool after you learn about chartering. (But you know that because it is the next step on the Roadmap.) So, I drafted an SHA based on what I heard. Our strategy was to introduce ourselves after arriving and before starting. We find it is best to confirm the purpose of the study and the measurements we would deliver at the end of the study.

We arrived at the site and were graciously met by the director's assistant, who was also the scheduling manager. I offered to meet with the sponsors, but the assistant said they were tied up. She would leave them a note. The scheduling manager confirmed we were to watch the intraoperative processes, so we went to put on scrubs and observe. She had us scheduled so that there was little chance to observe turnarounds. I volunteered to step out when the sponsors had a minute to chat about the week ahead and make sure we met their expectations.

Despite asking for a meeting as soon as we arrived, before the trip, and daily offerings to meet with the sponsors when I arrived, I could not get an audience with the sponsors until four days later. I did get a minute or two with the surgeon sponsor. I watched his case thanks to the director's assistant knowing I wanted to ensure we were on the right track.

Sharing Findings before Departing

I shared with the surgeon our preliminary findings, and he confirmed that was what they wanted. He also asked me to validate the reasons reported for delayed case starts. This was a new request because this supported us also observing turnarounds of ORs. As in so many failures, there are data in the process that show something is not quite right. After receiving the surgeon's request, I immediately left the OR to find the other sponsors to offer to do this in addition to the original metrics. This is something we do often, and there are usually data to help me help the client, so I asked the director via e-mail to share the data on delays. I got no response after two requests. I was a bit concerned now that we may be viewed as ignoring this new request from the sponsoring surgeon. So, I let my colleagues know I could do this, but the director had not responded to indicate that he received my request for data.

On Friday morning, five days later, I met with the scheduling manager and another surgical safety manager to discuss the week. I still had not had the chance to meet with the other sponsor, so I took this opportunity to confirm with his "right-hand person" what we did and when our report would be received. I showed them the preliminary report with the measures that we had. They remarked this was exactly what they wanted and seemed very pleased. The director's assistant seemed especially delighted in the findings because they confirmed what she thought was happening. We know there is usually someone in the client's organization who has an understanding of many of the issues and answers, but the person struggles to find a way of getting others to listen and act.

Clear Definition of the Issue and What Was to Be Measured Are Key

This story has several benefits for learning process improvement. One, the obvious one, is that a clear definition of the issue and measurements should be confirmed. Second, process improvement leaders who excel are ones who seek those who already have a good understanding and may just not have been able to share. In a top-down culture for decision making, these people surround the change leader if the leader can draw them out, that is, if they have not already left the organization due to frustration. The scheduling manager was one of those stars. Sadly, she remarked twice during the week when I showed up that I was there to fire her. My colleague and I shared notes Thursday night on how we were going to compile the observations. My colleague had previously shared a well-laid-out form with the measurements clearly detailed. We agreed to enter our observations into this report.

The week ended with observing the last case on Friday. I returned to the scheduling manager's office to bid adieu and was told that she had left for the day. I headed off to the airport feeling good about what my colleague and I had observed and recorded.

My colleague and I received a call from the project executive that the client wanted a preliminary report. On review and some editing of the report, the project executive said she had what she needed. After she met with the client to share the preliminary report, the client wanted some tweaks made before the final report. We thought this was promising confirmation that our work met their needs. We made the tweaks, which included adding some turnaround information (as we expected), and prepared to share the final report. The final report had a title slide, the purpose and objectives, and on the third slide, the answer to all measures. The balance of the report contained facts and analysis supporting the findings and offering suggestions.

The Final Report and Surprise

The final report was done with the project executives at the client's site and with my colleague and I joining by teleconference. The plan was for us to cover the first three slides succinctly, share some of the turnaround information requested after the preliminary call, and then open it up to questions. I expected the director and perhaps the surgeon to be leading the call. Surprisingly, a director we had not known to be a sponsor described herself as the client and asked us to begin.

A process improvement leader's bad day was starting to unfold. The newly introduced sponsor did not let us finish the first slide before she said we were focused on the wrong issue. She said some of our findings were taken out of context, despite the fact that we had not yet even covered our findings during this call.

I share this story because it has so many lessons in it, and I want you to avoid this at all cost. Peter Block, in his book *Flawless Consulting*, states there are four steps to achieving a strong consulting agreement.[2] We never got to the third step, which is what the client needs to do. All the client had to do was spend two minutes looking at the measurements we were collecting. Hindsight is 20/20. Being clear about roles and responsibilities was another responsibility.

A process improvement leader ensures in the chartering process, and in preparing people for change, that the sponsor is known. One last lesson is that we touched a nerve with the client who fielded the final report. Our report mentioned an observation that the nurses were complaining about how much time they were spending reading bar codes to manage inventories and to charge customers. For implants, they had to enter the same information in up to four different places. We found out that this client was the sponsor of the system that required the nurses to enter the data. Should we have known this and adjusted our report? I guess if we knew both this information and that she, alone, was the deciding client sponsor, then maybe we should have. Ah, such are the joys of leading change.

In summary, obtain confirmation that your measures are customer centric. It is that simple. Figure 6.1 shows a better way to ensure success. We want to make this so easy for you that we include a charter. All of the templates in this book may also be downloaded at http://www.rpmexec.com.

The Charter Template

The Issue Statement

This work is clearly defined by stating the issue, the customer, the process to be changed, the product or service the process delivers, and what a

Charter Title:			Role	Responsibility
1. Issue Statement Elements	Business Case:		Executive Sponsor:	Senior level manager who selects Work. Has authority to solve cross-functional issues.
a. Customer name:				
b. Characteristic to improve:			Signature	
c. Process name(s):			Champion:	Leader who owns the process and manages staff. Prime responsibility with Project Leader for success.
2. Product/Unit: *Name of what is produced in the process*			Signature	
			Clinical Leader	Decision-maker for clinical issues
			Signature	
3. Defect: *How we sense a failure in the product or service*			Process Owner(s):	Responsible for the design, continuous improvement and sustaining the process.
4. Metric(s) to Improve — Current Baseline — Goal (S.M.A.R.T.) — Date to Achieve			Signature(s)	
			Project Leader:	Leads the team and execution of the methodology. Shares prime responsibility with Champion for success.
			Signature	
5. Financial Impact Metrics: — Type of Impact — Traceable — Non-Traceable			Mentor/Coach	Coaches and mentors sponsor, champion and project leader in their roles
$ Annualized Amount			Signature	
6. Scope: Process Begins and Ends when.... — 7. Scope: What must be included or excluded is...			Team Members	Key contributor to Work. Participates with Project Leader in methodology and responsible for success.
			Core Member	
			Core Member	
			Core Member	
			Core Member	
			Core Member	
			Core Member	
High Level Project Plan: Rick Morrow			Core Member	

Phase	Planned Start Date	Planned End Date	Actual Start Date	Actual End Date	
Define/Charter signed					
Measure/Baseline obtained					
Analyze/Root Cause validated					Subject Matter Expert
Improve/Improvement piloted					Subject Matter Expert
Control/Sustainability plan					Subject Matter Expert
					Author name:

Figure 6.1 The charter template.

defect is in the product. If the work is to design something new, the defect is the gap in what the design is to fill. Once the defect is known, determining metrics is much easier.

The Measures or Metrics

Always start with a customer-centric metric and ensure the metric is relevant to the defect. For instance, if the issue is to reduce the delays in surgery, then a metric should measure the delays. As we detailed in the story of the assessment of the OR delays, the charter would have prevented any confusion.

Outcome and Process Measures

The measures or metrics might include both an outcome metric, such as the count of delays, and a metric of the inputs. One input we usually include in these studies is the service level or percentage of time an item is available. There is a correlation between lack of stock and having delays in surgery. Remember that in leading change to different outcomes, we benefit from measuring inputs. In achieving higher reliability in healthcare, measuring and managing the inputs is most important before their variation results in an unfavorable outcome.

Goals

The amount of change desired is detailed by filling in the goal statement. It may help to set the goal if we know where we start. A baseline performance level in each metric "grounds" us in reality. In healthcare, we often do not have a measurement system, or one that we trust, so often baselines are determined later in the work. The goal is the amount of change we are hoping to achieve. The goal should be SMART:

- *S*pecific to the issue, product, and defect.
- *M*easurable.
- *A*ttainable: A change leader is cruel to expect a team to defy the laws of nature.
- *R*elevant to the customer.
- *T*ime bound: We need a time when the goal should be reached.

Progressive Goals and Successive Successful Approximations

Progressive goals are often used and should be detailed in chartering. A change leader knows that, especially for difficult projects, setting SMART progressive goals to get to the ultimate goal is wise. Change is hard enough for many, and achieving successive successful approximations to the goal is rewarding and provides renewal. Successive approximation is a conditioning of people to progress in behaviors to achieve the desired final outcome. In other words, stop rewarding earlier successes while rewarding new successes.

Measures and Goals to Build a Safer Culture

In performance improvement, we might reward a staff member who brings up a concern about patient safety to a supervisor; our ultimate goal is for the staff member to feel safe enough to address the situation. When the person has gained confidence in speaking to a supervisor about an issue, we next begin to encourage the person to act on his or her own. We measure the quality of judgment to ensure the person is making the right decisions. Once the staff member begins to act on his or her own with good judgment and not rely on the supervisor to act, we cease rewarding the staff member for coming to the supervisor. It is important in change leadership not to reinforce moving in the wrong direction. This can set change back and gives the wrong impression that the change leader may be changing the vision when in fact the change leader is not. Again, honesty is the best policy always. If with new information the change leader decides to change the goal, then she should share it quickly with reasons. She should also show how it might affect the team and stakeholders.

The progress principle is a perfect term for leading change in complex work of long duration. The term was coined by Teresa Amabile and Steven Kramer in a *Harvard Business Review* article. They find that, "Of all the things that can boost inner work life, the most important is making progress in meaningful work."[4] Is this a change leader's motto, maybe?

Hold Off on Financial Metrics Until …

It is important to note that we do not mention financial metrics before we mention outcome and input metrics or process metrics. Often, the process improvement team and sponsor are interested in financial impact. However, financial impact is *always* a function of changing a nonfinancial metric. Unless you actually make money, which only governments do, making money is a bit of a misnomer. We "make money" by changing revenue or costs in healthcare or any business. Thus, we list metrics that change revenue and cost and then list financial metrics calculated from changing process or input metrics.

Reducing inventory is an example of how an improved process measure will result in an improved financial measure. We may want to reduce the amount of money we have in inventory. There is nothing inherently wrong with that because all inventories are waste. We help healthcare organizations reduce inventory just about every week. Inventory is a result of a process that is not flexible enough to provide a supply just when the customer needs it, and healthcare has few suppliers that are on site, as in some industries. Consigned inventory, which is actually inventory owned by the supplier until used by the healthcare organization, is still waste and also should be reduced. It is naïve to think suppliers do not try to capture the money they have tied up in consigned inventory at your site. Lean practices drive both supplier and customer to reduce inventory. Reducing the amount of money we have in inventory frees up money to spend on providing healthcare. To reduce inventory dollars, using U.S. currency, we have to reduce a nonfinancial metric. This could be by reducing the quantity, the price, or both. We work to change one of these variables and then "dollarize" the impact. If the item costs $1 and we reduce 1,000 items, then we reduced inventory by $1,000. We did not directly reduce it by $1,000. We had to change one or more of the other variables.

Scope the Work

After detailing the metrics, we need to scope the work. Will this be a change that spans the entire health system or just one unit in one building? The question of scope is split into two areas:

- Defining the start and stop of the process to be changed
- Defining what is in scope and out of scope, which helps create bounds for the work and is consistent with the progress principle

A process improvement scoping strategy is often used to achieve the change in one area, say a pilot or test area, and then replicate the work to achieve the change across the entire organization.

Charter "Signatories"

The next feature in chartering is listing the sponsors, champion, process owners, leader, coach, team members, subject matter experts (SMEs), and others, such as a process expert or clinical leader when it comes to healthcare. This tool would have saved the day in so many projects.

Sponsor

The sponsor's role in change is as the ultimate decision maker. The sponsor's name goes at the top due to the importance of this role. We list other stakeholders on the charter, including the process owner and perhaps the clinical leader. All of these roles could be filled by one person or others. The charter is actually the first tool followed by the stakeholder analyst (SHA). We lead with the SHA only when we are not clear who the sponsor is. Once the sponsor is found and the work clearly defined using the information detailed in the charter, we are now ready to perform the SHA in a better manner. Until we know the details, including the process, the product, the defect, and the scope, we cannot be confident we have the correct stakeholders.

Chartering Is Iterative

The chartering process is iterative.[5] We may think our first time through the charter that we have a clear definition of the issue and consensus. We then speak with the customer about the metric, and the customer does not agree that the metric describes the change needed. Once we get the metric to be customer centric and have the customer's approval, we return to the defect and other issue elements and correct them. Do not be frustrated, especially if you are drafting a charter without the customer with you and you do not get it right the first time. The document drives the dialogue between team, customer, and sponsor to ensure in the end there is a clear understanding of the change, amount of change needed, and most important, consensus. The completed charter is shown in Figure 6.2.

A tip I have for you is to have the charter template "in your back pocket" at all times, maybe on your smartphone as an app, in your purse, or by memorizing the essential elements. I do not know how many times someone has started rattling off a great idea, and I want to capture the issue clearly. Writing down what someone is describing, especially when that someone is the chief executive officer (CEO), shows respect for the person's idea and can speed the process improvement. Being clear right from the start may get you to that warm beach in the winter.

Charter Title:	Increase Patient Capability to Follow Discharge Instructions		Role	Responsibility
1. Issue Statement Elements a. Customer name:	Patients	Business Case: Patient surveys show a lower level of satisfaction than our competitors. Our reimbursement will be affected if we don't meet threshold levels.	Executive Sponsor:	Senior level manager who selects Work. Has authority to solve cross-functional issues.
b. Characteristic to improve:	Information shared by nurse to patient or advocate		*Signature*	**Wendy Sitty**
c. Process name(s):	Discharge		Champion:	Leader who owns the process and manages staff. Prime responsibility with Project Leader for success.
2. Product/Unit: *Name of what is produced in the process*	Information and instructions on safe care and possible changes to be aware of.		*Signature*	**Freddie Silver**
			Clinical Leader	Decision-maker for clinical issues
			Signature	**Dr. Welby**
3. Defect: *How we sense a failure in the product or service*	Patient or advocate confused about instructions.		Process Owner(s):	Responsible for the design, continuous improvement and sustaining the process.

4. Metric(s) to Improve	Current Baseline	Goal (S.M.A.R.T.)	Date to Achieve	*Signature(s)*	**Elway Pode**
Initial readback accuracy by patient of instructions given by nurse	22%	80%	90 days from project start	Project Leader:	Leads the team and execution of the methodology. Shares prime responsibility with Champion for success.
				Signature	**Adam**

5. Financial Impact Metrics:	Type of Impact	Traceable	Non-Traceable	Mentor/Coach	Coaches and mentors sponsor, champion and project leader in their roles
Readmissions due to instruction confusion	$ Annualized Amount	$36,000 per Readmission		*Signature*	**Janelle**

6. Scope: Process Begins and Ends when....	7. Scope: What must be included or excluded is...	Team Members	Key contributor to Work. Participates with Project Leader in methodology and responsible for success.
		Core Member	Jan
		Core Member	Layla
		Core Member	Mark
		Core Member	Mike
		Core Member	Brenda
		Core Member	
High Level Project Plan: Rick Morrow		Core Member	

Phase	Planned Start Date	Planned End Date	Actual Start Date	Actual End Date		
Define/Charter signed						
Measure/Baseline obtained						
Analyze/Root Cause validated					Subject Matter Expert	Jeff
Improve/Improvement piloted					Subject Matter Expert	Pat
Control/Sustainability plan					Subject Matter Expert	Donna
					Author name:	

Figure 6.2   A completed charter.

Sign the Charter

The signatories should literally sign the charter to show their personal commitment. It may give them pause to read the charter carefully and ensure the team has the issue, metrics, goals, and other fields correct.

A signed charter also enables the team by giving proof of the importance of the effort.

The charter template is in Appendix 4 and is ready to use in your process improvement. An electronic version is also available at http://www.rpmexec.com.

Key Points

- Chartering is the most important tool because it clearly defines the improvement needed.
- Chartering is often iterative. As you input fields, another field later in the charter may help you discover more clarity is needed for an earlier response.
- The signatories should literally sign off to show their personal commitment.
- A signed charter enables the team and tells all that this PI is important.

Practicing Skills: Chartering

Your healthcare organization is a good one, but your patients report being confused about instructions during the discharge process and when they return home. The patients call the nurses to clarify instructions often. A recent study by one nurse manager showed that only 22% of the time did patients read back to the nurse her instructions correctly. The impact financially of even one readmission is estimated by finance to be about $32,000, all things considered. Wendy, the chief nursing officer, is supportive of a team to improve the understanding of instructions given to the patient. Measuring understanding is tough, so she suggests considering the method that the nurse manager used. Freddie Silver, the unit manager, has volunteered to join Wendy in supporting this team. He is a real champion of change. Discharge instructions have a significant impact on patient safety, and we think Marcus, the physician leader, would be happy to answer any questions by speaking for the physicians. Dr. Welby can act as the nurse and physician leader. Mr. Elway P. Ode is the day shift manager; most of the discharges occur during the day shift. Confidentially, he just does not seem to want to change. We are glad that Freddie will support the team and help remove barriers that Elway may put up. Adam, our performance improvement leader, has agreed to lead the change on this one, and he will be supported by Janelle, our master black belt. (A master black belt is a highly skilled and experienced performance improvement leader.) The team includes the key stakeholders, including our patient representative. We will have a few subject matter experts who know all about handoffs and regulatory requirements.

Take the role of Adam and draft a charter based on the information to show your sponsor for eventual approval by all listed as signatories on the charter. A possible charter is on my Web site, http://www.rpmexec.com.

Notes

1. www.todayinsci.com, *Classification and Biology*, 2. Science quotes on: | Classification (46) | Mathematics (262), 1970.
2. Peter Block, *Flawless Consulting. A Guide to Getting Your Expertise Used*, Pfeiffer, New York, 1981.
3. B.F. Skinner et al., Differential reinforcement (shaping) response is gradually changed across successive trials towards a desired target behavior by rewarding exact segments of behavior. http://en.wikipedia.org/wiki/Shaping_(psychology).
4. Teresa M. Amabile and Steven J. Kramer, The power of small wins, *Harvard Business Review*, May 2011.
5. Peter Pande, Robert P. Neuman, and Roland R. Cavanagh, *The Six Sigma Way: How GE, Motorola, and Other Top Companies Are Honing Their Performance*, McGraw-Hill, New York, 2000, pp. 197–204.

Chapter 7

Stakeholder Analysis

Purpose of Stakeholder Analysis

I want you to learn process improvement in a very linear and methodical way to make it easier for you to apply the knowledge and obtain real results. I am teaching you the fundamentals just like a good coach teaches piano or a sport. In learning piano, a person is first taught where to place fingers on the keyboard and then practices scales. In basketball, a person learns how to dribble much earlier than how to hit a three pointer. In Change Leadership, one of the most critical fundamentals is stakeholder analysis (SHA). The purpose of doing the SHA is to reduce resistance to future changes. The SHA accomplishes this by first identifying stakeholders, who might not buy into the change, and a strategy to reduce the resistance.

Are you the advocate of the upcoming change and do you want to lead the change to a brighter future, with minimal resistance, and with faith that the change will be sustained? Do you fear change is coming to you? Have you just witnessed yet another close call by a surgeon, who was stopped just before cutting on the wrong finger? Are you picking up this book totally frustrated at having great solutions that no one seems to want to hear?

Case Study in Stakeholder Analysis

Stakeholders include the targets of the change. They are the ones for whom the change is intended. Here is a story of nurses in a dramatic change in the perioperative services of the largest private hospital in the United Kingdom, The Wellington. The Wellington's chief executive officer (CEO), Keith Hague, had a vision of a higher-quality healthcare organization for patients who would be more satisfied. He launched The Wellington Hospital on a transformational (A transformation includes a focus on leadership skills, cultural change, and process improvement skills for all.) journey in 2010. In less than 8 months, significant improvements were achieved in nearly every major service line within the hospital by engaging his executive team and through every organizational level. The patient-facing staff, including nurses, therapists, admissions staff, porters who transport patients, pharmacy staff, dietitians, housekeepers, and staff in the surgical instrument sterilization department, were the most engaged. Also included in the process improvement was the "front-of-house" staff, who are often the first point of contact as patients and family enter the hospital.

Key to this improvement was naming a dedicated champion, Chris James. Catherine Hanrahan, chief financial officer (CFO), chose Chris based on his high potential. Giving up one of her best for the role of process improvement was a big decision by Catherine, but she saw the value to the organization, its patients, and Chris. Chris is now participating on Mr. Hague's executive team based on his accomplishments. In addition, the CFO of HCA UK, Jim Petkas, now has Chris expanding his role to spread the engagement throughout all six HCA hospitals at their request.

One way to measure a transformation that is intended to change the culture is to measure the number of people engaged in the work. From a percentage of total staff, 100% of major departments and 30% of all Wellington staff have been engaged. Even better, many of the staff have participated in more than one major project or weeklong projects. At Princess Grace Hospital in London, a part of the HCA Group, Sheila Enright, chief nursing officer (CNO), and Stephen Maxwell, CFO, *Measure, Manage* to the measure, and *Make* it work with Healthcare Performance Partner's (HPP) Steve Taninecz as their coach. At least one major project has been accomplished monthly that has been chosen based on priorities to improve outcomes. To get this much done in just the first five months, Steve and Princess Grace's first champion measure and manage the inputs, including:

■ People development: One hundred and seven individuals have received process improvement training.

■ Engaging the people who do the work and managers: Sixty three have participated in the projects by applying their new skills.

■ Taking a value stream approach to reach out to multiple areas that all must work together to improve patient care and operations: Nursing, surgical services, and outpatient services have been most active; thus their patients and physicians are reaping the most benefit.

The Wellington Hospital and Princess Grace Hospital have also reached out to their other sister hospitals and engaged staff for projects. The momentum in process improvement is building for this HCA health system in an amazingly tough environment: private hospitals in an environment of free healthcare.

Stakeholders' intellect is a terrible thing to waste in leading change. Chris tells the story of brainstorming for solutions to speed the patient's journey in surgery. The Wellington has theaters (operating rooms, ORs) on several different floors and patient rooms on still other floors. The time to access an elevator and transport the patient to theaters and back can take a long time. The porters are people who transport the patients, with a nurse joining the patient and porter for safety. Three people, including the patient, often wait for the elevator and then wait as the elevator often stops at each floor. The patients are often embarrassed as the elevator stops, the doors open, and people enter. Brainstorming occurred on countermeasures to improve this situation. The first idea was to speed the elevator. That was not achievable, but it created an idea to provide lift keys to block stopping. Speed was achieved.

In the book *Reengineering Health Care* by Jim Champy and Harry Greenspun,[1] the authors claim that any dramatic reform in health care must be by clinicians. Not engaging stakeholders who are targets is destined for failure, I guess. The key point is that by engaging the people in the process they are much more respectful of the very "targets" of the change, and we find this results in speedier change. We have found that including others outside the process is also beneficial. Using a "fresh set of eyes" and the tool of asking "why five times" unlocks creativity and may result in solutions never thought possible. Therefore, engaging those individuals in the process is necessary. Engaging key stakeholders is necessary. Engaging interested parties is recommended.

Mission and Values of the Organization

Sharing the vision and engaging the troops are aided by stating the mission of the organization at this point in their change. Values should be developed with change leadership principles clearly stating the leadership's desire for positive change engaging all stakeholders. The leader is wise to share the stability that comes from a better future state. Competing and dysfunctional value statements make no sense in organizations that desire continuous improvement. A good test to ensure consistency of message, constancy of purpose, as Dr, W. Edwards Deming states, is to ask the organization how the values support positive change. Be prepared not to receive correct understanding the first time. Above all, do not avoid asking the question. Perception is reality. As we discuss the critical importance of measurement in leading change, let us share a key point now. Measure the change in perception as you start your change.

Stakeholders

Before we share what engagement in process improvement is and why it is important, you must understand the term *stakeholder*. A stakeholder is anyone who might be one of the following:

- Customer
- Supplier
- Process owner
- Decision maker in the change
- Interested party
- Target of the change

I include a SHA template in Appendix 5 and an electronic version at http://www.rpmexec.com (see Figure 7.1).

I arranged the form to guide us in the correct sequence for SHA. The SHA will improve the flow of the change by reducing resistance. In SHA, the form actually teaches us the fundamentals of SHA as we progress left to right.

Overview of the SHA

For the SHA, we start with the organization's name and enter it on the far left of the form shown in Figure 7.1. The organization's name is a

Stakeholder Analysis

Project					Stakeholder role					Contributor names:			
Date													
Organization/ Location/ Area	Name (or group name)	Role or Title	Customer of the process	Process owner	Decision-maker/ Approver	Target of the change	Interested party	Supplier to the process	Current level of buy-in to change. Rate 0 - 10 with 0 being no buy-in - heavy resistance	Needed level of buy-in to change. Rate 0 - 10 with 0 no buy-in needed	Gap	Strategy to close the gap
Scheduling department	Bobbie	Scheduler				x			6	10	(4)	
Scheduling department	Petra	Manager, Scheduling		x	x				5	5	-	
Scheduling department	Michael	Scheduler				x			9	10	(1)	
Scheduling department	Gemma	Scheduler				x			4	8	(4)	
Operations	Carrie	Director of Operations			x				10	10	-	
Clinic	Adam	VP, Clinic	x	x	x	x			7	10	(3)	
Clinic	Sophie	Nurse Manager	x						8	9	(1)	
Patient			x						9	9	-	
Physician offices		Physicians					x		4	10	(6)	
											-	
											-	
											-	
											-	
											-	
											-	
											-	
											-	
											-	
											-	
											-	

Figure 7.1 Stakeholder analysis template.

high-level description of a group of stakeholders. Next, we drill down further to a person's name or a subgroup of the organization. This level could be, and often is, the name of a person. The SHA is done confidentially with your team, and respect is tantamount. We list the roles the stakeholder has. A stakeholder may have multiple roles. An example of a person with one role is a person who owns the process but is not the primary decision maker for changes.

We then rate the stakeholder's expected level of buy-in to future changes on a scale from 0 to 10 with 0 being no buy-in; in other words, the stakeholder is expected to put up heavy resistance. The needed level of buy-in for a decision maker, or a target of the change, can be helpful in differentiating stakeholders who are important to buy-in to changes from those for whom buy-in as not as important. An example is if an interested party has low buy-in. The team feels the needed level of buy-in is rather insignificant relative to the decision maker in this change.

We do not share the SHA outside the team, usually due to its confidentiality, and need to be truthful concerning how much buy-in stakeholders may have.

Measuring the Gap: The Level of Resistance

Measuring the gap between the current level of buy-in and the needed level is a relative measure of the stakeholders who may resist the most. These stakeholders need to be led in the change, and the strategy is now listed to reduce their resistance. We will give strategies for each stakeholder. For now, let us create an SHA. We invite you then to do one for an upcoming change you are considering. Better yet, use the SHA with your team. We think you will find the SHA one of the most important and valuable tools in process improvement.

Highlight the one stakeholder you expect will have the largest resistance to the upcoming changes. Now, think about the differential between what you are thinking needs to be changed and how this person might feel. It is a good idea at this time to consider engaging the person and finding out exactly how he or she feels about the issue. Perhaps the person feels the same way as you; now that you both know what each other knows and find you feel the same way, you will both do something about it to improve. Yes, sometimes the differential is minimal, if not zero. Change Leadership's SHA pays off with strategies to reduce the resistance and gets change flowing. One strategy is to interview the potential resistors to seek how they feel and ensure they understand the chartered work.

Three Stakeholder Analysis Scenarios to Know Up Front for Your Strategy

More times than not, you will find change is not so easy for some stakeholders. Do not make this condition difficult for yourself. Understand up front in your process improvement effort that your discussion with stakeholders will take one of three courses:

■ You and the stakeholders might already share an understanding of the issue and find the stakeholders want change. Therefore, there is little to no resistance to change.

■ The stakeholder is not yet convinced there is an issue or as much of an issue as you believe. Resistance or apathy early and throughout the process improvement effort affects the leader's ability to lead change.

■ All have agreement about the issue but disagreement on the solution or method of finding a solution. Resistance to the change or the process of determining the change results.

My intention is to give you methods to process improvement and leading change for all three scenarios. I am confident you will be successful in process improvement and leading change if you apply what I share in the order I share it. The most important measure of any teacher is if the student learns. Please measure me on this ability as you read and practice the skills.

Designing the "Circuit" to Achieve Flow and Manage Resistance

By now, you should be gaining competence and confidence in distilling your vision, identifying stakeholders and analyzing their potential buy-in to change, identifying where the resistance may come from, and starting your strategies to reduce the resistance to create better flow of coming changes. In other words, you should be designing a "circuit" to manage the resistance for the flow of change you desire. You do not have to eliminate all resistance, but you have to manage it to a level that allows change to flow at the rate you wish.

If you want more practice with a measure of how well you do SHA, try the following scenario: Pick a change that someone who works with you will certainly resist. Both of you think out loud as you list stakeholders and their roles and as you rate their buy-in. Reaching agreement is a good measure of your ability to do SHA well. If you tend to disagree on who the stakeholders are, work to include more rather than less. It is better to list those who might have a stake than to miss stakeholders. You are doing well if you have consensus on who are the decision makers, customers, and process owners. Missing who might be interested is a minor issue. In judging the current level of buy-in and the needed level, the key measure is if the same stakeholders are identified as the ones with the largest gaps. These are the ones for whom strategies are needed to reduce resistance. The absolute numbers are not important in the buy-in columns because we all judge differently. Any areas that team members differ considerably in judging should use the lesson, "If we both know what each other knows, then … ."

Difficult to Be Perfect

A physician friend of mine described his first day of medical school. The instructing physician opened with how smart the person must be who has been accepted into his prestigious medical school. The students, though not infallible, will learn medicine and perform the best that can be expected. The professor, in his arrogance, added, "Who is our equal to question?" Who would embrace change if the person has been taught from day one that one will be as good as he or she can be and better than others? This is as good as can be.

The source of change is not always the person who leads the change. We will not always be the one leading the change, so we need to learn how to both lead and follow. We will learn how to lead and follow by starting with change leadership fundamentals—walking the talk, shall we say. Anything else would be hypocritical and a waste of time.

Them Is Us Eventually

We need to know the stakeholders and their roles in process improvement. We will eventually be in every stakeholder role over our lifetime, sometimes simultaneously, so there is no end to the benefits of knowing how to do an SHA. While we understand that leaders play a role as sponsors of change and the people doing the process improvement work are the change agents, we also have to consider those who will be asked to change as a result of the improvements.

Empathy is a powerful emotion in leading change. Empathy is gained by understanding each stakeholder's potential experience in the drama as sponsors, change agents, and the people impacted. The people impacted may experience confusion, pain, and it is hoped, if we do our jobs well, joy. Are we the ones leading the change, managing the change, or being asked to change in this change? The majority of stakeholders are often the "targets of change." Jeanenne LaMarsh, president of LaMarsh and Associates, taught me about the targets of change. The targets make up the group that will be asked to change. They often have no decision-making authority, may have many issues with the change, and may put up heavy resistance when they are ignored, as they have been in other change management approaches. The Managed Change Model™ from Jeanenne's firm is one of the better approaches in change management. We will learn to consider the targets of change and how to engage them in helping us improve the process.

Let us learn SHA by doing.

Starting a New Clinic

The new clinic startup is progressing but a bit behind the plan. The "all-too-common" delays in construction are occurring—thank goodness in one respect. The vice president (VP) has taken this delay to conduct a failure modes and effects analysis on the scheduling process, ultimately determining the amount of bookings taken—and thus margin. She just does not feel that there are enough recovery area bays. Without enough bays, the clinic will literally have to stop receiving incoming patients and lose them to other clinics. Who is involved with the scheduling process? Who has a stake in its performance? What if we validate there are not enough beds? Who might have to change knowing bed availability includes more processes beyond the scheduling process? Let us use the form to answer these questions.

Starting at a macrolevel, let us list the first organization that comes to mind. The scheduling organization is a natural start, but it does not matter. Sometimes the customer may come to mind, and we could start there. See Figure 7.2 to know who the stakeholders are.

We populated the role of the stakeholders as we entered their names. Let us detail each role. The customer is the one who receives the product of the process. In our example, it seems clear the patient is the customer of the scheduling process. What about the physician who wants to treat the patient in the clinic? Does the physician value the schedule? Yes, we think so, and in many cases we have internal and external customers, the patient being the customer external to the organization. Does it matter if the physicians are employees of the clinic? This does not really hold for SHA. The fact that they value having a schedule is enough, regardless of whether considered internal or external. Thus, we do not differentiate external or internal in SHA (see Figure 7.3).

Stakeholder Analysis

Project: Date: Contributor names:

Stakeholder role

Organization/ Location/ Area	Name (or group name)	Role or Title	Customer of the process	Process owner	Decision-maker/ Approver	Target of the change	Interested party	Supplier to the process	Current level of buy-in to change. Rate 0 - 10 with 0 being no buy-in - heavy resistance	Needed level of buy-in to change. Rate 0 - 10 with 0 no buy-in needed	Gap	Strategy to close the gap
Scheduling department	Bobbie	Scheduler										
Scheduling department	Petra	Manager, Scheduling										
Scheduling department	Michael	Scheduler										
Scheduling department	Gemma	Scheduler										
Operations	Carrie	Director of Operations										
Clinic	Adam	VP, Clinic										
Clinic	Sophie	Nurse Manager										
Patient												
Physician offices		Physicians										
											-	
											-	
											-	
											-	

Figure 7.2 Clinic SHA stakeholders.

Now that we have brainstormed and listed all of the stakeholders, let us use the template to guide us in finding where we need to focus to improve our chances of achieving the changes. Notice I avoid using the typical negative-sounding resistance term. Change Leadership is not just about reducing resistance. It is as much about increasing the engagement of those who want change. It is far better to have an army with you than to try and reduce resistance alone. Creating more open support for change is what we will share. We will also consider the "underground resistance" movement as a strategy when the culture is just not quite ready for everyone to be open. As you can see, we will have strategies for you when it is time.

Stakeholder Analysis												
Project			Stakeholder role						Contributor names:			
Date												
Organization/ Location/ Area	Name (or group name)	Role or Title	Customer of the process	Process owner	Decision-maker/ Approver	Target of the change	Interested party	Supplier to the process	Current level of buy-in to change. Rate 0 - 10 with 0 being no buy-in - heavy resistance	Needed level of buy-in to change. Rate 0 - 10 with 0 no buy-in needed	Gap	Strategy to close the gap
Scheduling department	Bobbie	Scheduler				x					-	
Scheduling department	Petra	Manager, Scheduling		x	x						-	
Scheduling department	Michael	Scheduler				x					-	
Scheduling department	Gemma	Scheduler				x					-	
Operations	Carrie	Director of Operations			x						-	
Clinic	Adam	VP, Clinic	x	x	x	x					-	
Clinic	Sophie	Nurse Manager	x								-	
Patient			x								-	
Physician offices		Physicians					x				-	
											-	
											-	
											-	
											-	
											-	
											-	
											-	
											-	
											-	
											-	
											-	
											-	

Figure 7.3   SHA with roles.

Time to Assess Each Stakeholder's Buy-In

Now is the time to assess the buy-in of each stakeholder or stakeholder group, as in this example for which patients do not need to be identified by individual. Your team will assess each stakeholder's current willingness for the changes expected. We do not know at the start of a project what the changes will be exactly. What the team is rating in the initial SHA is the willingness to change. After we find the contributing factors and issues with changes, we will develop the actual changes. We will use this SHA again at this phase in our change leadership to rate their willingness to the specific changes devised (see Figure 7.4).

Stakeholder Analysis												
Project			Stakeholder role						Contributor names:			
Date												
Organization/ Location/ Area	Name (or group name)	Role or Title	Customer of the process	Process owner	Decision-maker/ Approver	Target of the change	Interested party	Supplier to the process	Current level of buy-in to change. Rate 0 - 10 with 0 being no buy-in - heavy resistance	Needed level of buy-in to change. Rate 0 - 10 with 0 no buy-in needed	Gap	Strategy to close the gap
Scheduling department	Bobbie	Scheduler				x			6	10	(4)	
Scheduling department	Petra	Manager, Scheduling		x	x				5	5	-	
Scheduling department	Michael	Scheduler				x			9	10	(1)	
Scheduling department	Gemma	Scheduler				x			4	8	(4)	
Operations	Carrie	Director of Operations			x				10	10	-	
Clinic	Adam	VP, Clinic	x	x	x	x			7	10	(3)	
Clinic	Sophie	Nurse Manager	x						8	9	(1)	
Patient			x						9	9	-	
Physician offices		Physicians						x	4	10	(6)	
											-	
											-	
											-	
											-	
											-	
											-	
											-	
											-	
											-	
											-	

Figure 7.4 Stakeholder analysis with buy-in.

- Current level of buy-in to the change
- Needed level of buy-in
- Gaps identified
- Change strategy created

There are a few common strategies for those with a large gap. Resistance will be felt if one does not have a strategy and execute on the strategy to reduce resistance. The number one strategy is to inform the stakeholders about the process improvement. Elicit their feelings and invite them to share how these feelings got that way and if they have solutions. We do not want to jump to solutions, and letting them share ideas may increase the buy-in.

Why? This is because many people are frustrated because no one valued their intellect.

Other strategies include putting the resistor on the team. Engaging him or her helps each party understand each other better and allows you to manage "bad press" that might have been more gossip than fact. Resistors are often on the outside and unaware perhaps of why the process improvement is really needed. In his book, *Flawless Consulting*, Peter Block shares another strategy. Ensure shareholders know what is expected of them to make the change work.[2] Delaying the inevitable will increase resistance. Engage potential resistors early.

Key Points

- SHA is a must.
- Strategies are key to leading change when people resist.
- The SHA may expose that the charter is not quite finished. The team may need to add charter signatories to manage resistance. The team may also benefit by adding the process owner to the team.

Notes

1. Jim Champy and Harry Greenspun, *Reengineering Health Care*, FT Press, Upper Saddle River, NJ, 2010.
2. Peter Block, *Flawless Consulting. A Guide to Getting Your Expertise Used*. Pfeiffer, New York, 1981, pp 139–159.

Chapter 8

Finding the Root Causes, Improving, and Controlling

CIRCULATE among followers consistently.

Abraham Lincoln[1]

Explore Together

This chapter is about finding the root causes. If we know the root causes, we are better able to target solutions and improve the process.

Doctor Livingstone, I Presume?

To circulate among followers really means circulate among the people in the process. Lincoln's intent was not just to circulate among those with his same interests. As we circulate, we should consider being among others physically as well as mentally and emotionally. Explained in the opposite, do not expect to explore a process in a remote room. That would be like Scottish explorer Dr. Livingstone saying he explored faraway lands in his flat in Britain. Dr. Livingstone understood the mentality of the natives of Africa and their differing goals, expectations, and where they were emotionally. Although the physical location may not change, change leaders understand that the mental and emotional states vary constantly and can be a challenge in leading change. One must appreciate the right time for the right changes to be successful.

Dr. Livingstone also had an effective method to change minds that allowed him to succeed. Let us explore Dr. Livingstone's ways and benefit from his success in change leadership.

Livingstone had qualities and approaches that gave him an advantage as an explorer. Others attempting to explore Africa were often not trusted as potential slave traders and overzealous missionaries forcing change on the natives. Livingstone usually travelled lightly, and he had an ability to reassure chiefs that he was not a threat. Other expeditions had dozens of soldiers armed with rifles and scores of hired porters carrying supplies and were seen as military incursions or were mistaken for slave-raiding parties. Livingstone, on the other hand, travelled on most of his journeys with a few servants and porters, bartering for supplies along the way, with a couple of guns for protection.[2]

Explore Together with Empathy and Patience

Livingstone preached a Christian message but did not force it on unwilling ears. He understood the ways of local chiefs and successfully negotiated passage through their territory. He was often hospitably received and aided, even by powers in the tribal community.

Dr. Livingstone explored and engaged with the natives. He understood their needs and their wants and was successful in getting what he wanted— safe passage to find the source of the Nile—as well as his second motive, which was to change the spiritual beliefs of the natives. One should know that Dr. Livingstone initially considered missionary work. His success in exploration moved him to more exploration, but he also succeeded in leading change among the natives. The abolition of slavery is perhaps the greatest change to which Dr. Livingstone contributed. Well before the United States abolished slavery, Britain led its reversal of such an atrocity.

Building the Team

In exploring together, we emphasize the word *together*. Process improvement leaders know how to build a team with the right people. This does not mean just those who share our beliefs and values. A change leader circulates among those who often hold different opinions than he or she does. A change leader recognizes that there are reasons others do not share the same opinion, and perhaps it is because they know something the change leaders do not know. A good team is a team that has the same vision, perhaps, but diversity in the reasons for the current state.

Case Study: Patient Feeds Go Missing

The issue was to find why enteral feeds were not in stock for patients. The process was to have a stock of feeds that come in one-liter tubes in each of the patients' rooms. The nurses were complaining to the pharmacy that they were not providing feeds. The pharmacy was complaining to the dietitians that dietitians were the problem. The team, composed of people from all three disciplines, went to work.

The team circulated among the people in the process early in their project. They explored together and found that each person had a different view of the issue and cause. What they discovered was that all three disciplines involved with ensuring patients get the correct feed had a variation in process. An example of variation involved the nurses. Late at night when a patient was admitted, there was no dietitian available. One nurse would call the "on-call" person to obtain access to the feeds access. Another nurse would borrow from another patient, and yet a third nurse tried to store some in her area for these circumstances. The most common "fix" was to borrow. This practice was rampant among the nurses. Nurses would run out of feeds in one patient's room and immediately start borrowing feeds from another patient's room. It was not long before a different patient's feed inventory was eliminated, and that patient's nurse borrowed from a third patient's room.

Work-Arounds in the "Factory of Hidden Defects"

The "work-around" had been going on for years. Dr. Deming calls this behavior the "factory of hidden defects." His point about work-arounds is that people will continue working around the root cause of a problem for a greater good. If the work-around continues for a time, people will become too accustomed to the work-around and begin to not even notice or complain about the problem, in this case running out of feeds. The work-around becomes the way people work. Changing people's behavior becomes more difficult when the work-around is no longer seen as a reaction to a quality abnormality. Therefore, another lesson learned is to start change early, before work-arounds become the way people work.

Fortunately, the pharmacy manager, Melissa Monahan, discerned the work-around was not the way to work. She had different experiences from previous employment and could see the borrowing as a work-around. As a sponsor of the effort, she took a different path. Melissa wanted the work-arounds stopped for the good of her staff and the good of all others, including the patient.

Exploring Using the "Five Whys"

The team set out on its mission to have the right feed at the right time to the right patient by exploring together the reasons. They circulated all week among the people in the process and discovered many reasons for the feeds being borrowed. They used the tool of asking why five times to get to the root causes. They learned this technique in their training. See Figure 8.1 for the roadmap where this tool is found.

Here is how this root cause tool found on the roadmap helps drill down to the root cause. The team starts by asking the first question. Note that this is not blaming or asking who did what. That type of questioning will hurt your change leadership effort next time. It is root cause analysis, not root who analysis.

The team asked the nurses why they borrowed feeds from other patients. Nurses borrowed feeds from one patient for another patient.
Why?
Because the patient ran out of his or her feed.
Why?
Because the treatment room where the supplies were to be delivered did not have feeds for the patient.
Why?
Because the porter did not bring any feeds for the patient.
Why?
Because the patient was a new admission.
Why were there no feeds for a new patient?
Because the nurse found it easier to borrow from a patient nearby than to try to page the manager who was responsible for the pager to find someone who could go to the pharmacy, find the correct feed, do the paperwork, run the feed upstairs to the nurse, try to find the nurse who called, and then hand off the feed.

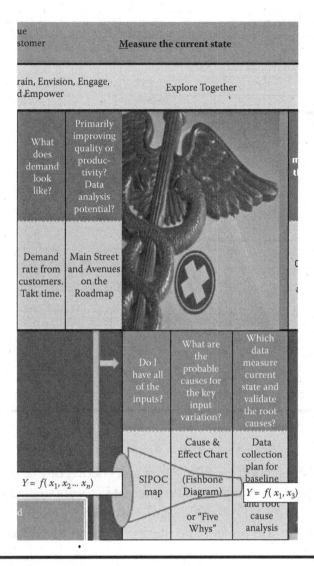

Figure 8.1   Ask why five times.

Asking why five times is a wonderfully simple and, most important, effective exploration tool in process improvement. My mother said I learned to ask why early in life. I think all three-year-olds do.

Explain

Explain means to take the root causes and connect them to the problem. A process improvement team can lose focus on the charter and its measures if the team members do not connect the activities to the charter occasionally.

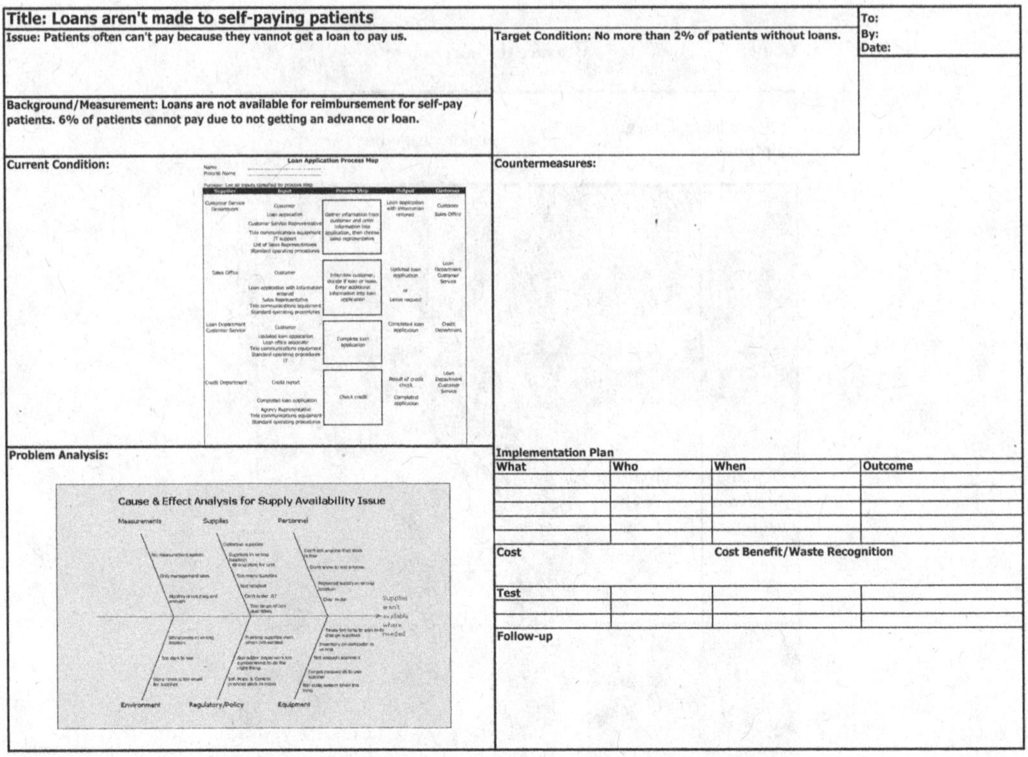
Title: Loans aren't made to self-paying patients
Issue: Patients often can't pay because they vannot get a loan to pay us.
Target Condition: No more than 2% of patients without loans.
To:
By:
Date:
Background/Measurement: Loans are not available for reimbursement for self-pay patients. 6% of patients cannot pay due to not getting an advance or loan.
Current Condition:
Loan Application Process Map
Countermeasures:
Problem Analysis:
Cause & Effect Analysis for Supply Availability Issue
Measurements
Supplies
Personnel
Environment
Regulatory/Policy
Equipment
Implementation Plan
What
Who
When
Outcome
Cost
Cost Benefit/Waste Recognition
Test
Follow-up

Figure 8.2 A3 storyboard.

Explaining also is aided by filling in a storyboard of the effort. An A3 size piece of paper is a common way to create storyboards and thus engage others in your project. An A3 storyboard is shown in Figure 8.2. This A3 is a great way to explain the project and status. Next on the Roadmap is to start improving the process.

Experiment

> The suggestions of the operators should definitely be included in this stage. … The results must be understandable, capable of being communicated, the analysis should not require too much time or expertise, and the analysis should reliably detect the signals.[3]
>
> **Donald Wheeler**

Experimentation is fundamental to change. Process improvement experimentation must also be practical. In agricultural experimentation, it might take a year before results are known. In process improvement, we are looking to know now or tomorrow. How often has a change that you wanted occurred exactly right the first time? You experimented, although perhaps initially you thought the change would go easily the first time. Thus, we find experimentation is mandatory because we did not get the change we wanted the first time. So, let us learn experimentation so we are better prepared for the inevitable as we lead change. Dr. W. Edwards Deming was one of the world's leading experimenters. He and Dr. Shewhart are credited with developing two of the first methodologies for process improvement, as we learned in a previous chapter. Now is the time that plan-do-study-act (PDSA) and plan-do-check-act (PDCA) add value. PDSA and Deming's revision to PDCA are perfect for this phase. To be good at process improvement, you need to be at least good at experimentation.

The first step is to plan the experiment. We plan in this phase to validate a root cause. Many people confuse plan to be the first step in process improvement. They miss the point that Deming and Shewhart, like all good experimenters, start with a hypothesis. An example of a hypothesis is that there is a correlation between a high number of admissions and missing patient feeds. The "do" in this experiment is to perform the experiment. It might be to increase the number of admissions at night and see the frequency of missing feeds. The "check" is based on whether the do actually had an effect. If the quantity of missing feeds increased, something to do might be what the team actually did. "Act" is the last step. I share with you what they did. Often, the experiment creates additional questions. The team needs to explore the various findings and explore for multiple solutions. Jumping to the first idea may miss opportunities for better solutions.

Explore builds on experimentation. Explore goes deeper into what one is finding in experiment.

Explore

> The primary objective (of experimentation) is exploration.
>
> **Donald Wheeler**

To explore after experimentation means to explore alternative solutions. The team in this case study actually did. Brainstorming is another tool on the Roadmap and is valuable in this phase due to its ability to create solutions that one person thinking alone may have missed. The rules of brainstorming, such as do not debate, are easy, but I find few teams do it well. They miss the opportunity to explore other thoughts and suggestions. For the sake of the team, I suggest always brainstorming in Explore or risk the sponsor or someone else becoming frustrated at a lack of creativity and effectiveness.

Brainstorming for Solutions

The team brainstormed for different ways to ensure feeds for a new admission. They imagined the spaghetti diagram of the nurse, the manager with the pager, the person who could go to the pharmacy and run the feed up to the floor, and all the people affected if the nurse borrowed from another patient instead of working around the issue.

What they discovered was a simple fix. They explored how medicines were provided for newly admitted patients, thinking that there must be a process for this critical "supply." They found there was a process: a small local supply that a nurse could pull from with proper control and documentation. The team experimented putting a small supply of the most common feeds in one location per hospital wing, explored the results, and found a simple and effective solution.

Once the team has brainstormed for solutions and validated them by experimentation, the team is ready to choose the best solutions or countermeasures. This is where Change Leadership can pay off. No one wants a team to fall apart at this stage because each individual has his or her favorite solution. Once the team has enough solution ideas, the team will move to gaining consensus on the best solutions.

Building Consensus

The team was taught what consensus is and what it is not. Consensus, as we know it, means that everyone comes to a decision and commits to the decision. There is no underhandedness or resistance once the consensus is reached. Consensus does not mean each person feels the decision is the best. A good experimenter may actually work to disprove his or her hypothesis to more strongly test and explore alternatives. However, once consensus is reached, the team can trust that all will move forward in the same direction and expend their change leadership energies on the next issues.

Resistance

The process improvement story continues. The team, surprisingly, found some resistance among the very people they were most trying to help: the nurses. More precisely, the nurse managers were the ones most resistant to the new local supply. One nurse manager was offered a chance to have the small supply (eight tubes) on her floor. The team had determined her floor was a good spot because many admissions occurred on her unit. The nurse manager, one of the hospital's most experienced and successful change leaders, having led several projects herself, politely but sternly said no. This was a bit uncharacteristic of her because in the past she had always said yes to our teams.

She spoke to the team and explained the reason for her resistance. She asked the team if they had thought about where most of the new patients requiring feeds are located. The team regrouped and found that the intensive care unit (ICU), or intensive treatment unit (ITU) in some countries, housed more new patients requiring feeds than her unit.

When I asked her about her quick decision, I was reminded of another lesson in process improvement: know your local history to know your stakeholders better. The lesson here is that even the Change Leaders in an organization may resist change when a team does not understand the past. The nurse manager had willingly said yes to a number of requests for space in the past. She had readily volunteered space for common supplies and space for common equipment that other floors also use. What she found was that there were burdens, such as inventorying the supplies and equipment, ensuring maintenance tickets were written, and helping others find the supplies when they came to her unit. Another contributing factor was more about timing. She was getting ready for her annual leave (vacation), and she did not have time to explore with the team as much as she would like. She is a great coach, but even great coaches run short of time to coach. Timing also is important when confronting stakeholders. Even the best change leaders can be in situations in which they are not able to help lead change. Patience has its virtue. Comedians may say, "Timing is everything." It is not everything in process improvement, but it is sure important.

The team's brainstorming did not immediately result in everyone believing a small local supply was the best countermeasure to reduce the borrowing. Other ideas included adding more stock; a process to alert pharmacy when a new admission occurred, even after hours; and having the person with the pager coached to be supportive and faster at getting the feeds up to the floor.

Additional Benefits from the Process Improvement

This project had many side benefits, including enhanced safety of patients. As the team explored and experimented with new methods of ensuring feeds were always available in the right place and at the right time, they discovered that at least once a feed had been borrowed from an isolation area. This is a risk to others because the feed was in an area where pathogens could have been transferred to others. An infection did not happen, but one can see that work-arounds are often risky as well as wasteful. I share how to prevent work-arounds in the discussion of stopping a process when a quality abnormality exists. The work-around is the opposite of this practice. Toyoda, the founder of Toyota, discovered the benefit of stopping a process when it first begins to vary. It is far better to stop the process immediately to find its root cause than let it run and then fix the process with a Band-Aid.

Train, Enable, Empower, Hold Accountable

Training in the Improvements

If people know what each other knows—training is the first step in getting people to know what each other knows. The good change leader is also a good trainer. Training should always start with an objective of skills desired by the student and knowledge attained. Using the vision statement protocol, we should envision a future state for the student and exert our energies in training accordingly.

Enabling others to participate in the change process occurs best after training. Engaging people in your improvement before they know the "end in mind" may actually backfire or create resistance to achieving your vision.

Case Study: Enabling and Engaging the Customer in the Process

The team wanted to help the hospital staff with a positive change. The members wanted to increase the compliance of healthcare professionals (HCPs) in washing their hands before and after entering a patient's room to reduce the risk of healthcare-acquired infections. The prior efforts failed, and one effort in particular tried to defy the practices of high-reliability organizations, the practice of keeping responsibility where responsibility lies. This is with the person doing the work. Dr. Deming and Toyota found success in improving quality by engaging the worker in knowing his or her quality of work versus relying on others after the process to know. The worker doing the work should do inspection. The hand hygiene practice being promoted was to engage patients first in inspecting if healthcare providers washed their hands on entering their room. The teams I led found this practice resulted in no significant improvement or sustained improvement. In fact, we found that it allowed those responsible not to engage as often as necessary when HCPs did not properly practice hand hygiene. One can imagine the angst and resistance from the very people the "Speak Up" campaign was trying to help: the patients. How do you feel about telling your nurse or physician to wash his or her hands?

I have been fortunate enough to work throughout Europe and Asia. I have also been fortunate enough to bring my wife, children, and friends with me. My wife's best friend, Lisa , who is a friend of mine from high school, came to London with us. This was her first visit. She loved visiting Hard Rock Cafés. One of her goals was to visit the London Hard Rock Café and have her favorite sandwich while looking at the memorabilia. The Hard Rock was quite a bit out of our way, if anyone knows where the Hard Rock Café is in London, but this trip was for her. We got there late, and the restaurant was very quiet. I was glad we missed the crowd and happy that we got a table immediately.

On ordering, our server said she could not get the burger because they were out of it. The server said Lisa could have the smaller burger. Lisa was disappointed. Lisa is also a woman who gets what she wants, and she thought about it and questioned why she could not get the burger she wanted because it was made with two smaller burgers (she thought). The server said the larger patty was out of stock (here we go again with inventory problems.) Lisa then got a bit annoyed when she suggested the kitchen combine two patties with the condiments she enjoyed on the burger she wanted. This seemingly logical solution was resisted highly by our server. The server rejected her solution out-of-hand, saying, "No, it could not be done. You will have to choose another item on the menu." Let me share a bit more about Lisa. Lisa is not a diminutive, shy little girl. Lisa stands about six feet tall, is a successful businessperson, and has overcome significant personal and business challenges. For the server to resist so strongly and destroy Lisa's vision of a memorable night enjoying her favorite sandwich was not wise. Lisa complained to the server strongly and tried again, to no avail.

There Are Good Times, and There Are Bad Times

Now, if you know what we know about arguing with your server before you get your food, you can feel like my wife and I felt, and probably would do as we did. You would coach Lisa to cease and desist immediately. My wife and I shared a vision of our food in the kitchen out of sight being adorned with added ingredients we shuddered even to think about.

Enable

Enable in this phase means to give the people the resources necessary to do the process the way it should now be operating. I have seen far too many solutions fall away when we did not enable the people in the process with the time and resources needed to sustain the gains.

Standard work is another tool on the Roadmap. It is basically the right way to do a task. There is standard work for housekeeping, admitting patients, and a host of other tasks. People must be shown the instructions, or at least made aware that there is a right way to do work and a wrong way. Know the right way to sustain the gains and have patients and physicians who are more satisfied.

Empower

Empower in the improve and control phase is critical to sustain. What if the solution for patient feeds is to put a small number of feeds in a common controlled area, and we did not give the people the right to replenish? Of course, we may not want them to negotiate their own multiyear contract with a new supplier of feeds, but many would handle this process for us.

Hold Accountable

Everybody was sure that somebody would do it.

The process improvement team should be taught process control, enabled to measure the process as it flows, and empowered to make decisions within boundaries. The standard work used in training people in the change is also effective in holding people accountable. There have been several studies linking healthcare-acquired conditions, and infections, let us say, with variations in how work is done. Evidently, some are not following the standard work of those whose patients do not get infections. We need a way of knowing who is doing what to reduce the variation. Then, we ensure training is done well and the student has learned.

The Just Culture is not a blame-free culture. Healthcare professionals may know Just Culture is not a blame-free culture. James Reason contrasts a Just Culture and a blame-free culture as one where if people come to work incapacitated due to substance abuse, the person should be held accountable. It is not society's fault.[4]

Times Not to Speak Up?

There is a time to speak up and times when tact ought to be considered. To get HCPs to wash their hands, we advise not to confuse the roles of the HCP and the patient. Change leaders know that confusing responsibility for quality and safety does not work. Sure, it may be an important and sometimes effective tactic to inform the patient that the patient should assume that their caregivers, housekeepers, and others entering their room may not wash their hands. The patients have every right to ask them to wash for their own safety and the safety of others. But, we should never rely on the customer to inspect hand washing. The workers need to be their own inspectors. Workers and managers should not rely on patients to do their inspection and coaching for them. This inspection and coaching are what the 3Ms (measure, manage to the measure, make it easier) are about, and we will share how the 3Ms work.

Last, our Roadmap helped us navigate the process improvement journey quicker and more easily. It is not time to celebrate. It may seem odd that we have celebrate on the Roadmap. It is not by mistake. We need to reinforce positively those individuals and teams who work to improve processes continuously. In America, individual certification is often desired. In other cultures, this may not seem to be for the good of the many. The process improvement leader should seek what team members value. For many, it is simply a better work life. For others, it may be a little recognition. Whatever it is, do not forget to celebrate to tell everyone that process improvement is the behavior we reinforce.

Key Points

■ Explore together builds teamwork, reduces resistance, and should end with a better study than not exploring together.

Standard Work Procedure									
Process Name:		**Discharge**			Signoff or initial acknowledgement		Date:	Recorded by:	Revision Date:
Key		Safety	Critical	Quality Check	Supervisor names				
Step #	Process Steps	**Time (seconds)**			Layout and Graphical Job Aid				
		Time (seconds)	Key	Safety Equipment Required	Moment				
1	Park trolley outside patient room								
2	Enter room								
3	Wash and glove			Sanitise	2				
4	Clear room								
5	Take dirty linen, equipment, and waste to sluice								
6	Sanitize hands			Sanitise	3				
7	Collect clean linen and take to room								
8	Sanitize and gloves on			Sanitise	2				
9	Clean bathroom top to bottom								
10	Reglove and Sanitize			Sanitise	3				
11	Clean bedroom, dusting high and low, surfaces, etc.								
12	Make bed								
13	Towels in bathroom/amenity								
14	Complete vaccuum								
15	Sanitize hands			Sanitise	5				

Figure 8.3   Standard work.

■ Explain connects the root causes found in explore together with the charter and project goals.

■ Experiment is key to checking how countermeasures may improve a process or a design.

■ Exploring alternative countermeasures and solutions may result in more improvement.

■ Building consensus is vital, and the stakeholder analysis may be used again to understand who might resist consensus.

■ The control phase relies on people to be trained in the change. Standard work is an effective template to hold people accountable by making clear rules and responsibilities. (see Figure 8.3).

Notes

1. From *Lincoln on Leadership* by Donald T. Phillips. Copyright © 1992 by Donald T. Phillips. By permission of Grand Central Publishing. All rights reserved.

2. David Livingstone. http://en.wikipedia.org/wiki/David_Livingstone.

3. Donald Wheeler, *Experimentation, Understanding Industrial Experimentation*, SPC Press, Knoxville, TN, 1990, pp. 1–3.

4. James Reason, *Managing the Risks of Organizational Accidents*, Ashgate, Surrey, UK, 1997.

Chapter 9

Utilizing the 3Ms: Measure, Manage to the Measure, and Make It Easier

Introduction

Now you are ready to learn how to lead process improvement in healthcare by remembering three important lessons. Process improvement that works and lasts requires:

- *M*easuring
- *M*anaging to the measure
- *M*aking it easier

Measure

Utilizing the first M is often enough to get an improvement started. There is a story of a manager writing a number on the floor but saying nothing. People had no idea what he was doing. The next day, he wrote a different number and again said nothing. Soon, someone figured out the puzzling behavior. He was writing the prior day's production output on the floor. Once the staff realized the "game," they worked together to improve the process and beat the prior day's numbers. It became fun, and the improvement started all because of a measure.

Practicing Measure

Try measuring as in the story and see how it works in your area. If you do not manage anyone, this does not matter. Measuring works for anyone. For this exercise, try measuring something not working well in a common break area. Put a number on the wall of how many dirty dishes are left in the sink by others. Or, maybe put a sticky note with a count of how many times the coffee pot or water cooler is found empty. Use one of the charting methods further in this book to share the measure daily and really have some fun with measuring. Let me know what happens (http://www.rpmexec.com).

How many times have you shared a measure with a team and heard, "I had no idea. If only we knew." Think of the top two or three outcomes of patient care for your organization. Mortality should come to mind if you are in an acute care hospital. Next, write down the measure of each objective. If you are struggling trying to figure out exactly the measure, that is not uncommon. I cover the most common measures in healthcare because they are often not well understood. Last, what is your current performance in each of the measures for each objective? I am not expecting you to have them all memorized, so look around for the measure to be posted. Are you struggling to figure where to look? Do not be alarmed. Workers can see the measures in a Toyota vehicle assembly plant, a consumer customer service call center, and Kohl's department store. They can see the objectives, the measure, and the current state daily. Your organization may not be there yet. You will know exactly how to achieve this for yourself and your organization and have them set up by the time you finish this book. The first M is the most important of the Ms for without Measure, there is little to manage to, and one never knows if it is easier if we do not know where we started.

Measurement is key to improvement. Measurement alone can often bring about change because it makes people aware of the need for change. A Change Leader can often get the change desired simply by doing the 3Ms (measure, manage to the measure, make it easier). And the first M is not an option. Michael Porter and Robert Kaplan remind us of the management axiom, "What is not measured cannot be managed or improved" in their article, "How to Solve the Cost Crisis in Health Care."[1] This axiom is a perfect lead-in to the second M.

Measurement matters. When clinicians see their numbers, they act to improve them, using their professional pride and competitiveness to find solutions.

Randall D. Cebul, MD, Director, Better
Health Greater Cleveland

Manage to the Measure

Simply measuring something and not managing based on the measure is fruitless. For example, hand hygiene charts are posted quarterly on walls in the unit's break area. There is seldom any evidence that anyone pays attention to them. Often, the chart is dusty and not current. It is clear that the measure of hand hygiene compliance gets little attention and does not result in any significant change. In his principle of operator self-control, Joseph Juran found the person doing work should be empowered in three abilities:

■ The person doing the work has the necessary knowledge, skills, and tools to do the job.
■ He or she has the ability to regulate the process.
■ He or she gets feedback on how he or she is doing.

Make It Easier

The greatest change will still fail if it is not easy enough to apply. "Water flows the path of least resistance." If it is easier *not* to change, change is destined to fail. The 3Ms are the most valuable three letters in process improvement. Doing all three Ms well is the best recipe for change to succeed.

I can tell you every change I have led for which processes controlled by humans succeeded because of the 3Ms. This was true whether it was eliminating wrong-site surgery, sustaining hand hygiene compliance, achieving record high on-time performance to demanding customers like Toyota and big box retailers, or preventing catastrophic vehicle failures, measuring, managing to what the measurement was telling us, and making changes easier.

Visual Management

Visualize your workplace. Look around your area for measures that tell you how the quality, safety, and productivity are right now. Like most, you may struggle. Try the PC (personal computer) at your station. Can you find any visual aids about how things are managing now? How about a chart on today's census? You probably have that; it is a good example of visual management. Visual management is something that we can sense that tells us what is important, how we are doing, and where we want to be. Another example in healthcare is a monitor in the intensive care unit that shows a patient's vital signs. It tells us now what is important, how the patient is right now, and goals, or at least boundaries of acceptable status.

I work at Healthcare Performance Partners (HPP) in healthcare quality and safety consulting, and I love my job, my colleagues, and clients. Charles Hagood, Marshall Leslie, and my friend from working on hand hygiene compliance, Dr. Dave Munch, recruited me to join them at HPP, the world's foremost healthcare performance improvement consulting firm. Everything about HPP seemed right, especially how they treated their team and promoted the value of measuring early in the work. The entire HPP team promotes and requires the use of visual management in every project. Many of us have worked in high-reliability organizations where we knew instantly how our customers were feeling, how the processes were working, and if there were any quality issues, and we knew it visually. Having worked in high-reliability organizations, I learned that real-time monitoring and process control is vital so the frontline staff can intervene and prevent failures.

At Eaton Corporation, we made safety devices that had to be calibrated to prevent electrical shock. The circuit breaker is called a ground fault circuit interrupter. The product's purpose is to stop the electricity before a fault in the circuit allows electricity to hurt anyone. If the calibration is not done, the breaker may not function. What if one got past us into a box and was shipped to be installed in your home? Visual management was clear. If any breaker did not pass through the calibration system, an alarm would go off—not next week, not tomorrow, but right now.

Measuring Example

Yesterday, I counted the number of pages I have to see how I have progressed in writing this book. I counted the pages to manage my time to ensure finishing the book on time for Kris and CRC Press. After work, I read and write. I have written most of my working life but started more as just a reader. To write, I have to read because I am humbled each time I write when I realize how much there is to know about just about anything. I have always also used measuring when I read, come to think about it. I remember measuring the amount of books I read in early grade school per section; I wish I could remember the name of the reading series. It was set up to let the teacher measure progress, and I had fun managing my progress to get to the next series. Yes, as geeky as it sounds, I also measured and managed to the measure to compete.

Managing to the Measure Example

I really liked playing baseball, but I could not hit. Being the second-shortest boy from first through eighth grade did not convince me that sports was my thing. When I wanted to help my son learn how to hit, I did it by reading and watching experts. I read that Pat Murphy, coach of Notre Dame and Arizona State, conducted a baseball camp. Adam went there and learned how to measure progress by measuring hitting fundamentals. I like to think that reading Sports Illustrated Baseball and working with Adam on the hitting drills well before Pat Murphy's camp helped at least a bit. Adam and I measured and managed to the measure and success came. He led his age group in hitting virtually every year. Do not look for a book from me on baseball, though. Remember what I said about how little I think I know?

Make It Easier Example

Water flows the path of least resistance. Electricity flows the path of least resistance. People will often take the path of least resistance. I had a piano teacher who also believed people would take the path of least resistance until she had me as a pupil. I loved learning the piano in first grade, until I discovered percussion around fourth grade. My interest in piano fell sharply as I took up drumming. I would not practice piano nearly enough, and my teacher was becoming annoyed with my lack of practice and obvious difficulty in playing the pieces. Finally, one day she confronted me: "Rick, isn't practicing easier than listening to me harp on you to practice?" She had a point. Practicing was the path of least resistance until I found an even easier path of least resistance: I quit piano. So, why not try to find the path of least resistance in process improvement?

I measure, manage to the measure, and make it easier to do anything that is really important to me. I have been married for over thirty years to Jan. I am delighted to have great clients and a place to work where I measure my contributions and what I learn daily. This book has been a work in process for several years, but it was not important enough until recently, and no one was measuring me on finishing it. The publisher and I both are measuring now. After measuring where I am to achieve the 250 or so pages to improve skills in process improvement, I think we are right where we need to be. The measure that I used is takt time.

Takt Time: A Measure of the Pace Needed to Meet Customer Demand

My takt time to finish this book is two pages per day. Takt time is a good measure for writing a book, and its value is found throughout healthcare. What is the pace that a lab needs to work to process all samples? What is the rate of patients, on average, a family practitioner needs to achieve to satisfy his or her patients? What is the production rate needed by your pharmaceutical company to avoid back orders? How can 167 prescription drugs be on back order, as was true in mid-2011? Maybe we could have measured demand or drug production better? Takt time is not the only measure, of course, but its value is often missed in healthcare operating room (OR) scheduling, running labs, discharging patients, and much more.

Calculating the takt time in writing this book is easily done. Takt time is the ratio of the number of days I want to make available to write this book divided by the number of pages remaining. For example, 256 pages is our nominal page plan. I want to spend two nights and one weekend afternoon in writing. Let us call these sessions. The time available was twenty weeks, or 20 weeks × 3 sessions per week = 60 sessions ÷ by 257 pages demanded = 60/257 = a takt time of 0.233. This means I have to create a page every 0.233 sessions. This equates to about four pages per session, 1/0.233 = X pages/1 session. In other words, think of the publisher "pulling four pages from me" every session.

I therefore need to average four pages per session. Of course, some days I will do more, and some days I will do less, but on average, I will get this book to you on time if I do twelve pages per week. Of course, there is a lot more to publishing a book than writing. Therefore, I create a team, and we all measure progress every session to ensure we meet demand. Each of us must meet the takt time of 12 pages per week, regardless of our role. We manage to the measure when variation occurs, such as getting an idea of how we can help you learn the 3Ms by using a new experiment. This is when we decided to show you how impactful the 3Ms are with the public. When we find something too difficult, we "make it easier."

Illustrating the book is a difficult task. My son, Adam, did some of the illustrations. We found that illustrations could not be done by one person in the takt time required. What did we do? Change takt time? Well, we only had two variables in the equation, time available or the number of pages. We could not sacrifice the number of pages because we would risk failing to meet your expectations of this book. So, the only other variable was time available. We could try to speed up the illustrators, but quality might have suffered. What is another way of making more time available? Time available is a function of two variables, actually. Time available = time to do a task × the number of resources doing the task. How about adding resources to increase the time available? Of course this was the answer.

The number of resources to meet customer demand can also be found using the measure of takt time. If the illustrator can do two pages per session and we need four pages per session, then the number of illustrators we need is four pages per session/2 pages per person = two illustrators needed to make takt time.

In our work with clients, we focus first on taking out waste before we suggest adding resources. One way to define lean is using fewer resources for a given task. In reducing the wait time in the emergency department (ED), demand is often reduced first because patients come to the ED when a clinic is better for them and more convenient. In this case, we reduce the denominator, demand. We now use takt time to ensure staffing in the clinics is sufficient and to determine how many are now required in the ED. Therefore, we often reduce the numerator and denominator.

This is how healthcare organizations are coached to meet the demand in their ED, labs are helped to reduce their back orders, and just about any healthcare service is advised when there are issues in satisfying demand.

Measuring: The Most Important M

Measure is the most important concept in this book. Start measuring what is important, and that alone may be sufficient to lead change.

I also share that without measuring, little is achieved and even less sustained.

Honestly, what in the past has been sustained that humans control? How many of your successes, whether organizing your desk, getting staff to wash their hands, or training and promoting team problem solving, has been sustained without measuring? I am almost embarrassed to say that it is this simple to see a common thread. Yet, why do we have to reinvent this wheel repeatedly? Process improvement leaders and teams measure results. They measure not only the outcomes but also the vital behaviors that lead to the desired outcomes, such as leading a perioperative team to measure the behaviors up to and after the procedures.

Applying the First of the 3Ms and Seeing the Value

Pick a task that you want to occur that is not at the performance level you expect. Choose a task that will give us data frequently so you still have time to learn the other two Ms instead of watching corn grow. In addition, it should be one for which you are not sharing the measure of performance with those doing the tasks or at least not in a timely manner for the task being performed.

We want a task where you can see failures occurring frequently so we can see the tremendous value in measuring. If you cannot think of one, take hand washing using alcohol-based dispensers. Other tasks that might work for you are refilling the office copier with paper, opening the door for others, and something as simple as always greeting each other at the beginning of the workday before barking orders or requests. If you work alone, think of a task frequently done at home or at your local pub or community center.

Start with simply observing people doing the task inconspicuously to avoid influencing the behavior that you want to measure. I will use hand hygiene because it is needed everywhere and the events are easily observed. In addition, your patients, staff, and everyone visiting will get an immediate benefit: lower risk of healthcare-acquired infection (HAI). We can thank Dr. Semmelweis again.

Setting Up Your Experiment

Purpose: Measuring if measuring has an impact on behavior.

Setup: Find an area where you can observe hand cleansing without being conspicuous. A high-traffic public area like a reception desk, patient rooms where the door is usually open, and a cafeteria are all good candidate areas.

Find a dispenser in a reasonable spot where people can easily access it. This is a hint of the third M: make it easy. So, let us jump ahead and make sure it is convenient to do the task as we focus on the first M, measure.

Measuring the Baseline

Measure the baseline to know if measure has affected the rate of hand hygiene. Use the hand hygiene data collection sheet (Figure 9.1), which is also found in Appendix 6. Make as many copies as you wish to take with you to observe. We make the template to fold in half to make it even less conspicuous.

Create a measure. The simplest measure is often a count. For example, count the number of times someone refills the copier after using it versus having to refill it because it is empty. Or, count how many times someone opens or holds open the door for another or how many people say hello before discussing work. For hand hygiene, count the number of times someone does not wash on entering and exiting a patient care area or a cafeteria line before he or she starts touching the salad bar utensils (see Figure 9.2).

The team achieved exactly what it needed in a measure to show the problem: Nurses were wasting time leaving the room because of a lack of supplies where they needed them. Sometimes, measuring can result in other wins. Some OR directors work to reduce the amount of times a door to an OR is opened. Opening a door allows air to exchange, which might allow pathogens inside the OR. The chart in Figure 9.2 may lead the team to a reduction in surgical site infections.

The next-simplest measure is to calculate a ratio using a count such as discussed and divide the count by the number of times the task occurs. A ratio may be better when the number of occurrences varies significantly period to period. In the example of a chart for counts, it does not make sense to create a ratio because the data were gathered by each case. Figure 9.3 is a chart of the ratio of customers entering a cafeteria over the

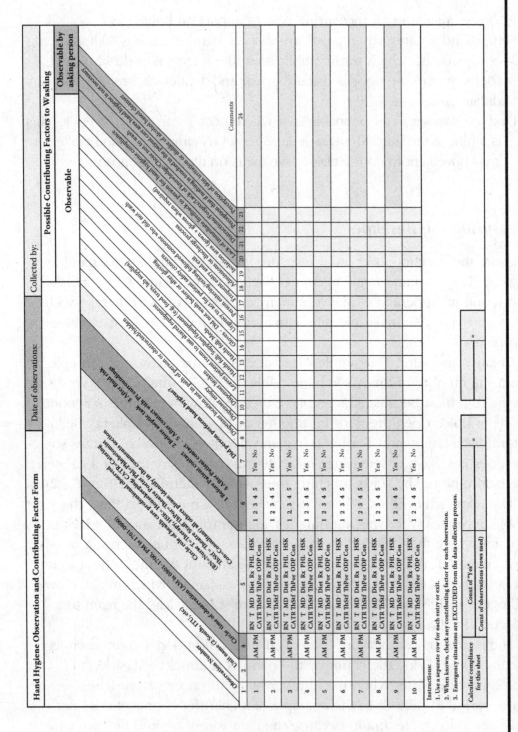

Figure 9.1 Data collection sheet.

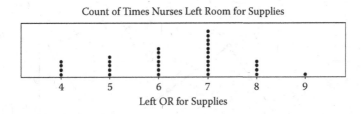

Figure 9.2 Chart 1 of count of times nurses had to leave the OR for supplies.

entire day who washed their hands. The number of customers varied significantly, and a simple count might suggest compliance varied differently. A ratio or percentage is a better statistic than a simple count when the number of people in the study varies.

The chart in Figure 9.3 is effective in hand hygiene compliance because we count the times healthcare professionals washed compared to the number of times they should have washed. Figure 9.3 is an actual chart of hand hygiene. These data were collected before the hospital embarked on its hand hygiene compliance initiative. The only chart the hospital had prior to this chart concerned compliance for the month. The chart in the past was shared only in monthly meetings and not on the floors or departments. We provide a chart in Appendix 8.

Statistical Process Control Charting: Turning Data into Information

Another way to measure a process occurring every day is a statistical process control (SPC) chart (see Figure 9.4). An SPC chart on hand hygiene

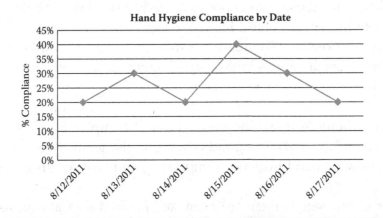

Figure 9.3 Hand hygiene compliance.

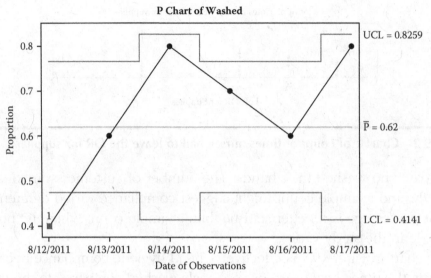

Figure 9.4   SPC chart of hand hygiene compliance using Minitab software.

compliance also alerts us to when compliance is significantly improving or worsening so we can celebrate or take action. You will learn how to use SPC in utilizing the 3Ms in a further chapter. For now, just be familiar with how the same data can be shared. Managing to the measure benefits from charts such as these.

The average compliance is .62 or about 62%. Notice the chart in Figure 9.4 has two other lines. The top line is an upper control limit. An upper control limit defines the upper range expected if the compliance continues as before. The lower control limit is the lower line at .4141. Statistically speaking, compliance for these data is not expected to be above the upper control limit or below the lower control limit. Seeing compliance above this line is improbable, but possible. The reason is that the lower control limit is based on what the compliance was in the past. If compliance goes below this line, something has changed beyond what is normal. Hand hygiene compliance lower than normal suggests exploring together and explaining the cause of compliance being so low. The same is true if compliance goes above the upper control limit. This is good news, and the team should investigate to understand why hand hygiene is improving and ensure this change is sustained.

Peter Drucker suggests there are a few key methodological concepts that add value in charting. The key point is to transform data into information.[2]

Charts are a powerful method to show data as information. A control chart like the one shown in Figure 9.4 also shows fluctuations compared to what the process fluctuation is normally. Drucker adds the value of such displays of data is helpful. "As long as fluctuations stay within the normal distribution of probability … no action is taken. But the exception, which falls outside the accepted probability distribution, is information. It calls for action." There is no better method than SPC to show the fluctuations compared to normal fluctuations.

For your experiment, observe people at times that represent what commonly happens. We can assume that the baseline time and then the times when you measure are similar with no other significant variable that may affect the behavior that you are measuring. Ideally, you can set a baseline and start experimenting in the same session, but this is not necessary.

Create the chart now to see if measuring has an effect. I created a chart for you; it is in the Appendix 8.

Practice now plotting the data as if you are observing and scale the vertical axis for what you think the count or ratio will be. A good experimenter will make a prediction of the measure before actually observing. This is a good time to place wagers with those who are joining you in our little experiment and have a little fun.

Sample Size

Determine a minimum time to observe. If you want to think in terms of sample size, here is an important lesson all too often confused in healthcare. Sampling is about representing the population. The sample size is about the confidence we have in estimating differences.

Some suggest that larger sample sizes better represent the population. I disagree. When we ask people to sample large numbers, the burden of data collection often results in them taking shortcuts in gathering the data to achieve the sample size. Sampling too many recently resulted in a hospital not getting the charts to the floor because it took so long to collect all the data that the team did not have time to enter it. Maybe it would have been better to have fewer data and charts posted daily than to have no charts until much later, after all the data entry was complete. The desire for convenience overtakes the desire to represent the population across the variables that a sample should cover. I have seen people go to the biggest group, the biggest container, the highest-volume time of day to get the largest sample in the least amount of time. Sample size gives us a level of confidence in our findings. There can be no shortcut to representing the population.

Hand Hygiene and the 3Ms

Recently, our team began measuring hand hygiene on an inpatient unit. The observers were doing well observing nurses, physicians, housekeepers, therapists, dietitians, and other healthcare professionals washing their hands. Here, 50% of nurses, 3% to 10% of doctors, and a representative number of therapists were observed, reflecting the balance of entries and exits to and from a patient's room each caregiver. However, my team started having too much fun observing and wanted more observations. The last days of data showed a disproportionate number of nurses in the data. This particular unit had a well-trained nursing staff who washed at a rate above most hospitals due to its leader's coaching in its importance. The compliance rate started increasing only because the observations were not representing the rate at which each healthcare professional was entering rooms.

Observe at the same time for the same amount of time on a day when the other variable that may affect what you are observing is usually a good practice. Do whatever makes sense to have the measurement be the only variable that changes between your baseline and when you start measuring.

Ready to Observe

You are just about ready to start observing. Make sure that there is an area to post your chart measure in full view of the person doing the task. It would be somewhat silly if the hand hygiene compliance were only shared off the floor with your Quality group and top leadership (sorry if this is happening in your organization.) Think of this as yet another benefit of reading this book. Dr. Deming also promoted that the person performing a task should be allowed to know his or her quality and be his or her own inspector. You may have a quick win if you are already measuring and posting the chart soon after the time of the data collection and the behaviors.

For a hand hygiene experiment, experiment in your cafeteria. Consider a dispenser on a stand immediately in front of the trays or dishes with an area to post a chart directly above the dispenser.

Alternative Experiment

Replenishing paper in a copier is another good choice for experimenting. One way to fail is in those organizations where the copier is in a dark, out-of-the-way place with walls already plastered with human resource mandatory postings on labor laws that no one ever examines. Make a data collection sheet, and while you are at the copier, *please* refill it. Walk the talk.

Start observing: Plan your method of observation so you do not give away that you are measuring behavior. Now is probably a good time to share the story so often used in healthcare, that of the Hawthorne effect.

The Hawthorne Effect

Between 1924 and 1933 at the Hawthorne Works outside Chicago, Illinois, experimenters gathered productivity data while changing the illumination level. The original researchers believed the changes in productivity were more a result of workers being studied than the changes in illumination. Therefore, the term *Hawthorne effect* is used often to describe short-term improvements during observation that are not sustained after observation ceases. Hand hygiene compliance has increased initially during a healthcare organization's initiative, only to revert to lower levels after observations have ceased. In my work on hand hygiene, I found that in the absence of an automated measurement system, the decreasing observation can correlate with decreased compliance. However, if the measurement from observation continues and is shared, compliance can be sustained. We did not observe compliance maintained when sharing the measurement ceased. Is a behavior changed and sustained because of just observation? Does it also need measurement?

Or, is the more important question, how we can maximize and sustain desired behavior change while minimizing both observation and measurement? Both are not value added to the patient and staff. The patient does not usually want to pay us to observe and record hand hygiene, but that does not mean we should not do it. Some tasks are vital to support the value-added tasks, such as providing products and services. Although we prove the 3Ms are necessary to sustain gains in human-controlled and variable processes, measurement is not value added and should also be minimized.

I will give you a solution. The design of a measurement system includes optimizing the measurement system for sustaining and improving behavior. The study of reproducibility as a way of measuring the quality of the measurement system is the answer to knowing if the balance of observation with the 3Ms and sustained behavior has been achieved. Think of it this way: A department can earn the right to observe and measure itself in hand hygiene compliance when the hand hygiene compliance measured by the unit staff or physicians matches the compliance measured by a trained third party. Once the accuracy and precision have been reproduced, the amount of observation and measurement could be reduced. If the two groups measuring start to deviate, perform a measurement system analysis. The usual answer is to increase the observation and 3Ms until the desired accuracy and precision are reached again. This is also a good time to let the unit know what was learned and to search for reasons and countermeasures to continue to decrease both observations and the 3Ms.

Desire to Increase Productivity

At the Hawthorne Works[3], management wanted to increase productivity. The experiment was to be observed in real time by engineers and researchers who would record the productivity rate. Their experiment was to test if better lighting would increase productivity. The first step the researchers took was to increase the lighting levels. Then they went to the factory floor and counted the production to calculate the productivity rate. They then compared this rate to the previous rates before the lighting was increased. counting the production to calculate the productivity rate. The researchers noticed an improvement in productivity when the lights were brighter. Could this indicate that an increase in light increases productivity? Yes, they thought. On more observation, they wanted to validate that the light levels would increase productivity. Therefore, they turned the lights back down to the original level. Lo and behold, productivity increased again. This was not what the engineers expected to happen. The conclusion from the experiment was that the variable that caused increases in productivity was the extra attention the workers were receiving by having the researchers on the floor with them. Remember Lincoln's practice of spending time with the troops in the field and how this experiment supported Lincoln's method. In Toyota and other facilities, they practice the same methods for similar reasons.

The Hawthorne effect was born from this study. For years, we believed that productivity increases when workers are engaged and treated with respect. The Hawthorne effect has been credited for changing from an autocratic culture of "shut up and listen" to a true collaborative one in some healthcare organizations. In addition, productivity has gone up.

Utilizing the 3Ms by Changing the Measure

I can tell you firsthand how management interaction with employees in the process affects productivity. Around 1986, Alan Houser, Wayne Boatman, and I wanted to improve the plant where we worked. We had heard about the Toyota Production System (TPS), and a Harley-Davidson plant a few hours north of us had improved productivity and reduced inventory considerably by applying TPS. We started applying the concepts and found that they improved our quality and productivity. We did something else, though. We spent lots of time on the floor engaging workers in creating better-flowing processes.

Bob Kayma and Ed Lechleiter were industrial engineers who helped lay out the first flow cells. Bob and Ed did something unheard of. They took teams of employees off the floor and out on the lawn to engage them in designing their own work area. We also had a big change for the workers that had us very anxious about resistance.

Incentive Piecework as a Measure

We knew that incentive piecework negatively affected quality. We needed to find a way to replace the piecework incentive with incentives that promoted quality and productivity. We tried the first autonomous work cells in which employees were trained, engaged, enabled, and empowered to lead their small unit. Now that we had people helping each other by flexing to other stations, the piecework incentive was not possible by individual. We had a dilemma. How do we equalize the pay for the extra value we were getting with these new methods? We sat down with the union, shared data, and spoke to a lot of workers. In the end, our experiment was to pay the team the average of what the group was earning on individual incentive. Naturally, some people lost take-home pay and some gained. We were surprised how little resistance we got.

Productivity went up to record highs despite eliminating incentive standards; this was without increasing total salary expense. We eventually eliminated the piecework incentive system. Many of the quality issues it caused by reinforcing just volume without regard to quality disappeared.

More on the Perverse Incentive Measure

Here is how perverse the incentive pay was. One person could make extra incentive pay by leaving out a few parts, which allowed him to complete his task faster. Inspectors would later find the defects, and then someone else would repair the devices. Here is where it gets really perverse. The repair person would also be eligible for piecework incentive to repair the devices.

Measuring only good production versus total pieces leaving a bench also reinforced quality. Measuring only services and products that are valued is always the right thing to do.

Length of stay (LOS) is quite a measurement, isn't it? How many times have we seen healthcare professionals focus on reducing LOS only to have readmissions increase? Watch what you measure—you may just get it. Isn't this the same issue we saw at the plant? Reinforce volume regardless of quality, and one gets volume regardless of quality. Reinforce bed turnover, and beds will turn over.

French Restaurant Dining

Dining in a French restaurant is an experience for first-time visitors from America. One will have a story about how leisurely, quiet, and slow the experience is. What frustrates many Americans dining for the first time virtually anywhere in Europe is the experience in paying. You see, in Europe your server will not deliver your check to you until you ask. In a restaurant in the United States, your server will often place the check on your table before you finish your dessert. Servers are often annoyed when diners stay because they are measured on turning tables over, and tips come from new diners, not diners sitting. In France and the United Kingdom, tips are truly optional because servers are usually paid by the restaurant owner for value delivered. Tips are often politely to rudely returned, in fact. We behave as we are measured.

The Hawthorne Effect Revisited

The end of the story at the Hawthorne Works is perhaps being rewritten. Someone claimed to have found the original data. The statistician reran the analysis and found a correlation with day of the week. Regardless, we will look at the role measuring productivity has on productivity.

Case Study in Timeliness in Sharing the Measure

How important is timing and frequency of sharing a measure in healthcare? Does a 20% improvement in hand hygiene compliance interest you? How about changing the culture in a large perioperative services unit in less than six months?

The 20% increase in hand hygiene compliance was appreciated at one of the world's finest hospitals, Cedars-Sinai in Los Angeles.[4] Jennifer Blaha is the master black belt (highly experienced performance improvement specialist) at Cedars-Sinai and wanted to see the effect of simply increasing the frequency of posting hand hygiene compliance on people's behavior. The unit was being observed daily, but the results were shared only monthly. The unit had achieved an increase in compliance but had plateaued with a stable rate. The compliance was not increasing or decreasing. Jen began posting the hand hygiene charts in the unit weekly versus monthly in addition to initiating an elevator marketing campaign. Guess what happened to compliance? The rehab unit achieved and sustained a 20% increase in compliance.

Jen had also begun posting the hand hygiene more frequently in another unit. While this unit also saw an immediate improvement in compliance, staff were not able to sustain the performance. I wonder if the second M, manage to the measure, might be needed. We will visit this again in the following chapters. Regardless, Cedars-Sinai went on to achieve record high hand hygiene compliance and has sustained these levels for over three years. Dr. Semmelweis would be very proud.

Key Points

- Utilizing the 3Ms goes hand in hand with being a Change Leader.
- Charts are an effective way to share data and turn data into information.
- Simple charts can be all that is needed.
- There are more advanced control charts that give extra value to exploring, explaining, and experimenting.
- Watch what you measure because you may get it. Perverse measures drive the wrong behavior.

Notes

1. Michael Porter and Robert Kaplan, How to solve the cost crisis in health care, *Harvard Business Review*, September 2011, pp. 46–64.
2. Peter F. Drucker, *Management Challenges for the 21st Century*, Jossey-Bass, San Francisco, 1999. Copyright © 1999 by Peter F. Drucker. Reprinted by permission of HarperCollins Publishers.
3. Western Electric history. http://www.porticus.org/bell/westernelectric_history. html#Western%20Electric%20-%20A%20Brief%20History.
4. Case Study of Hand Hygiene at Cedars-Sinai Medical Center, LA, California. Used with permission: Cedars-Sinai Medical Center.

Chapter 10

What to Measure

Introduction

Change Leaders, we know, have created a vision. They also have determined a way of measuring when the vision is achieved. This is an outcome measure relevant to the outcome desired from the change. Dr. W. Edwards Deming found that to achieve certain outcomes, especially those that occur infrequently or far in the future, it is useful and often necessary to measure the inputs. These inputs are the ones that need to change to achieve the outcome desired. Examples in healthcare are numerous.

Hidden Factory of Rework and Swiss Cheese

Dr. Deming and James Reason help us know what to measure in process improvement. Dr. Deming coached process improvement leaders to measure the inputs to a process to achieve the outcome desired. The graphics in Figures 10.1 to 10.4 may help you understand. We will use wrong-site surgery (WSS) and we use this frequently to achieve an understanding of why measuring the process is key to changing an outcome.

Eliminating WSSs is one of the best examples of needing to measure the process inputs that vary or may even go wrong. Fortunately, WSSs do not occur frequently enough to observe them happen. It is not practical to use the frequency of their occurrence to assess if changes have been

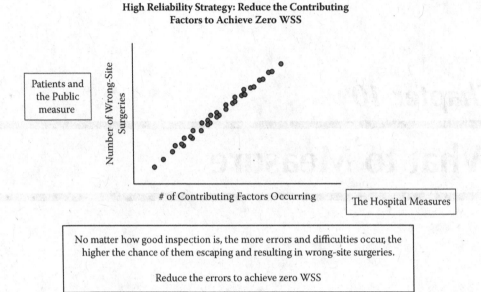

Figure 10.1 Theory of escaping defects, W. Edwards Deming.

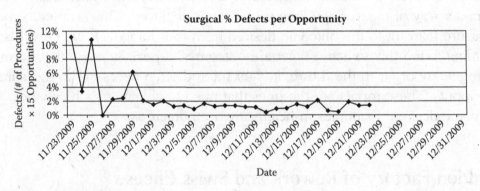

Figure 10.2 Chart of reduction in defects in surgical processes.

successful in reducing surgeries that go terribly wrong. Even though WSSs are one of the top three sentinel events most frequently reported to the Joint Commission, some healthcare organizations have never had one.

How do you lead a team to enact changes when the changes may never be seen in the outcome measure? You change the inputs. In Six Sigma, an equation often used describes what Dr. Deming did to improve the quality and safety in many different industries.

$$Y = f(x_1, x_2, x_3, \ldots, x_n)$$

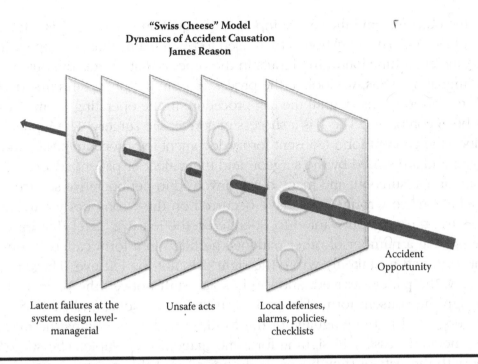

"Swiss Cheese" Model
Dynamics of Accident Causation
James Reason

Latent failures at the system design level-managerial

Unsafe acts

Local defenses, alarms, policies, checklists

Accident Opportunity

Figure 10.3   James Reason's Swiss cheese model of escaping defects.

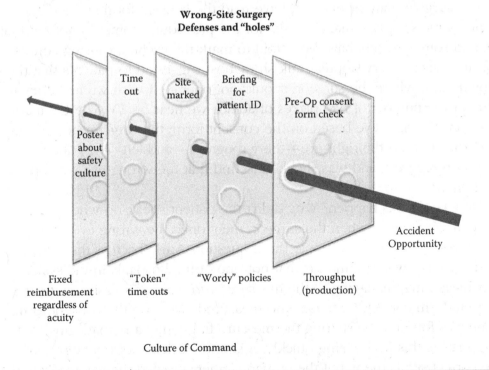

Wrong-Site Surgery
Defenses and "holes"

Time out

Site marked

Briefing for patient ID

Pre-Op consent form check

Poster about safety culture

Accident Opportunity

Fixed reimbursement regardless of acuity

"Token" time outs

"Wordy" policies

Throughput (production)

Culture of Command

Figure 10.4   "Swiss cheese" model for wrong-site surgery.

Y is the outcome, and the *X*s are inputs. The equation reads as, "*Y* is a function of the *X*s." This equation is then used to teach teams that an output and outcome are a function of the inputs in the process that creates the outcome. In eliminating WSSs, we look at the processes from the physician's first decision to perform surgery until the last procedure in the operating room (OR) has been completed. The *Y* is a successful correct-site surgery. The inputs include the consent form (consent forms document the procedure, site, and patient and are signed by the surgeon and the patient or patient advocate), patient input, surgeon, and many others involved in perioperative services.

What can go wrong? WSSs have occurred on the wrong body part. In one case, the surgeon wanted to operate on the left eye. Later that day, after seeing a number of other patients, he filled in a form called a consent form and mistakenly wrote the right eye, not the left eye. The day of surgery, the patient arrived, and the hospital staff noticed the patient did not sign the consent form. The patient, nervous, anxious, and perhaps not very good in the language of the form, signed as one signs the many documents necessary in signing for a mortgage, for example. The surgeon met with the patient (few hospitals do not require this premeeting), who may have been one of several patients he was operating on that day.

The surgeon may or may not have read the consent form and left to scrub. Some surgeons mark the site for the procedure, some do not mark at all, and some patients have been told to mark themselves, causing confusion for all. In fact, a very popular talk show host suggested to patients that they should mark where the surgeon should not operate. I wish we had a measure for the number of bad pieces of advice we hear on TV. The OR team prepared the right eye based on the consent form; the surgeon performed the procedure on the right eye—the wrong eye—and left. The patient awoke in recovery and was shocked to find that the wrong eye was operated on.

How could this happen? Why didn't the patient speak up when signing the consent form or when the surgeon mentioned the wrong eye during the premeeting? The answers to these questions varied across the WSSs we studied. What was common is that not one of the hospitals in the system was measuring, managing to the measure, *and* making it easier to get the consent form correct. Of those who measured errors on the consent form, none was found to be sharing the measure frequently and managing to it. Fortunately, this is changing quickly. Again, the science of operating on the correct site is there, but the human element created the variability and wrong outcome.

Getting Started: Preparing for Change, Chartering, and Stakeholder Analysis

Case Study: 3Ms Improving Surgical Safety

We have been measuring WSSs for a long time, and little has changed, despite the World Health Organization (WHO) surgical safety checklist, the Joint Commission's Universal Protocol, and that no one intends to do harm. Success has been made, though, at Lifespan, Rhode Island's major healthcare system, whose teams applied the 3Ms (measure, manage to the measure, make it easier) for process improvement.

Dr. Mary Reich Cooper, senior vice president and chief quality officer at Lifespan and sponsor of my work, reports zero WSSs since implementing the changes. The system had five wrong patient/site/procedure events in 2007–2009 according to Dr. Cooper. The team at Rhode Island Hospital (RIH) included Diane Skorupski, director of the OR; Dr. Ed Marcaccio; Dr. William Cioffi; and every manager and staff person. RIH is the largest hospital in the state and a trauma 1 hospital with over twenty-five operating rooms. My teammates were an obstetrician-gynecologist (OB-GYN), Dr. Erin Dupree, who is trained as a Lean Six Sigma green belt; and Kate Ranft, who is trained in change management and has a PhD in English. We worked with three Lifespan hospitals and researched everything we could find on WSS. We appreciate the states of Pennsylvania and Minnesota, which provided public information on occurrences of WSS.

The project at Lifespan was in a highly charged environment—leading change to reduce the risk of wrong-patient and -site surgery across the system. The stakeholder analysis template guided us in indentifying all stakeholders, prioritizing where resistance may occur, and developing strategies to engage stakeholders and manage resistance.

The Measure Is Invented

We started with measuring the number of WSSs, which included wrong-patient surgeries that had occurred. We found no measures currently in place. No one expected a chart measuring the number of WSSs. To Dr. Deming's point, measuring an infrequent outcome like WSS is not very useful. We dug deeper for other measures that might correlate with the errors in the past. We looked for evidence of audits that might have recorded relevant measures. We held focus groups to learn the level of awareness of the staff and physicians in measures that might hint at issues. We not only did not find any measures, but also few staff remembered anyone gathering any information relative to WSSs. In fact, we found no ongoing measures within the hospitals of anything to do with quality and safety.

Let me be clear about Lifespan's measure compared to most hospitals and ambulatory surgical centers where I have worked. They are statistically no worse than many other healthcare organizations based on the number of procedures they perform. And, few others are measuring what we started measuring in Lifespan in 2009—the year of the last WSS at Lifespan. I knew then that we could make a big difference in this very rare, but inexcusable, mistake. We use this case and its significant success in changing a culture and eliminating errors to learn process improvement's 3Ms: measure, manage to the measure, and make it easier.

Measuring the Errors to Reduce the Risk of Wrong-Site Surgery

We had to find the defects along the way that may slip through defenses some day and result in a wrong-site surgery (WSS). It is not one defect that causes these events. Often, an interaction between two defects results in an error. We thought if we could apply Dr. Deming's methods to measure the defects, we would reduce the number of defective units, surgeries in this project.

Healthcare, like many organizations today, is complex. Complexity can be described by how many people, variables, environments, regulations, and reliability issues are present in the system. We had to find a way to focus on the vital few, or fewer in this complexity, and start measuring those inputs. A failure mode and effects criticality analysis gave us the method to filter down to the vital variables to measure defects.

We found about fourteen variables, and some of these may seem quite trivial to those who are not involved with perioperative processes. In studying WSS, we saw that site marking, consent forms, and the energy it took to get staff and physicians to concentrate during the time-out that should occur immediately before "knife to skin" were some of the fourteen. A time-out is a method to get everyone to focus and inspect the site, side, patient, and other variables. It is the last chance to prevent an error. We created a data collection sheet to record the occurrence *and* quality of these variables. What we mean by quality is best described using an example.

Culture is hard to measure, but we can measure behaviors. Is the culture in the OR conducive to people helping each other prevent defects? I have

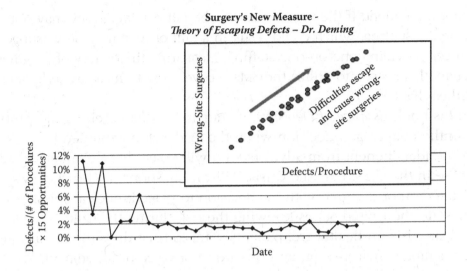

Figure 10.5   Surgery's new measure.

witnessed time-outs done by a nurse in the corner, and no one is paying any attention. At Lifespan, they got so mindful during time-outs, they actually physically pointed to and touched the site, just like two pilots who point to and touch the dial to adjust altitude to ensure they are really concentrating on what they intend to do. Getting back to what we mean by the quality of an action, Lifespan would measure how many calls it took to get something to occur, such as a time-out, versus whether the action occurred or not. Do you see the degree of difference? This gave Lifespan much more power in analyzing and improving.

We now chart in hospitals and ambulatory surgical centers similar charts like the one in Figure 10.5. Although not Lifespan data, this chart reflects the significant reduction in errors and defects possible. Measuring the defects and managing to them is exactly what Dr. Deming intended. Lifespan is leading the way in surgical process improvement to reduce the probability of a WSS.

Measuring the Quality of a Decision

At another health system, a process improvement team needed to correct poor decisions in assessing the risk of a patient falling. Some hospitals have a "no restraint" policy often used for patients who may injure themselves getting out of bed. These hospitals may provide one-on-one staffing to monitor the patient. If they cannot assess the fall risk well, they may not provide the staffing, which could result in a fall, or they may be wasting resources providing one-on-one staffing. Measuring the quality of judgment is yet another reason to utilize the 3Ms. I cover how to measure judgment in a further chapter.

In his book *Essence of Decision*,"[1] Graham T. Allison relates the problem in the quality of a decision when the leader is surrounded by "yes men." Leaders benefit from advisors who will voice disagreement, as was the case in the Cuban Missile Crisis. Allison questions if Khrushchev's advisors did not disagree with his decision to place a nuclear missile so close to the United States knowing the risk during the Cold War of a nuclear crisis. In healthcare, patients want to trust the surgeon, are in a very strange environment, and often do not voice disagreement. We come back to how process improvement teams can improve the culture if people are comfortable in challenging others, even charismatic leaders who may have the authority to fire. There are solutions, and the 3Ms guide teams and leadership in improving cultures as well as processes and outcomes.

Practicing Measuring

Let us practice measuring an outcome that is easier to measure and see the effect from changes you will make. Pick an outcome that you can measure frequently in a day that provides an opportunity to see the tasks that lead up to the outcome. An idea is the time it takes getting visitors to where they want to go. The outcome is getting them to the correct place in your building the first time with no wrong turns or mistakes. Another metric might be arrival in the least amount of time given the pace the visitor wants to travel. A good outcome metric in this last scenario might be the seconds elapsed from the time the person needs help until the person is where he or she wants to be. Note the time is when the visitor first needs help, not when you recognize you need to help. Outcome metrics should be customer centric, not business centric. Tasks along the way may start with recognizing someone needs assistance.

Healthcare members do this better than just about anyone else, I think. I see housekeepers, nurses, receptionists, volunteers, and executives stopping whatever they are doing to help a visitor navigate an often-confusing path to where the visitor wants to go. I have seen chief executive officers (CEOs) speaking with chief nursing officers (CNOs) stop dead in their tracks and help someone with directions. Other tasks can be pointing out the signage, contacting others by phone, writing directions, and more.

Setup

Set up a table to record the outcome metric and input metrics each time a visitor needs help. Record the data in a reasonable increment. For the scenario mentioned, minutes might not be granular enough to see changes. Time can be aggregated up, so maybe start with measuring any time metric in seconds. Another metric might be whether an error in direction is made. A count of errors gives us both a time and a defect metric. Let us keep this first practice simple and record the number of wrong turns or mistakes the visitor makes in getting to the destination and the errors in giving direction and signage caused by misunderstanding by the visitor. A simple interview follow-up of the visitor can obtain these data without being too obtrusive, and the visitors may actually be impressed with your effort to improve what we have all needed—getting directions in a building or neighborhood. I even have trouble finding the way out of my family physician's office treatment room area. See Figure 10.6 for a data collection tool. I include a larger one in Appendix 8 for your convenience.

After recording your data on a reasonable number of events and probably discovering some other "opportunities" to improve during this little exercise, analyze the outcome and input metric data.

■ Total the input errors for each visitor assisted.
■ Compare the number of errors for outcomes when the visitor reached the destination correctly the first time with the number of errors made when the visitor did not reach the destination so well.
■ Do you see more errors for the bad outcomes? This simple exercise illustrates the theory of escaping defects. What if we would have had no input errors? The outcome is self-evident, of course, but even reducing the errors getting the visitor to the destination increases the probability that the visitor will reach the destination correctly the first time.

Are there any quick wins? Just by measuring, we often get some great ideas of what to improve. Perhaps a sign would be a little clearer? Or a map

Visitor (Remember patient confidentiality rules, so use something like a number or destination)	Outcome metric – Number of wrong turns in getting to the destination	Errors in giving directions (Count the times that you change your instruction, regardless of reason)	Signage – missing, wrong, confusing, too many signs, blocked	Visitor taking a wrong turn (Turning differently than the directions that you gave or the signage directs)
1	4	2	1	3
2	1	0	3	1
3				
4				
5				

Figure 10.6   Data collection for directions.

in your pocket to give to visitors or to help you give directions? Measuring has so many benefits to process improvement. Why does anyone resist it?

Please share your experiment with me at http://www.rpmexec.com, and I will share with others and give you credit. We can keep it confidential if you prefer. Regardless, I hope you see the difference in measuring inputs and outcomes and how reducing the errors in the inputs can have a favorable effect on outcomes.

A Change in One Area May Affect Other Areas

We need to be aware that measuring several outcomes may be necessary, depending on the project. An improvement in one area seldom occurs in a vacuum. It may have an effect elsewhere. Therefore, we need to consider measuring the outcome we expect to change and outcomes that may change because of changes made. We need a counterbalancing metric when a singular focus on one metric may result in an unfavorable change in another metric. A balance is needed. In an Agency for Healthcare Research and Quality (AHRQ) study of high-reliability organizations (HRO), the following statement was made: "Anything can be measured and measures can be quite simple, but sometimes multiple measures are essential to track system performance."[2]

Inventory Management

Inventory management is an example of when we may need to measure two or more outcomes. Healthcare organizations often experience wastes when supplies run out. In one hospital, a person had to leave the OR an average of seven times per patient case to get something outside the OR.

Sometimes, the most common supply, such as saline to irrigate an incision site, is in short supply. We often find that someone was charged with reducing inventory, which is quite easy. The outcome is also easy to measure and is usually the amount of money in inventory.

In inventory reduction projects, I have seen people go after the big dollars with arbitrary goals such as to reduce the amount of inventory dollars by 50%. The team may have looked at the items with the most dollars in inventory and translated the goal to be a 50% reduction in count to get to the 50% reduction in dollars, euros, pounds, or whatever the currency is. The team identifies an item and then cuts the inventory in half. You know that there is something missing here. One should measure how many are needed and at least another variable, the responsiveness of the supplier to replenish, before changing the amount in stores. Here we have four measures, at a minimum:

■ Inventory investment (count and maybe currency)
■ Demand quantity
■ Frequency of replenishment
■ Time to replenishment

Did you think of another critical metric? An outcome metric should be customer centric. Does a patient really care how many pounds of saline are on the shelf? What do patients care about? They care that the OR team has the saline when needed. Thus, we have a "balancing" outcome metric that process improvement leaders who are successful often measure. Service level *and* inventory reduction should always be measured together. These are classic balancing outcome metrics that process improvement teams need to understand and be confident enough to use. Sometimes, resistance will come based on the measures. Not all measures will be politically correct, but that does not mean you should completely ignore the metric. The number of times a surgeon is late for a case is a sensitive metric. A good Change Leader can minimize the resistance to get the measurement working for the organization.

Balancing Metrics, Be Careful What You Measure!

A surgeon may be frustrated because she runs out of nonblunt sutures and starts measuring the number of times she runs out. Nonblunt suture? I heard this term for a week by surgeons operating in a major medical center as they sent nurses out to get them. Seems like an odd way of naming a suture. Isn't the prime function of a suture to be sharp enough to pierce the skin? Did you ever hear in a steak house, "Get me a nonblunt steak knife?" When did healthcare stop calling a sharp suture simply a suture and anything purposely not as sharp as blunt?

Balancing metrics often results in resistance. A Change Leader has to be aware that simply how change is measured can result in extreme resistance. For instance, Finance may feel that inventory reduction has been stalled too long because the clinical staff kept playing to the fear that patients may die if inventory is reduced. The chief financial officer (CFO) tells the inventory reduction team to "get in there and reduce the inventory and focus on that metric." The same argument works the other way.

Regarding the nonblunt sutures, the state inspectors had come in and told the hospital to use blunt sutures to reduce the risk to the surgical team from getting pricked from sutures. *Stick* is a term describing an accidental puncture. It was a stick that caused the pathogens to enter Dr. Semmelweis's colleague and resulted in him getting puerperal fever. His death in turn triggered Semmelweis's understanding that something on a surgeon's hands was killing mothers that the surgeon touched. The OR director, fearing for her career, increased the stock and told her team this was a NOOSE. No, we do not mean that she was going to hang someone if the surgeon did not have her desired suture. NOOSE is a term to describe an item that should be "never out of stock, ever." Healthcare has them all over: saline in an OR, dressings in an emergency department, syringes in a lab, consent forms in a surgeon's office, gloves in an isolation area, and alcohol-based hand cleaner near every patient care area. Measuring the inventory *and* availability of NOOSEs is a very wise practice by supply chain managers. I show you how to measure NOOSEs and just about anything in healthcare in further chapters.

Measure What the Customer Measures

A good rule of thumb is to measure whatever your customer measures. Resistance will come soon and strong if the measure you are using in process improvement is not appreciated by the stakeholders. As much as I respect a physician I worked with, he and I continue to have different views of what to measure in surgical safety. He wanted to measure the number of surgical cases (a case is defined as all procedures performed in a single trip to the OR) that had zero slips, lapses, and mistakes. I wanted to measure and share with the client the number of slips, lapses, and mistakes. I could estimate the average number of cases with zero defects by dividing the number of slips, lapses, and mistakes by the number of cases, but we both knew that this was not precise because a large number of defects in any one case results in the average number of zero-defect cases being lower than actual.

Calculating the number of cases with zero defects takes a lot more effort in recording because we have to record all defects for each case versus simply measuring the number of defects for the day or whatever period is used to chart the defects. This goes back to the issue of not getting a measure for hand hygiene from the hospital that collected many observations because it was not easy enough to measure. My other argument for not focusing so much on the number of zero-defect cases is an argument of customer centricity. I do not think a patient values as much a metric about how many defect-free cases the surgery center has had. The patient cares that there are no errors or zero defects along the way. Only a fool expects inspection to catch all errors.

I would think of James Reason's Swiss cheese model when I am going in for surgery because I do not trust the defenses knowing defects happen. And, the type of defect means a lot to me, if not more than the number. I will choose a surgeon who has forgotten to wait until everyone is silent when he is doing a time-out over a surgeon who has marked the wrong incision site.

Base the Measure on Correlation with the Outcome

What we measure should be based on importance to the outcome. This is the key point to customers as well as teams. The energy to reduce resistance can also be better applied by the Change Leader if the importance to the outcome of each metric is estimated. Getting resistance on how to measure something that we think might be important is one thing. If I am getting resistance in measuring a primary function, I am willing to devote more energy to reducing that resistance.

Now is a good time to add another benefit of the 3Ms, specifically, make it easier. I hinted at this benefit when I discussed trying to measure defective cases and how hard it is to collect the data to calculate the percentage of defective cases. Make it easier to measure for if measuring is too difficult, the person leading the team and team members will meet with much resistance. How many times is measurement not achieved because the resistance to the effort to measure is the argument? In the chapter on how to measure, I make it as easy as possible to measure. Just because something we know is important to measure is hard to measure, this is not justification not to measure. Mike Fenger, formerly the chief quality officer and my boss at Motorola, coached us all that although it may be hard to measure, keep trying to find a way. Dr. Deming acknowledges numerous times that what is most important may not be measurable. That does not mean it is not important, and it does not mean the Change Leader is off the hook to measure. We must find a way to measure.

High-Reliability Organizations: What Do They Measure?

A measure could be zero failures reaching the customer. I share more after some definitions. Healthcare executives are hearing a lot about HROs. Everyone seems to want to become one, whatever they think HROs are. As a patient, I think healthcare also should become an HRO. So, what is an HRO? What do they measure? What can a process improvement leader do to help an organization become an HRO?

Let us give credit to authors who have studied companies and industries that many refer to as HROs. My favorites are James Reason, Karl Weick, Kathleen Sutcliffe, the Orladys, and David Marx, to name a few. We would be remiss for not mentioning Dr. Deming, Dr. Shewhart, Sakichi Toyoda, Taiichi Ohno, and companies; SKF is a Swedish manufacturer that pioneered many of the concepts HROs practice today. Let me add the U.S. Navy; United Airlines, which has not had a pilot-caused error fatality since 1978 and pioneered in the aviation industry crew resource management (CRM); and others noted in the work of the authors mentioned.

Healthcare benefits from the work commissioned by the AHRQ. I draw from their work, *Becoming a High Reliability Organization: Operational Advice for Hospital Leaders*.[3]

Karl Weick and Kathleen Sutcliffe believe HROs are mindful of variation occurring and ways failures occur and thus are more able to prevent accidents than those not mindful. They find five elements to being mindful:[4]

- **Sensitivity to operations.** Preserving constant awareness by leaders and staff of the state of the systems and processes that affect patient care. This awareness is key to noting risks and preventing them.

■ **Reluctance to simplify.** Simple processes are good, but simplistic explanations for why things work or fail are risky. Avoiding overly simple explanations of failure (unqualified staff, inadequate training, communication failure, etc.) is essential to understand the true reasons patients are placed at risk.

■ **Preoccupation with failure.** When near misses occur, these are viewed as evidence of systems that should be improved to reduce potential harm to patients. Rather than viewing near misses as proof that the system has effective safeguards, they are viewed as symptomatic of areas in need of more attention.

■ **Deference to expertise.** If leaders and supervisors are not willing to listen and respond to the insights of staff who know how processes really work and the risks patients really face, you will not have a culture in which high reliability is possible.

■ **Resilience.** Leaders and staff need to be trained and prepared to know how to respond when system failures do occur.

Should we measure the organization's mindfulness if it is that important? How do we measure mindfulness? Should we measure the five elements and consider mindfulness an outcome to a greater outcome, which is safety? Do HROs measure the elements?

In reliability and safety work, the five elements are definitely measured. Role playing, "war games," and other exercises help us become more mindful, and practice is important. Pilots spend a lot of time in flight simulators experiencing errors and defects for a couple of reasons: (1) They learn how to counter the issue, and (2) they become more mindful of the issue.

Measuring these specific considerations, general orientation, impact on processes, and ultimate outcome is what Dr. Deming intended in his theory of escaping defects. We can use the $Y = f(x)$ equation again. Exceptionally safe, consistently high quality of care $= f$ (Specific considerations, General orientation, Impact on processes). If you want it, measure it.

For us in this book, suffice it to say a process improvement leader will do well measuring these if charged with leading an organization to become an HRO. The following measures are from the AHRQ study. Many of the specific initiatives described include descriptions of how progress was measured over time.

■ **Measuring leadership.** Jeff Selberg, former CEO of Exempla Lutheran Hospital, shared these discussions of leadership's role in creating a high-performance culture.[5]
  – Are you committed to your own growth as you grow your organization?
  – Are you creating the environment so that the right and, most of the time, the wicked questions are asked?
  – Are you engaging in patient-centered versus ego-centered conversations?
■ Are you embracing challenges that stretch your capacity as a leader?

A Safety Culture and How to Measure

The aviation industry has its HROs. Even though lives have been lost, the volume, complexity, and uncontrollable factors (including weather) make air travel arguably safer than most other modes of transportation. The culture in HROs is a "safety culture." James T Reason, in his book *Managing the Risks of Organizational Accidents,*[6] shares what a safety culture is and its four critical subcomponents:

■ A reporting culture
■ A just culture
■ A flexible culture
■ A learning culture

The interaction of these four subcomponents equates with the term *safety culture.*

I do not know how to measure culture, but I have measured the behaviors in reporting, judging and coaching, flexing with variables that occur prior to failures, and behaviors of instructing and coaching before, during, and after surgery. These cultures are pervasive in HROs. These behaviors are seen in HROs every second of the day. The people in HROs behave this way regardless if someone is watching. They manage to the measure. Any behavior that is not safe is managed. This is managing to the measure. HROs also make reliability increasingly easier as they become more reliable. An HRO is a continuous improvement organization at its highest level of meaning.

Measuring the Inputs versus Just the Outcomes

James Reason finds that measuring the intrinsic safety of a system is not best done measuring outcome data. A better method is to measure the process. As in our work in reducing WSSs and catastrophic failures in vehicles where the events rarely occur, outcome data are an unreliable method because they are too late and too infrequent. As Dr. Deming shares, the way to prevent bad outcomes is to measure the process variables that correlate with outcomes. Control these variables, and one controls the outcomes. Think of these as the vital signs. Vital signs are those measures that can predict health. Improving the vital signs improves the outcome.

An outcome desired by many improvements, regardless of industry, is financial gain. Notice that the financial metric follows the outcome and process metrics. These efforts and measures all have an impact that can be translated into money. For instance, reducing medical errors saves the patient time and money and sometimes his or her life. Reducing this most common error also reduces the healthcare organization's costs and may even save its existence when the cost of litigation and lost revenue is too great for the organization to survive.

Therefore, a Change Leader's greatest convincing argument is often to translate improvements in process metrics and outcomes into financial impact. A Change Leader is wise always to consider financial impact, even if deciding later not to mention financial impact. A Change Leader may actually increase resistance if he or she tries to use money saved as the reason to reduce errors in surgery. Others may be so enraged by mentioning financial impact when the true purpose of the change is to protect patients and staff that they may rebel and not even start the change process.

In many changes, the financial impact is a Change Leader's tool, and he or she should use it. The cost of healthcare today is one of the biggest issues in America, the United Kingdom, and across the globe. We have to change to something different because we cannot continue to go deeper into debt and receive the same amount of care. Presidential candidates have used healthcare's financial implications as a reason for change.

Measuring the Culture

I have never found a means to measure culture directly; we successfully measured behaviors in the OR and relevant behaviors before and after surgery. Those behaviors were measured for every case and every procedure within a case, and immediate feedback was given by many to correct the behaviors before they resulted in failures.

There are stories of surgeons becoming angry and throwing knives. I have never witnessed such an event, but I have heard from many experienced and reputable surgical team members these events have occurred. I have also heard that little, in fact nothing, had been done to address these behaviors in the past in some institutions. These are the same institutions where no measurement or recording of the event probably took place. To change to a culture of safety, we decided to measure the four subcomponents of a safety culture.

The WHO Surgical Safety Checklist is a valiant attempt to reduce the risk of error in surgery. There are three process steps measured in the checklist.[7]

- The sign in step includes measuring if the patient and the surgeon are in agreement on the surgery to be performed and if the staff is aware of possible risks, such as allergies to medicines.
- The time-out step is arguably the most important step to measure in the prevention of wrong patient, wrong site, and wrong procedure. The behaviors expected inside the OR are often predictable during the time-out. The time-out's purpose is to ensure the correct patient, procedure, and site are known before the surgeon makes the incision or entry. If the culture is one of teamwork, the time-out will have all members paying attention during this quick but effective minute spent.
- If the culture is top down and authoritative with limited value on teamwork, the time-out may not even occur. A circulating nurse may be responsible to ensure the surgeon performs the time-out, and this nurse may be berated for reminding the surgeon to perform the time-out. I have seen in even the finest hospitals a surgeon totally dismiss doing the time-out while the circulating nurse goes through the motion of a time-out. Measure these behaviors, manage to these measures, make it easier for the surgical team to perform the time-out correctly, and WSS can be eliminated. Rhode Island hospitals have not had a WSS since enacting a checklist that not only measures if the time-out was done but also how well everyone behaved during the time-out. If the surgeon required several prompts by the staff to do the time-out, these prompts were measured, charted, shared with leadership, and addressed with the surgeon.

Total Quality Measurement System for Perioperative Process. Preop and OR Critical-To-Quality Factors

Pre-op site mark (surgeon's initials) **on or as close as anatomically** possible to the surgical site upon arrival in OR
Surgeon initiated Time Out Independently without prompt
Surgeon initiated Time Out after prompt from a team member
Surgeon initiated Time Out after more than one prompt from a team member
Surgeon Refused to do the Time Out after prompt
Surgeon Refused to do the Time Out after prompt and the situation was escalated up the chain of command
Did not initiate a Time Out and was not prompted by a team member
Team members ceased conversation Independently without prompt
Team ceased after prompt by a team member
Team ceased after more than one prompt from a team member

Figure 10.7　Measuring behaviors to measure the culture.

■ Debriefing is a powerful communication and learning step. The military will debrief after war games and battle to become more mindful and improve.

The checklist and job aids created for each role on the surgical team make it easier to do the right thing. An example of how to measure behaviors in is Figure 10.7. The desired behavior is listed first. Subsequent rows show an increasing degree of undesired behaviors. The mildest nonconformance usually is when the behavior is missing initially, such as the surgeon initiating the time-out after one prompt by a team member. The most severe behavior is refusal to do the behavior and no member prompting the behavior. No one speaking up is considered worse than the responsible person refusing despite a team member reminding the person. The reason is that besides the responsible person refusing, the reporting culture, as mentioned by James Reason as practiced by HROs, is also missing.

The following quotation is from a National Transportation Safety Board (NTSB) presentation by the honorable Jim Hall, former chair of the NTSB: "We've found through 30 years of accident investigation that sometimes the most common link is the attitude of corporate leadership toward safety."[8]

We used data from past failures across the US hospitals that publicly reported to reduce the resistance to change. The NTSB also considers a corporate culture to be triggered at the top of an organization and measured at the bottom.

The only thing we have to fear is fear itself.[9]

Franklin D. Roosevelt

Change Leaders recognize the fear of change and address it head on. Franklin D. Roosevelt, in his inaugural address before he took the oath of office as president of the United States during the depths of the Depression, spoke this famous line, often quoted by process improvement leaders: "So, first of all, let me assert my firm belief that the only thing we have to fear is fear itself—nameless, unreasoning, unjustified terror which paralyzes needed efforts to convert retreat into advance." How many times have you found resistance to change when those resisting do not even know the reason for their fears or their information is false?

FDR continues: "In every dark hour of our national life a leadership of frankness and vigor has met with that understanding and support of the people themselves which is essential to victory. I am convinced that you will again give that support to leadership in these critical days." Again, we repeat the need for process improvement team leaders to be frank with the people, and the people will understand and lend support to the changes necessary. "If they know what I know, they will feel like I feel, and they will do as I do." FDR continues: "With this pledge taken, I assume unhesitatingly the leadership of this great army of our people dedicated to a disciplined attack upon our common problems. This Nation asks for action, and action now." A process improvement leader informs his or her "army," engages the stakeholders, acts, and acts now, not later.

So how do we measure risk that leads us to realize fear and reduce the very fear that creates the resistance to change, especially the paralyzing fear of change? The next chapter answers our question.

Key Points

- Measure the input variables, the Xs, to improve the outcome.
- Balance measures to achieve the right change, not to sacrifice one outcome for another.
- Measure the five elements of mindfulness and manage to the measure.
- HROs measure and operate on mindfulness and measure and manage to the behaviors that are safe.
- Making it easier to be mindful and build a safety culture is key to achieving a safety culture.

Notes

1. Allison Graham, *Essence of Decision: Explaining the Cuban Missile Crisis,* Little Brown, New York, 1971.
2. S. Hines, K. Luna, J. Lofthus, et al., *Becoming a High Reliability Organization: Operational Advice for Hospital Leaders* (Prepared by the Lewin Group under Contract No. 290-04-0011), AHRQ Publication No. 08-0022, Agency for Healthcare Research and Quality, Rockville, MD, April 2008, http://www.ahrq.gov/qual/hroadvice/hroadvice.pdf.
3. Ibid.
4. Karl E. Weick and Kathleen M. Sutcliffe, *Managing the Unexpected Resilient Performance in an Age of Uncertainty*, Wiley, New York, 2007. Reprinted with permission of John Wiley and Sons, Inc.
5. http://www.ahrq.gov/qual/hroadvice/hroadvice3.htm
6. James Reason, *Managing the Risks of Organizational Accidents*, Ashgate, Surrey, UK, 1997.
7. http://www.who.int/patientsafety/safesurgery/ss_checklist/en/
8. http://www.ntsb.gov/doclib/speeches/sumwalt/SCEG_pre.pdf
9. "Only thing we have to fear is fear itself": FDR's first inaugural address, 1933. http://historymatters.gmu.edu/d/5057/.

Chapter 11

Measure Risk to Achieve High Reliability

Introduction

High-reliability organizations measure risk. Then, they prioritize the risks and act to prevent failure. The tool they use is aptly named: failure mode, effect, and criticality analysis (FMECA). FMECA was originally documented in 1949 by the U.S. military. (FMECA is found in MIL Spec MIL-P-1629.)[1]

Resistance can come from fear. Fear may come from what the change brings to the person resisting, to the future, to the organization, to the patient or customer, or to any other stakeholder.

The National Transportation Safety Board's (NTSB's) vice chair, Robert L. Sumwalt, summarized the NTSB's findings in over thirty years of accident investigations. "The safest carriers have more effectively committed themselves to controlling the risks that may arise from mechanical or organizational failures, environmental conditions and human error."[2] Most important, we used FMEA (failure mode effects analysis) to help lead the culture change in the operating room (OR).

FMECA is a reliability evaluation technique to determine and measure the effect of system and equipment failures. Although FMECA is an essential reliability task, it also provides information for other purposes. The use of FMECA is called for in maintainability, safety analysis, survivability and vulnerability, logistics support analysis, maintenance plan analysis, and failure detection and isolation subsystem design. This coincident use must be a consideration in planning the FMECA effort to prevent the proliferation of requirements and the duplication of efforts within the same contractual program. These failures are classified according to their impact on mission success and personnel/equipment safety.

There are two steps to an FMECA:

■ Failure mode and effects analysis
■ Criticality analysis (CA)

We will concentrate on FMEA because it is one of the first tools in designing a process or product and the foundation of FMECA. The purpose of FMEA is to measure risk, prioritize that risk, and then prevent failure with an action plan and control plan. FMEA is a process improvement team's tool to engage the stakeholders in the change. FMEA is the culmination of the thoughts of the stakeholders and subject matter experts of how a system can fail, the effects of those failures, and the priorities in making the changes. FMEA is also a Change Leader's tool to improve a change and the change process. Stakeholders engaged in completing the FMEA may well discover potential failures in the change. The FMEA assists the Change Leader and the Stakeholders to reduce the potential failures in the change.

The FMEA Form

Look at the FMEA form in Figure 11.1. The form is well known in HROs and virtually every company in the auto industry, aviation, aerospace, electrical safety, nuclear, and many other industries. I explain FMEA and how it measures risk and prioritizes risk by explaining each column of the FMEA form. FMEA is a measurement tool for change. Measuring outcomes and inputs is easy in the FMEA. Notice the column for the input. This FMEA form makes it easier for you and your team to connect how the inputs and outcomes are related. Not every FMEA has a column for the input, and there are variations to FMEAs, but this FMEA form will look familiar to anyone who has used FMEA in healthcare, automotive, aviation, NASA, and nuclear industries. Not listing the inputs misses a chance to "connect the dots" of inputs failing and results in poor effects (outcomes). We have clearly identified the connectivity of inputs to the possible outcomes via each row on the Excel file.

Failure Mode and Effects Analysis

					Prepared by:			
System or process name:			Process Owner Name:					
Core team member			Date latest version:		FMEA Date (Orig)			
Sequence	**Process Step or Function**	**Input**	**Potential Failure Mode**	**Potential Effect(s) of Failure**	S E V	**Potential Contributing Factors to Failure**	O C C	**Current Process Controls Prevention**	**Current Process Controls Detection**	D E T	R P N
Sequence	Include step from Process Map in all rows for sorting	Include input from Process Map in all rows for sorting	Failure or symptom evidenced in the output	Impact on the customer requirements	How severe is the effect to the customer?	Causes to input failure. Add row for each cause within step/Input	How often does cause or FM occur?	Existing controls that prevent the cause or the Failure Mode	Existing controls that detect the cause or the Failure Mode before defects escape	How well can you detect cause or FM?	Risk Priority #
1											
2											
3											
4											
5											
6											
7											
8											
9											
10											
11											
12											
13											
14											
15											
16											
17											
18											
19											

Figure 11.1   FMEA form.

The Process Step or Design Function

The FMEA begins by identifying a system and then subsystems listed in the header. The perioperative process in healthcare could be such a system, with intraoperative processes as a subsystem. Within the process are steps. In a design effort, the process step column converts to a function of the design. A piece of imaging equipment has one primary function and that is to develop an image. We will stay with the example of perioperative services to explain the FMEA process and form. Dr. DuPree and I use an input that was a contributing factor in 60% of the wrong-site surgeries we studied: site marking. Site marking identifies where the incision is to be made on the patient.

Input, Failure Modes, Effects, Causes, and Scoring of Risk

The next column on the FEMA form lists the inputs to the process. In our example, we consider site marking as a critical input for preventing an incision in the wrong area. We list failure modes in the next column. A failure mode is how a failure of the input is evidenced. A common failure mode for site marking is not marking the site. It is important to list all failure modes for each input. Another failure mode for site marking is marking the wrong limb. The failure effect is the outcome that goes wrong, wrong-site surgery, in this example. The next column is the first of three measures, what this book is about. Severity is a measure of the impact the failure mode has on the customer or patient in our example. The higher the severity to the patient, the higher the severity value is. There are tables healthcare organizations may use to calibrate the severity measure, with a nine or ten reserved for catastrophic failure. See Appendix 9 for tables that you can use or modify.

Catastrophic failure is a loss of personnel or equipment. The next column lists the potential causes for the failure. Again, we may have multiple causes for each failure mode. The team should exhaust all causes, knowing that a prioritization will occur in the FMEA process to focus on the vital few causes. The second measure, occurrence, is in the next column. Occurrence refers to the frequency of the cause occurring and resulting in the failure mode. Data are sometimes available and should be used in FMEA. However, FMEA is to be used first in designing a process so data will not exist. Comparable relevant data should be used however subjective it may be and replaced as data become available. A high occurrence relative to the entire FMEA for this system refers to a cause that more frequently occurs relative to other causes.

Existing Controls

The next two columns are related. They are to list any controls in place that will prevent the root cause resulting in a failure mode and thus an unfavorable effect. Often, the FMEA will have nothing in this column because no control exists to prevent failure. The next column is more likely to be populated, especially in healthcare, where often inspection is the only control in place. We cannot always control a surgeon's marking of a site if we are in the OR setting up a case. But the team can detect and control the process by requiring the surgeon to mark the site prior to the patient entering the OR. The last of three measures, detection, is the FMEA's way of measuring the ability of detecting if a root cause occurred that may result in a failure mode and unfavorable effect. This measure often confuses people doing FMEA for the first time. The detection value will be lower when our ability improves in detecting a root cause prior to failure.

Risk Priority Number

The most important value in an FMEA is the Risk Priority Number (RPN) because the larger RPNs suggest the highest risk to focus improvement efforts. We often will sort the FMEA in descending RPN to bring the most important risks to the top. The RPN is simply calculated by multiplying the three values of severity, occurrence, and detection. Remember that the higher the value for each of the three variables, the higher the risk. To make calculating the RPN even easier for you, I include an Excel FMEA template at www.rpmexec.com which calculates the RPN.

I also have a column to list how we might detect variation in the input. The detection column is one of the three characteristics used to calculate the RPN. Detection is often the most important variable in the RPN in healthcare. The severity and occurrence may be the same for different cancers, but cancers with tests that can identify them have a lower RPN because the detection value is lower. Remember, the easier it is to detect an input starting to fail, the lower the detection value will be. Heart disease can be cured if inputs going wrong are measured (detected) and caught in advance. Diet, smoking, obesity, cholesterol, and other inputs once measured can be used to detect heart failure risk. Modifying and controlling these inputs can prevent heart disease and even cure it in some individuals. We use a template to better connect inputs to outcomes. The inputs are what may vary and fail. Again, improvement comes from managing the inputs and to prevent failure.

In healthcare, FMEA is in its infancy. Many hospitals have started using FMEA to prioritize their risks and improve processes to reduce the risk. In my work to prevent wrong-site surgery, we used FMEA from before our first on-site visit, added to it as new information occurred, and used it after we handed off the project to prioritize continuous improvement of their new quality and safety management system.

One FMEA Every Eighteen Months Sends the Wrong Message

At least one accrediting organization requires one FMEA to be done every eighteen months. Actually, this requirement sends the wrong message to many. It gives healthcare organizations a false sense of security when they interpret this to mean that one FMEA every year and a half is sufficient for patient and staff safety. The saying, "Beware: You get what you measure," warns us that this one FMEA every year and a half is not enough to achieve high reliability because healthcare is one of the most complex industries in the world. Healthcare is complex because it has an abundance of inputs and variation, lacks measurement of many of these inputs and outcomes, and lacks detectability of inputs that are starting to vary and fail. Healthcare needs FMEA more than most industries.

Why isn't healthcare a leader in the use of FMEA? Maybe it is because of the fragmentation of this industry. There are thousands of healthcare organizations in every developed country in the world compared to the aviation industry, which has two major airframe manufacturers who can promote the use of FMEA in their processes and demand FMEAs from its suppliers. The same is true in the automotive industry and electrical safety products industry, where I first learned and benefitted from FMEAs. Maybe healthcare is so far behind in benefitting from FMEA because of one of the reasons I wrote this book: resistance to measure how healthcare might fail a patient. Keep in mind that healthcare deserves much respect in measuring. Measuring the patient's vital signs is so ingrained in healthcare that the same industries which are HROs use the term *vital signs* to describe key measures to gauge the health of their processes and products. In Motorola, those at the Corporate Initiatives Group responsible for consulting in quality launched a quality improvement campaign named Quality Vital Signs under the direction of Mike Fenger, chief quality officer. Motorola Solutions leads the world in the sales of first responder communication devices, such as police and fire radios. If you work in a hospital, chances are your staff use Motorola devices, whether it is for clinical reasons or simply to trigger staff to bring more supplies to the OR. Motorola Solutions and the former Motorola Automotive unit, which turned around the quality of OnStar for GM, used FMEA extensively to create highly reliable communication devices.

FMEA for Information Technology

Even information technology (IT) in Motorola Automotive began using FMEA. Bill Cooper, IT manager for the Automotive Group in Seguin, Texas, and I led teams in design and manufacturing to improve the quality of automotive safety products, including OnStar and BMW Assist, a similar system to protect occupants of vehicles via communication of critical parameters and accident information. We were working to reduce zero-kilometer failures of the OnStar device. Zero-kilometer failures are failure modes that occur before the vehicle leaves the factory. You can imagine this is embarrassing to any supplier and highly frustrating to the vehicle manufacturer; GM and BMW were threatening to develop other suppliers, and Motorola was at risk for the first time since developing Telematics, the technology that makes OnStar and BMW Assist work. The engineers had used FMEA to design the product and processes to make OnStar. They had submitted the FMEAs to GM and BMW prior to shipping the first devices years ago. However, it is clear the FMEA and subsequent design and process improvements missed something.

Data Can Be a Component in Today's High-Tech Equipment

The team discovered that data errors occurred within the device causing the failures. Data in a Telematics device are a critical "component." I put component in quotation marks because components prior to microprocessors being installed in devices were seen as screws, metal, electrical resistors, and so on. In Telematics, data allowed the device to function. An example of data working as a component was the "wake-up" feature. Data in this feature included the identity of the vehicle where the Telematics unit was installed. If the data that identified the device were faulty (say it was actually another device and thus another vehicle), the intended device may not wake up and function. One function is to contact the police if an accident occurs. Help may not arrive, or arrive as quickly, if the device did not function.

But There Never Has Been an FMEA on Data Components

I asked Bill to bring the FMEA to the team so we could learn about the failure modes and potential causes of the effect of data components being wrong and not waking up the device. Bill looked a bit embarrassed. Bill knew what I did not know. FMEA was not required by the manufacturers for data components, and IT had never done an FMEA for any reason, despite the fact that data downloaded into a Telematics unit are as valuable as the hardware that holds the data. In fact, Bill Cooper coined the term *data component*, which is commonly used today in Telematics, to elevate the importance of designing a device that has a process to download data into it to function.

Why wouldn't a designer want to use the same proven method of using FMEA that has improved the quality and safety of everything from the simplest devices to space travel? I do not think it is any coincidence that the group that makes first responder radios and other safety equipment is also the business that helped develop Six Sigma in the 1980s when its quality started to suffer. This business unit is by far the market leader still and has now also won the Malcolm Baldrige Award. It was the first time Motorola won that Six Sigma first became known outside of Motorola.

FMEAs Do Not Always Prevent Catastrophic Failure

You may know that NASA and its partners used FMEA extensively and used it on the same systems that experienced catastrophic or mission-ending failures: *Apollo 1*, *Apollo 13*, and the space shuttles *Challenger* and *Columbia*. What experts know is that without FMEA, we never would have had many successful missions. In a *Wall Street Journal* article by Betsy McCaughey,[3] she countered a Medicare study and an editorial by another author suggesting that many surgeries on older Americans are wasteful because "32% of elderly American patients undergo surgery in the year before they die." Betsey added, "That's like saying Babe Ruth struck out 1,333 times so he must have been a poor ball player—even though he had a .342 lifetime batting average." NASA engineers describe rocket launches as sitting on top of a controlled explosion. Space travel is not without risk, and the safety record is as high as it is because of tools like FMEA that measured the risk, prioritized actions, and then used measurement of the input variables to know when to act to prevent failure.

The shuttle *Challenger* disaster highlighted the value of FMEA. The failure was technically a result of leakage eroding an O-ring, allowing gases to escape and ignite. Scientists and engineers had identified the risk of cold ambient temperatures allowing conditions resulting in the erosion of the O-ring. What failed that day was the ability of engineers and management to stop the launch despite knowing the risk. One could suggest it was what every Change Leader has to overcome: resistance. The decision makers resisted listening to the engineers, who said that the input, ambient temperature, had varied that day to a level never yet seen at launch. The engineers had measured the amount of O-ring erosion after each launch, knowing from the FMEA that there was a probability of erosion that could result in catastrophic failure. They had correlated ambient temperature to have an effect on the amount of erosion.

Lesson of 3Ms: Must Manage to the Measure, Not Just Measure

The *Challenger* disaster is a lesson of 3Ms (measure, manage to the measure, make it easier). Measurement had occurred. NASA and Morton Thiokol engineers were measuring the amount of erosion of the O-ring and measuring the ambient temperature the day of launch. What failed that day was the second M, manage to the measure. The measures were disregarded by management. Despite clear evidence that colder temperatures increased the risk of O-ring erosion with personnel and vehicle loss as a possible effect, NASA management failed to manage to the measure. They launched, and the shuttle program's first catastrophic failure occurred. NASA ultimately used the third M, make it easier, for engineers to be heard and management to make the correct decision to launch. A panel was set up to make it more difficult for decisions to ignore valuable tools like FMEA and measurements of inputs that may vary beyond limits.

HROs have hundreds of FMEAs, amounting to thousands of ways a system can fail. FMEA is used so pervasively in HROs that one cannot use a fastener in a safety circuit breaker without having an FMEA on the risks of that fastener failing. The FMECA, according to the original documentation in the military, "is an analysis procedure which documents all probable failures in a system, determines by failure mode analysis the effect of each failure on system operation, identifies single failure points, and ranks each failure according to a severity classification of failure effect."[4]

> We find no sense in talking about something unless we specify how we measure it; a definition by the method of measuring a quantity is the one sure way of avoiding talking nonsense.
>
> **Sir Hermann Bondi**[5]

> Whenever you can, count.
>
> **Sir Francis Galton**[6]

The risk of a change, or not changing (which is more appropriate for a book on leading change), measures the potential impact on achieving the mission and patient, physician, and staff safety. Yes, the Change Leader often reduces resistance to change by informing stakeholders of the risk and impact to them if change does not happen. Paralyzing fear must be addressed, and the FMEA is a way to inform and engage stakeholders to reduce fear, which often comes from an inability to measure the impact.

Facilitating an FMEA

Leading FMEA is easy with practice. Judging what is an input versus a failure mode versus an effect and cause can be difficult. I help you by adding definitions on the FMEA form provided. You can also ask an experienced facilitator to get your team started. One is of great benefit to get the team going if everyone is new to FMEA. The facilitator can leave after the team shows confidence and competence. "Calibrating" the team by giving some examples relative to the process always helps.

Judging the RPN is a function of judging the severity, occurrence, and detection. I include tables in Appendix 9 that can be used as is or modified.

The next lesson in measuring is how to know if change is really occurring. This is most critical. This gives the Change Leader and the stakeholders confidence that change is happening.

Key Points

- FMEA is an important and valuable measuring system.
- FMEA prevents failures by thinking how a system can fail, acting to prevent failure, and controlling the system to sustain function and performance and minimize risk.
- FMEAs in healthcare are just starting, whereas they are extensively used in HROs.
- FMEAs must be shared; people must manage to what they suggest: manage to the measure. Thinking about risk without acting is not worth much except sleepless nights.
- FMEAs are relatively easy but can be time consuming without strong facilitation.

Notes

1. http://www.assistdocs.com/search/document_details.ctm?ident_number=86479
2. Robert L. Sumwalt, Safety leadership, presented to South Carolina Gas and Electric Board, June 19, 2008. http://www.ntsb.gov/doclib/speeches/sumwalt/SCEG_pre.pdf.
3. Betsy McCaughey, Cooking the books on grandma's health care, *Wall Street Journal*, November 1, 2011.
4. *Potential Failure Mode and Effects Analysis (FMEA) Reference Manual*, 4th edition, Chrysler, Ford Motor Company, General Motors Corporation.
5. Sir Hermann Bondi, Relativity and common sense, 1964. http://www.todayin-sci.com/QuotationsCategories/M_Cat/Measurement-Quotations.htm.
6. In James R. Newman, *Commentary on Sir Francis Galton*, 1956, 1169.
7. Science quotes on: | Statistics (66).

Chapter 12

Measurement as a System

You, in this country [the USA], are subjected to the British insularity in weights and measures; you use the foot, inch and yard. I am obliged to use that system, but must apologize to you for doing so, because it is so inconvenient, and I hope Americans will do everything in their power to introduce the French metrical system. ... I look upon our English system as a wickedly, brain-destroying system of bondage under which we suffer. The reason why we continue to use it, is the imaginary difficulty of making a change, and nothing else; but I do not think in America that any such difficulty should stand in the way of adopting so splendidly useful a reform.

Baron William Thomson Kelvin[1]

Overview

The opening quotation is relevant for our subject, I think. Making it easy to measure is to change to the metric system. The metric system's common denominator of ten seems so much easier than the English measure divisible by twelve for feet to inches. The reason we have not switched despite over forty years of saying we should is the resistance to change. Maybe we could apply the learning from this book to convert finally to the metric system? Well, remember chartering about a SMART goal (see Chapter 6)? Is this really attainable? Who wants to lead this change?

This chapter helps you ensure that the measures you are taking are correct. This is not the easiest chapter to read due to its sometimes-technical nature. Please read the first few pages to understand what a measurement system is. Then, you may want to skim through the balance of this chapter for now to appreciate the value when you really need it later. This is a "how-to" book and this chapter delivers its value when you have a variable that you are not quite sure how to measure or you are concerned about the quality of the measurements you are taking. The next chapter on how to measure is very much dependent on the concepts and techniques covered in this chapter. Do not be embarrassed by someone finding error in how you measure.

Measuring outcomes and process measures is sometimes easy. A measurement system may exist. So often, it seems in healthcare no measurement system exists, and the team must lead the creation of one. Do not worry; I teach you step by step how to use an existing system or make one. Examples of measurement systems include errors in admissions documentation, emergency department (ED) wait times, inventory time supply, hand hygiene, handoff communication quality, and financial impacts across the organization from quality and waste issues.

Designing a measurement system starts with a purpose. The charter taught previously clearly defines the purpose, so please consider starting with the chartering process to design a measurement system. The charter walks us through the process of defining clearly the issue, the outcomes and process variables, and the metrics needed to measure changes in the outcomes and process variables. We even have a goal that further connects the issue with the measurement system.

Measurement as a System

What is a measurement system? Let us define a measurement system word by word. We have covered the word *measurement*. A *system* is a network of components that work together to achieve a function. In a measurement system, the components work together to assess a variable. Think of a system in healthcare terms. Measuring a patient's blood pressure requires a person, a training program, a cuff that goes around the person's arm, a stethoscope, and a procedure. The person who trains others in taking the reading may also be considered part of the measurement system. The cuff and stethoscope can be replaced by an automatic blood pressure reading machine, but we wanted to start with the manual method of reading blood pressure to avoid the error of thinking a measurement system has to be an automated electronic method. It does not. A good measurement system is everything needed to measure accurately and precisely.

Measuring the Quality of a Measurement System (Measurement System Analysis)

Every measurement system is composed of a measuring device and something to measure. Some are more complicated than this with multiple components. A blood pressure measurement system as pictured in Figure 12.1 has these components:

- Patient
- Nurse or other qualified person trained in taking a measurement
- Arm cuff
- Finger cuff
- Meter
- Electrical power
- Procedure
- Stethoscope, optional in this system

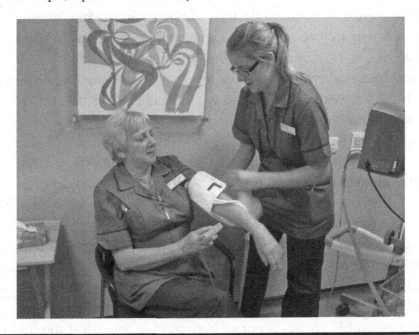

Figure 12.1   Components of a measurement system taking blood pressure.

Each of the components is necessary to measure blood pressure. There are multiple ways the measurement can be inaccurate. The patient's blood pressure may also change between readings, but if the change in readings is not the patient's actual pressure changing, we have variation in the measurement system. This is an error in the measurement system. Any variation not attributable to the item or service being measured is error.

Qualities of an Acceptable Measurement System

> No two things are alike, but even if they were, we would still get different values when we measured them.
>
> **Donald J. Wheeler**[2]

A quality measurement is one that measures only what is being measured. The measurement system itself should not influence the measurement. Have you stepped on your bathroom scale, read the measurement, and stepped on it again and the scale shows a different weight? Did your weight really change that much in the two seconds between each weighing? The variation in weight is a result of a lack of quality in the measurement system. A quick way to lose credibility in healthcare is to have a bad measurement system.

We step on a scale to weigh ourselves; we do not like the answer, so we weigh ourselves again. What are we thinking? If we do not like the answer, we blame the measurement system. Do you weigh yourself twice if you get the weight you expected or desired? Probably not. This practice is common in healthcare. Perhaps you had a nurse take your blood pressure and the nurse decides to retake it. A common reason a person takes the blood pressure reading twice is because the person felt uncomfortable with the first reading and retook the pressure. Did you ever wonder why they never seem to retake a measurement if the measurement is within an acceptable range, yet they seem often to retake a measurement when it is not within range? What makes them think that if the measurement system is flawed the first time for an unacceptable or borderline measurement, the first measurement is always accurate and precise enough if the first reading is acceptable?

During my last annual physical, this very thing happened to me in my blood pressure result. The nurse took my blood pressure. It was a bit higher than we both expected after a review of my chart. She dismissed it as perhaps because I was a bit anxious, announced the doctor would be in shortly, and left. My doctor reacted to the blood pressure similarly. My doctor retook my blood pressure, knowing now I was anxious, and it was significantly lower than what the nurse measured. The doctor said all is well and chalked it up to a bad measurement system. Did my blood pressure really change, in fact go down, knowing that the anxiety would have only increased my blood pressure more? There are several components to most measurement systems, and to get a high-quality measurement, we need to be able to identify any component that causes variation in measurements.

Measuring the Quality of a Measurement System: A Measurement System Analysis

Accuracy and Precision

The measurement should represent what is being measured and have enough precision to differentiate changes in what is being measured. The best way to understand accuracy and precision is to demonstrate.

Accuracy

Accuracy is the ability of the measurement system to find the true value. If a measurement system is not accurate, it is said to have a bias. In bias, a measured value is consistently lower or higher than the true value, such as your weight at home compared to the value at the doctor's office.

A measurement process is biased if differences exist in the average of the measurements made by different persons, machines, and so on when measuring the identical characteristic. The average of measurements is different by a fixed amount.

In taking blood pressure, if the systolic pressure is actually 127 mm Hg and the measurement system gives a systolic of 126 or 128, it may be considered accurate. If the system gave a reading of 140, we would say it is not accurate. The difference between what is actual and what is measured is important enough.

Precision

The precision of a measurement system is its ability to discern differences in what is being measured. If the systolic blood pressure is rounded off to the nearest ten, such as reading 120 or 130, we might consider this system is not as precise as one that reads to the nearest millimeter of mercury.

Repeatability

Repeatability is the ability to get the same value consistently on the same service or product using the same measurement system. If I measure your blood pressure twice with all the same conditions within a very short time frame, I should get the same blood pressure reading. If I get different blood pressures, I have not repeated the measure well, and thus there is a repeatability error in the measurement system.

Reproducibility

Reproducibility is the ability for two different measurement systems to achieve the same value. Poor reproducibility is when two different people or measurement systems, such as automatic versus manual blood pressure reading systems, get different readings.

The measurement system analysis (MSA) methods differ based on the type of data, variables or continuous data for discrete or attribute data. I teach you a way of measuring the quality of a measurement system for both types of data—and the simplest MSA for the discrimination needed. We apply what I teach: make it easier.

> It is really just as bad technique to make a measurement more accurately than is necessary as it is to make it not accurately enough.

> **Arthur David Ritchie**[3]

Designing a Measurement System

Figure 12.2 describes the process of designing a measurement system. The steps in the design flow down from the top middle columns. The inputs

Inputs	Process Map Steps for Measurement System Design & Analysis	Outputs
Customer CTQs Development needs	Purpose for measuring and standards	Purpose
Similar systems DOEs FMEAs	Determine environmental factors that may influence measurement system	Completed FMEA with action plan for influences
Similar systems Standards Expert advice Suppliers of systems	Design measurement system	Design
Standards Higher discriminating/quality measurement system	Calibrate system	Calibrated MS
Trained belt/expert Operators expected to use MS MSA methodology	MSA	Acceptable MSA Unacceptable MSA
Training plan Control plan	Train operators	Operators capable System capable
Measurement system Process or product	Implement	Truth in measurements
Standards Stability & Linearity cycles MSA	Control Plan	Calibration plan MSA Plan

Figure 12.2 Measurement system design and analysis process. CTQ stands for critical to quality. MS stands for measurement system. DOE stands for design of experiments.

show what is required in the design, and the outputs demonstrate what each step delivers. The team could benefit from this map if it has to design a new system or wants to understand the components.

Performing a Measurement System Analysis

Conducting an MSA is important for the team. Change is difficult enough sometimes without having your credibility questioned. Sometimes the MSA is as simple as validating the start and end times are well defined.

MSA helps determine if the measurement system is capable of

1. Classifying good from bad
2. Measuring process improvements

A team wants to measure the average wait time for patients who come to the ED on the weekend to ensure staffing levels are sufficient. The first step in an MSA is to know the purpose and then to define the boundaries of the measurement. We often measure elapsed times, and the MSA should define when the timing should start and when to "stop the clock." In this project, the team defines the clock start time to be when the patient signs in and stops when the patient is seen. Some of you are questioning if this is a truthful way to measure wait times. You might be thinking that it is not fair to stop the clock until a physician sees the patient. Some of you are comfortable to define the wait time as between sign in and triage. Triage is a French word that means separate or sift. Triage was used in World War I by French doctors to separate patients into one of three categories:[4]

- Patients who would live regardless of what care is received.
- Patients who will die regardless of what care is received.
- Patients who, if treated immediately, may have a better outcome.

Triage is a process in many EDs between the sign-in process and being seen by a physician to route the patient quickly for safe care. A patient with chest pains may be immediately routed for tests, as an example. If the purpose of your project is to ensure an early judgment of the care a patient may need, triage may be the best process to measure the end time. Know the purpose of your measurement to make the right decision.

MSA Can Be Really Easy

Your MSA in this example is fairly easy and starts with getting consensus with your sponsor when the clock should start and stop. You may also want to ensure how granular your measurements should be to discriminate differences in wait times. Perhaps rounding to the nearest minute in ED wait times that are now taking up to twenty minutes is granular enough. A statistic that is useful in an MSA to judge if the measurement system is good enough to assess how well a process is performing to what is required by the patient, customer, or process owner is percentage precision to tolerance (%P/T). I show you how this and other useful statistics are used to assess the quality of your measurement system and when to use each one to ensure your measurements are truthful.

After you apply the 3Ms (measure, manage to the measure, make it easier) and performance improvement and get the wait times down to three minutes, your MSA may suggest measuring in seconds to improve your process continuously. This is when the MSA statistic, percentage precision to total variance (%P/TV) or percentage contribution is the correct statistic to use. Once the ED wait times are better than what the patients demand, the MSA statistic percentage precision to tolerance is less relevant. We now need to be able to measure improvements regardless of patient expectations.

MSAs Are Critical in Utilizing the 3Ms

The last thing you want in leading change is to have your first M, measure, to be wrong. Critics and resistors of change will often question measurements to stop or slow change. The change leader needs to know the value of analyzing measurement systems and ensure that the measurements are correct.

Have you also thought about doing an MSA after seeing a billboard (one of those electronic signs that can be updated remotely) showing a local hospital advertising its ED wait times right now are eleven minutes? What does that really mean? We should do an MSA before we start measuring anything of importance. There are even legal consequences if the measurements we proclaim in advertising or research are not correct.

Another important MSA in healthcare can be in its supply chain. Procurement is receiving complaints from the clinicians that they are running out of supplies. The procurement team wants to study the suppliers' response times. The procurement team believes the suppliers' response time is too long. The team finds purchasers did not realize that the requested receipt dates set by the computer add an extra day due to batch processing.

Inaccurate Measurement Systems Can Lose You Customers

Not knowing your capacity in surgical services or radiology or any number of services may result in your staff turning patients and high-margin customers away. Turning away doctors who want to use the services of your healthcare organization can be a big loss to your margins. This can often be a failure of the measurement system. A chief executive officer (CEO) of a large hospital heard that his staff turned away two prospective professional football players who needed tests as a condition of their contracts. These football players were already well known, and a football player can be a significant user of healthcare services for many years. They also tend to be able to pay. You now know the CEOs' concerns and reason for change.

This issue was not just in the hospital's lab and test services. I saw first-hand how a measurement system's inaccuracy and lack of precision almost resulted in two surgeons being told the surgery center could not accommodate their requests for operating room (OR) time. The hospital staff looked at their paper-based scheduling system and saw that the recovery areas were too full to allow any more surgeries to occur. They were about ready to turn away the business. Instead, they looked at a new scheduling system that had just been put in place and saw that there was plenty of recovery space to allow the surgeries to occur. Of course, there could be other remedies to allow the surgeries if the recovery area was the constraint, but our point is the measurement system was flawed, and in the busy day, people were turning patients away due to the measurement system they had. This system had two flaws. The system was not accurate, and it was not precise. Accuracy and precision are two first tests of the quality of a measurement system.

A Measurement System Using Actual Data by Surgeon and by Procedure

The hospital team found that the system could not accurately estimate time for patients who required multiple procedures. The system would add the full time for each procedure as if the procedure required patient positioning and other setup that is not necessary once the surgeon has started one procedure. What would show as 3 hours to do two procedures might only take a few more minutes after the first procedure, say a total of 100 minutes to do both procedures. Thus, there was a significant amount of time available. What is even more complicated is that there are two groups of staff making decisions if time is available. The first group receives booking requests from the surgeon's office and tries to estimate the time procedures take and ensure that the surgeon has the allotted reserved time, called a "slot" or "block time."

They know the measurement system, the computer-generated total time for both procedures, is flawed. So, they become the measurement system, trying to estimate the time to know if the answer to the next question, if the surgeon has enough block time, results in enough time available. The block time practice is very common in surgery centers. We also find that the block times are often not used and not made available to other surgeons who may be looking for time to do surgeries. Not making a good estimate of the time required for procedures is described as being inaccurate. The times are inaccurate estimates of the total time required for both procedures. Next, I describe how a lack of precision can describe a measurement system's quality.

The standard times in the scheduling system were rounded up to quarter-hour increments. If a procedure took five minutes, the system might round it up to fifteen minutes. The original intention might have been in the patient's best interest. It may be better to tell the surgeon that there was not enough time versus allowing the surgery and then not having sufficient space in recovery when the surgery is complete and needing to transport the patient to another area to recover. Good intentions overriding improving effort to improve a poor measurement system, however, are not in the patient's, surgeon's, or hospital's best interest. Measurement systems need to be accurate and precise in healthcare. High Reliability Organizations know this and ensure their measurement systems meet their quality requirements. Measurement systems must be designed to meet the quality requirements.

This is how the team at the hospital improved its measurement system. The first step was to find all the elements of the measurement system. A critical element is the data used to estimate the average time each procedure took by each surgeon. The average time for the same procedure performed by two different surgeons can vary by over 100%. No one knew where the original estimates came from, and we believe they were standards supplied by the software firm in who knows what country and by what type of surgery center. We were fortunate to have the actual times for each procedure and combination of procedures for most surgeons. This helped us improve the accuracy of the scheduling system immediately. Eighty percent of the cases that had multiple procedures had data on the total elapsed time of the case.

We wanted to improve the precision as well as the accuracy. Resistance was heavy in the scheduling department. Previous attempts at getting the informal leader to try new ways had failed. I call these attempts "drive-by change attempts." Sometimes we test the waters for how much resistance we can expect by suggesting a few ideas as we walk by or through a department and see the reaction. When a team hears, "Oh no, that won't work," during these drive-by change tactics, we know change will come with more difficulty.

We started to improve the precision of the measure how long a procedure might take by calculating the variance of each combination of procedure and surgeon. Using the variance, we were able to estimate more precisely the time most cases would take if we wanted to schedule the OR and recovery area with enough time for 95% of the occurrences. We found that even with this estimate, the software estimate was still considerably higher than what the surgeon needed.

This measurement system is already much more accurate and precise just by improving one element in the system, the data. To test the new system, we used an actual day's schedule when the ORs were very busy. We simulated the recovery area needed using the new measurement system and found it measured what really happened well. We now knew we needed a process to take new bookings and find ways to achieve higher capacity so we did not turn any business away. The schedule is visual and easy to read (see Figure 12.3).

Another component in many healthcare measurement systems is us, the humans. This measurement system of bed availability relies on two components: the data that estimates the time for each procedure that is shown on the Excel sheet in Figure 12.3 and the person who should look at it and make the judgment. If either of the two measurements are missing, the measurement system fails. What can we do when staff don't use the

Time	Trolley Bay 1	Trolley Bay 2	Trolley Bay 3	Trolley Bay 4	Trolley Bay 5	Trolley Bay 6	Trolley Bay 7	Trolley Bay 8	Trolley Bay 9	Trolley Bay 10	Trolley Bay 11
7:00:00	1A	2A	4A	5A	6A	7A			Patient 13		
7:10:00											
7:20:00											
7:30:00											
7:40:00											
7:50:00											
8:00:00											
8:10:00											
8:20:00											
8:30:00											
8:40:00											
8:50:00											
9:00:00											
9:10:00											
9:20:00											
9:30:00											
9:40:00											
9:50:00											
10:00:00											
10:10:00											
10:20:00											
10:30:00											
10:40:00											
10:50:00											
11:00:00											
11:10:00											
11:20:00											
11:30:00											
11:40:00											
11:50:00											
12:00:00											

Trolley
Chair
Overnight

Figure 12.3 Measurement of bed availability.

measurement device despite incorporating the stakeholders' ideas and meeting their needs and desires? Read on.

Drawdown

Drawdown is another military invention, I hear. I am not sure where it was first coined, but it is often the only way to get people to make the change. I was a Lotus 1-2-3 user for many years. Lotus 1-2-3 is a spreadsheet application, and it revolutionized using math and making charts. Anyone working with numbers who needed to make charts and had a personal computer in the 1980s probably was aware of Lotus 1-2-3.

Then, Microsoft started selling its spreadsheet application, Excel. Eventually, my company's information technology (IT) group tried to get us to choose Lotus or Excel. One can imagine the resistance in shifting. I was very happy with Lotus, even after trying Excel, and I was running a site that demanded focusing on customers and my employees. Doing spreadsheet work was a part of my work life, but definitely it was just a tool to allow me to focus more on customers and employees. Why should I switch when there would be time wasted learning Excel? What is the third M? Make it easier, right? It was not easier to use Excel. It sure was not easier to have to learn the same functions in Excel when I already knew how to do everything I needed in Lotus. Did anyone ask me what I thought?

Over time, the IT group lobbied and eventually got the company to make Excel the standard. That meant that all of us "Lotus Lords" who knew Lotus like the backs of our hands had to switch. The IT group could not get everyone to switch voluntarily, and the group implemented a change management technique called drawdown. They took Lotus off our machines to force us to change to Excel. Drawdown is the term for when a leader reduces or decreases the resources, such as in a troop drawdown in a foreign country. The drawdown will result in a change because the old method is no longer available. This forces people to change to the new way or new location using the troop drawdown technique. I want to be clear here. I use drawdown as the last resort, preferring to get people to change willingly. But, not all change is favorable for each individual, as discussed in the first chapter. Sometimes a Change Leader needs to invoke a drawdown for the benefit of the organization. The good news is that Excel was not all that bad. One spreadsheet software fortunately became the standard so everyone could communicate and share.

There is another lesson here. Even a good change will result in resistance on minor issues with the change. For example, I still struggle with the changes in charting in the 2010 version of Excel, as do many of my colleagues. I think the creators of Excel could use this book and the 3Ms. I do not think they did a very good job leading us to the new changes in this version. They were evidently concerned enough that they provided an application that tells you how to do a feature based on the screen navigation for the prior version. Unfortunately, they did not do a very good job communicating they did this. I also do not think they measured client satisfaction with the new methods. Otherwise, they would have done something differently.

Measurement Systems That Add No Value to the Client

Are you also annoyed at Microsoft's error message that asks if you want to send information to Microsoft now that its software or system just failed? You have seen the box with a blue margin on it after your application has crashed. It starts with the words "Please tell Microsoft about this problem. … We have created an error report that you can send to help us improve Microsoft Office Outlook. We treat your report as confidential and anonymous." Of course it is anonymous. They do not want to give you access to the company. Did you ever wonder what happened to customer service phone support? The end of the message asks whether to send the report. Here are just more keystrokes and wasted time the company pushes onto the customer to help the company measure their lack of reliability. My takt time also had to be revised, discussed previously. I lost four hours of work due to Word crashing. I had four hours less time available while the page counts went back up for the pages I lost. When the numerator (which is the time I have available) decreases and the denominator increases because the page count increased to its value before the crash, Takt time must be even faster than just losing the four hours. Takt time, as you can see, is another measure for the lack of quality. Rework costs both time and supply.

Calibrating a Measurement System

Most measurement systems include a process known as calibration. Calibration "tunes" the measurement system to meet accuracy and precision requirements when the measurement system is first put in use and to maintain its accuracy and precision. Our bathroom scales are often not accurate because calibration is needed. I know some people purposely do not calibrate their scale at home because of change—they do not want to admit they need to change their diet and way of life, maybe? For years I would set (calibrate) my wristwatch to be about five minutes early. This is another example of inaccuracy. The precision was good because it was able to discriminate in seconds as well as I needed, but it was not accurate to the actual time.

Calibration has also been used to help Change Leaders. When people do not seem to appreciate the reason for change, the Change Leader may recalibrate his or her thinking. An example is in hand hygiene. The World Health Organization (WHO) has used a statistic to recalibrate the severity one puts on not washing hands. Many people report saying they do not think hand washing is important. When one hears that on average 247 people die every day in the United States due to healthcare-acquired infections, the WHO is attempting to get people to measure the severity differently: to recalibrate what severity really means when it comes to the effect of not washing hands.

Categories and Types of Data

MSA techniques vary based on the categories of data and types of data one wants in the measurement system. The categories are

■ Quantitative (numerical responses)
■ Qualitative (categorical responses)—variables for which an attribute or classification is measured

There are two types of data within the quantitative category:

1. Continuous (variable data) (any point on a histogram possible, such as in measured and decimal subdivisions)
    - Data that indicate how much or how many
    - Variable data can be subdivided into finer increments of precision:
        a. Time (seconds)
        b. Speed (feet/minute)
        c. Rate (inches/time)
        d. Dimensions (millimeters)

2. Discrete (attribute) (numerical responses from a counting process in which not every point is possible on a histogram)
   - Good or bad counts
   - Number of machines working
   - Shifts of overtime scheduled
   - Counted things (number of errors in a document, number of units shipped, etc.)
   - Percentage good or bad (percentage derived from counting)

Qualitative (categorical responses) are variables for which an attribute or classification is measured.

■ Yes or no
■ Good or bad
■ Meets the standard or does not

For example, measuring the process time to wait in the ED may be continuous data measured in minutes. Whether a hospital meets the standard by patients for cleanliness is judged using a qualitative category data.

Checklists as Measurement Systems

Many checklists used in healthcare, aviation, aerospace, and automotive industries use a yes or no response option. A checklist is often qualitative based on the binary response option. More difficult surveys may use a degree of response, such as a survey that asks to judge satisfaction with a service based on a scale from zero to ten, with ten being highly satisfied.

MSAs can be difficult for qualitative data. Judging the staff's friendliness is a judgment call with a hard-to-define standard. Remember, measurement is a way to compare something to a standard. In 2013, Centers for Medicare and Medical Services (CMS) will base some of its reimbursement on a healthcare organization's patient survey. The questions from Hospital Consumer Assessment of Healthcare Provider System (HCAHPS) are seen in Figure 12.4, as are the process measures. Note that CMS will use process and outcome measures in its system to reimburse hospitals in the future.

Every one of the HCAHPS questions is a qualitative measure. Doing an MSA on such data is fraught with chance for error. Healthcare organizations (HCOs) that can do MSAs on this type of data may be well ahead

TABLE 4—ACHIEVEMENT THRESHOLDS THAT APPLY TO THE FY 2013 HOSPITAL VBP PROGRAM MEASURES

Measure ID	Measure description	Performance standard (achievement threshold)
	Clinical Process of Care Measures	
AMI–7a	Fibrinolytic Therapy Received Within 30 Minutes of Hospital Arrival	0.6548
AMI–8a	Primary PCI Received Within 90 Minutes of Hospital Arrival	0.9186
HF–1	Discharge Instructions	0.9077
PN–3b	Blood Cultures Performed in the Emergency Department Prior to Initial Antibiotic Received in Hospital.	0.9643
PN–6	Initial Antibiotic Selection for CAP in Immunocompetent Patient	0.9277
SCIP–Inf–1	Prophylactic Antibiotic Received Within One Hour Prior to Surgical Incision	0.9735
SCIP–Inf–2	Prophylactic Antibiotic Selection for Surgical Patients	0.9766
SCIP–Inf–3	Prophylactic Antibiotics Discontinued Within 24 Hours After Surgery End Time	0.9507
SCIP–Inf–4	Cardiac Surgery Patients with Controlled 6AM Postoperative Serum Glucose	0.9428
SCIP–VTE–1	Surgery Patients with Recommended Venous Thromboembolism Prophylaxis Ordered	0.9500
SCIP–VTE–2	Surgery Patients Who Received Appropriate Venous Thromboembolism Prophylaxis Within 24 Hours Prior to Surgery to 24 Hours After Surgery.	0.9307
SCIP–Card–2	Surgery Patients on a Beta Blocker Prior to Arrival That Received a Beta Blocker During the Perioperative Period.	0.9399
	Patient Experience of Care Measures	
HCAHPS	Communication with Nurses	75.18%
	Communication with Doctors	79.42%
	Responsiveness of Hospital Staff	61.82%
	Pain Management	68.75%
	Communication About Medicines	59.28%
	Cleanliness and Quietness of Hospital Environment	62.80%

Figure 12.4   CMS process measures for healthcare.

of others who do not understand MSA. For instance, understanding the elements that affect a patient's judgment, such as how staff can affect the patient's measurement of services, can create variation in the measure. I can affect the way people rate my training by how I discuss the survey that they will get. Just by asking people to fill in the survey, I can change the measurement of my services. A classic example is a hotel survey. Who fills in a hotel survey? More than likely, it is someone who has had a horrible experience. If I can get more guests who are delighted with my services to fill in the survey, I can change the measurement, even though I did not change the service quality.

We will talk more about such effects, called bias, when we discuss sampling error. For now, just understand that there are two categories of data, with different types of data. MSAs need to be done on all data, regardless of category and type, but we need different MSA approaches for each.

Granularity

Granularity is another variable in measurement. Granularity refers to the degree of discrimination in the data. Let us understand discrimination first to understand granularity.

Discrimination

Discrimination is the capability to detect and indicate even small changes. Examples are:

■ Swim event stop watch times for a grade school compared to the timing required for an event in the Olympics. In the grade school event, seconds may be granular enough. In the Olympics, the measurement system is able to discriminate between ten thousandths of a second.
■ Days of inventory versus weeks on hand. Days are more granular.
■ Dollars versus cents.
■ Well trained or competent.

We suggest a gauge repeatability and reproducibility study (Gage R&R) when two conditions are met: 1. The data type is continuous and 2. High granularity in the data is present.

One way of performing a gauge R&R study is to use a computer and statistical software like Minitab. Minitab is a common software application and makes doing a gauge R&R study much easier.

Overview of Performing a Gauge R&R Study

A good way to do a gauge R&R without a computer is to follow these steps:

1. Gather a sample, or determine how to gather a sample, that represents the population the measurement system is expected to assess. I suggest including a range of samples representing both extremes of the population. An example is if you want to measure the time in the ED from sign in through starting the triage process. Take an example when the waiting room is empty and a time when the waiting room is very crowded because the times may be very short and very long.
2. Have two people with watches that can measure in seconds and are reliable (many smart phones have stopwatch functions) positioned so they can see the patients from sign in until they are seen in triage.
3. Ensure each person measuring knows when to start and stop the watch and have them practice on measuring patients in the environment. Correct any confusion.

4. Determine the most representative sample, such as time of day and staffing at nominal levels (levels that meet requirements) and that will span the range of times needed to be measured.

5. Have each person time at least five patients, if possible, from sign in until they are seen in triage by a qualified person.

6. Compare the times recorded by each person. Calculate the differences in each measurement. Judge if the differences between each observer are acceptable for the accuracy and precision needed.

7. If not acceptable, determine the reasons why and correct. Trial and correct until accuracy and precision are achieved.

For most situations, this MSA will satisfy the quality needed in your measurement system.

MSA for Blood Pressure Reading

Cardiologists have a number of "tricks up their sleeve" in taking blood pressure. By taking the blood pressure standing up versus sitting down, a cardiologist can measure certain conditions. Taking the blood pressure in each arm can also detect issues. The measurement technique in taking blood pressure can change the value of the pressure significantly. Some experts suggest that blood pressure readings should be taken while the patient is seated and has rested for two minutes or more. Seldom do these conditions occur. So, what is the quality of the measurement in these situations? Is the quality sufficient? These are the issues in measuring blood pressure. The person taking the reading, the time the patient has rested, and the equipment are elements of the measurement system. All can affect the quality of the measurement.

When the granularity of measurement needed is low, a simpler measurement using two measurement systems may be enough. In the swim example, having two parents clock the swimmer and comparing the two measurements may be enough to have confidence in the measurement system. There is no need to calculate the average and variance. If the two times are close enough for determining a winner, the measurement system is good enough. Periodically, someone should check the watch and method used to ensure stability over time.

MSA for Attribute Data

- How do we ensure one person judges a good result correctly?
- Can we use MSAs to certify a person is ready for a role for which judgment is required?
- How does a person being surveyed agree with himself or herself over time? Under different conditions? Against an expert?

These scenarios demonstrate why MSA is needed for even attribute type data.

Attribute Agreement Analysis

For qualitative data, there is a technique called attribute agreement analysis (AAA). It is a statistical technique like those mentioned and may be the best MSA when judgments must be correct and to a standard.

An example is judging the level of care placements for psychiatric and addiction services for both adult and child/adolescent populations. A Level of Care Utilization System (LOCUS) was invented by the American Association of Community Psychiatrists and used in healthcare to measure the risk of harm. An example of the judgment criteria for a moderate risk of harm is given next.

Moderate Risk of Harm

- Significant current suicidal or homicidal ideation without intent or conscious plan and without past history.
- No active suicidal/homicidal ideation, but extreme distress and/or a history of suicidal/homicidal behavior exists.
- History of chronic impulsive suicidal/homicidal behavior or threats and current expressions does not represent significant change from baseline.
- Binge or excessive use of substances resulting in potentially harmful behaviors without current involvement in such behavior.
- Some evidence of self neglect and/or compromise in ability to care for oneself in current environment.

Note: Used with permission by the American Association of Community Psychiatrists http://communitypsychiatry.org/aacp/contact.aspx

The Soft Drink Challenge with AAA

Here is a fun way to learn AAA (that is three As, not two). Can your measurement system differentiate two sodas? You are the measurement system, and many people claim to be able to measure the difference. Try it and report the results on my Web site at http://www.rpmexec.com. See Figure 12.5 for an example of the output. The instructions are included in Appendix 10.

An AAA tells us not only where the errors are but also suggests where to improve the measurement system.

- Poor repeatability (within appraiser)
- Poor reproducibility (between appraisers)
- Poor accuracy (wrong decisions)
- Taster's ability

The way to test a person's measurement quality in attribute data such as risk of harm is to set up scenarios spanning the range of risk and asking the person to determine the risk of harm. A standard is needed to know if the

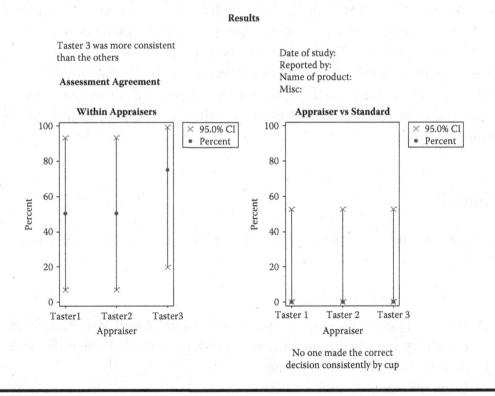

Figure 12.5   AAA for drinks.

judgment is correct. Another statistic in an AAA is the repeatability of the person. Good repeatability is the person making the same judgment, for the same scenario, more than once. To test if the person is consistent in judgment, that is "repeatable," we test the person using similar situations, but different to mask that they are the same. If the person judges the same situation differently, the measurement system is flawed, and one needs to find the contributing factors and correct them. Repeat the AAA until the person correctly judges.

Stability

Stability is another variable in measuring that we need to understand. Stability is getting the same measurement on the same exact service event or product over time. Any difference in measurement of the same event or product is a result of an unstable measurement system. In measuring our weight over a year's time, the scale may give us different readings. If we did not actually gain or lose weight, the scale has introduced error, or variation, in the measurement. The scale may have gone out of calibration because dust has collected over time and made the sensors less sensitive. Correcting poor stability is often achieved by recalibrating. In measuring anything over time, it is a good practice to check the calibration. A Change Leader's practice should be to check the stability of the measurement system before claiming victory.

Linearity

Linearity is a measure of the difference in accuracy or precision over the range of the measurement device. Examples include the ability to measure

- Long cycle events and short cycle events equally well. An example is the ability to measure the time patients wait in the ED when the wait time is short or extremely long.
- Large objects and small objects.
- Customer satisfaction in Asia and South America.

Overview of MSA for Continuous Data and High Granularity

Gauge Repeatability and Reproducibility

Gauge R&R is powerful in assessing the quality of a measurement system. This MSA methodology also guides the team in improving the MSA by tests of the characteristics.

However, it is most useful when:

1. You have continuous data.
2. High granularity and high discrimination are required.
3. The MSA is highly dependent on the quality of the characteristics (discrimination, stability, linearity, accuracy and precision).

$$\sigma^2 \text{ Total variation} = \sigma^2 \text{ What is being measured} + \sigma^2 \text{ Measurement system}$$

$$\sigma^2 \text{ Measurement system} = \sigma^2 \text{ Person measuring} + \sigma^2 \text{ Measuring equipment} + \sigma^2 \text{ Measuring technique} + \ldots$$

Example of a MSA and Steps

The team is trying to improve the strength of a glue to secure tubing used in surgery. The measurement system is a pull test in which the amount of force (continuous data) is measured until the tubing is stretched five millimeters. Five samples are selected every hour. The team is concerned that the tool used in measuring pull strength does not always give correct readings. They perform an MSA.

1. Calibrate the gauge or ensure that it has been calibrated.
2. Select the parts to measure, usually five to ten, from the process that represents the population well.
3. Select the people measuring (usually two to three people.)
4. Each person will measure each part at least two times to test repeatability.
5. Set up your schedule to measure. Be sure to present the tubings randomly to each operator.
6. Have them measure.
7. Analyze the data to determine the statistics of the MSA.
   - Control charts
   - Use several measures (% contribution, %P/TV, and %P/T)
8. Analyze results and determine follow-up action, if any.

Precision to Tolerance (%P/T)

Knowing Good from Bad

The percentage precision to tolerance is used to determine if the measurement system is capable of accepting or rejecting what is being measured according to the specifications.

- The specification width may be too tight or too loose.
- Calculates percentage of the tolerance (as indicated by the customer) taken up by measurement error.
- It is desirable to have the value less than 30%.

It is usually expressed as a percentage and is called the % Tolerance in Minitab.

Percentage Precision to Total Variation (%P/TV)

For process improvement beyond just knowing if a product or service is good or bad, use the percentage precision to total variation:

- It includes both repeatability and reproducibility.
- It is minimal to have the percentage precision to total variation less than 30%.
- The value desired is less than 20%.
- It is usually expressed as a percentage and is called the % Study Variation in Minitab software.

The percentage precision to total variation is the better measure to use for process improvement because it will detect changes in the process, not just how well the service or object being measured meets customer specifications.

Percentage Contribution

Percentage contribution is the best for understanding the performance of the measurement system. It addresses what percentage of the total variation (as indicated by the process) is taken up by measurement error.

- It includes both repeatability and reproducibility.
- The percentage contribution should be less than 9%.
- A value of less than 4% is desired.

The percentage contribution is perhaps even better than the percentage precision to total variation because the contribution is a more understandable measure of the variation caused by the measurement system.

Remember, measurement systems must be analyzed *before* spending too much time collecting data. Too many times, people collect data, sometimes spending money and time, only to find the measurement system is flawed.

It is important to use the MSA that best fits the accuracy, precision, and purpose.

Sampling

Sample selection is important; sample during normal production to capture the total range of process variation. Be cautious of data from systems if you did not measure the data that went into the system. Know exactly how the data were gathered or sampled, if any data were omitted or edited, and so on. An MSA is absolutely necessary for any data. The MSA does not have to be arduous.[5] Just analyze the system to make sure the data are truthfully representing what you are measuring and accurate and precise enough to help you make decisions. Do not even think about *not* validating your measurement system—it could be very embarrassing.

Should I Measure 100% or Sample?

Let us answer the question of whether you should measure 100% or sample using examples of projects almost every hospital has tried: measuring the wait times patients experience in an ED (also known as an ER or emergency room). First, let us understand what a population and sample are. A population is the entire set one wants to understand. A sample is a subset of the population.

We are sitting in the lobby and measuring the time it takes for every patient to be seen. This is measuring the population. We measure every patient that comes in, day and night. Perhaps we have other things to do, yet we still want to estimate the average wait time. We could go to the ED once an hour for ten minutes and measure the time for any patient who enters during that ten minutes. We, of course, would not be measuring every patient (the population) assuming patients arrive when we are not in the ED. To know all wait times in an ED population would be to measure every patient who enters the ED, every hour, every day. Sampling would be to measure fewer than the entire population of patients. Writing the words *entire population* is redundant because I could have just said population. But, I want to stress the definition of population as everyone or everything, and a sample is less than the population.

Sampling Quality

Sampling quality is simply determined by how well the sample represents the entire population. The most common question I get is, "How many samples do I need?" This is not the most important question. The answer is *to represent* truthfully what you are measuring.

Sample size is important to achieve the confidence we want in our decisions. Often, we want to compare two groups to see if there is a difference. In reducing catheter-associated urinary tract infections (CAUTIs), we may want to compare two standards of care. We take samples from both techniques of care and then analyze to see if there is a lower rate of CAUTI in one technique compared to the other. Sample size is important to estimate the confidence we have in the outcome if there is a true difference. A good rule of thumb is to gather at least thirty samples from each group to be compared. If we want to study the difference in CAUTI between treatment A and B, we would gather thirty samples of treatment A and thirty samples of treatment B. Most important still is if we represent both populations of patients and techniques.

Key Points

- MSA is critical to ensure the measures we are using are correct.
- Your MSA should be kept as simple as needed to have confidence in the measure. Do not overcomplicate your MSA.
- MSAs are based on data types. MSAs for continuous-type data are different from methods for discrete-type data.
- Minitab and other software make doing more complex MSAs easy.

Notes

1. http://zapatopi.net/kelvin/quotes/
2. Donald Wheeler, *Experimentation: Understanding Industrial Experimentation*, SPC Press, Knoxville, TN, 1990.
3. Arthur David Ritchie, *Scientific Method: An Inquiry into the Character and Validity of Natural Law*, 1923, 113.
4. M. Cipman, B.E. Hackley, and T.S. Spencer, Triage of mass casualties: concepts for coping with mixed battlefield injuries, *Military Medicine*, 145(2), 99–100, 1980. PMID 6768037.
5. Jeffry Bauer, *Statistical Analysis for Decision Makers in Healthcare*, 2nd edition, Taylor & Francis, Boca Raton, FL, 2009.

Chapter 13

How to Share and Communicate Measurements

A picture is worth a thousand words.

Charting

Managing to the measure is often facilitated by graphically displaying the data. There are a number of charts that can help the team share what is happening. I cover two of the most valuable charts:

- Pareto charts
- Statistical process control (SPC) charts

Pareto Charts

Pareto charts are bar charts that display the most frequently occurring variable to the far left, and bars are displayed in descending order. A helpful feature of Pareto charts is a cumulative percentage line. The bars show the variables in the order of importance, and the cumulative line allows the reader to assess how many variables make up x percent of the total. See Figure 13.1 for an example of a Pareto chart of the reasons for not washing hands.

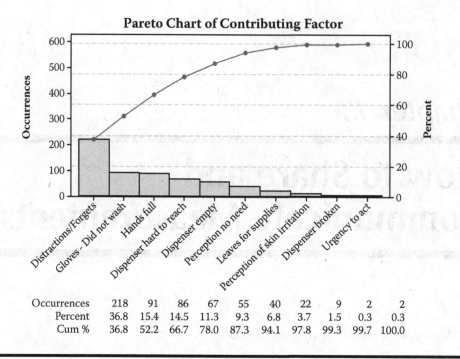

Occurrences	218	91	86	67	55	40	22	9	2	2
Percent	36.8	15.4	14.5	11.3	9.3	6.8	3.7	1.5	0.3	0.3
Cum %	36.8	52.2	66.7	78.0	87.3	94.1	97.8	99.3	99.7	100.0

Figure 13.1 Pareto chart of reasons for not washing hands.

The most frequently noted contributing factor in this hospital for not washing hands is that the person is distracted or forgot to wash. The second-most-frequent contributing factor is the frequency of entering and exiting a patient's room. If we wanted to reduce 80% of the contributing factors, we can use the table below the Pareto chart or the cumulative line to find where 80% of the contributing factors noted are located. In the chart, one can see that only four factors make up 78% of all reasons. If we were to eliminate these four factors, we would eliminate 78% of the occurrences when we did not wash our hands.

A Pareto chart helps the Change Leader focus on the vital few issues instead of wasting time on all possible factors. The measurement system used in determining the occurrence of each factor is important. Teams will use Pareto charts often in a complex change to focus the stakeholders continually and prove to resistors that progress can be made.

Pareto Analysis to Reduce Resistance

I use Pareto analysis to reduce resistance. I was getting resistance from a group to use the 3Ms (measure, manage to the measure, make it easier) to improve staff satisfaction. They did not want to measure the outcome, believing it was too difficult to measure staff satisfaction frequently. I asked them to list the reasons why it was difficult to measure employee satisfaction every day. We counted the frequency, or number of people, who listed each contributing factor and arranged the reasons in order of descending votes. The top reason was their feeling that this wasted time and a person would not give us different readings. What the people did not realize is that we planned to sample only a portion of the staff population. Therefore, no one person would be surveyed more than once a quarter. The next frequently noted reason was that the time was too great to survey so frequently.

Ask Why Five Times

We used another process improvement tool to reduce the effect of these top two contributing factors to not measuring staff satisfaction frequently. We asked why five times, or as often as necessary, to understand why they voted for these two factors.

Here is how it went:

1. Why do you think that it wastes time to survey a sample of staff on their level of satisfaction?
   An answer we got is that the current survey is six questions long.
2. We asked why it was six questions long.
   They said because they not only wanted to know the satisfaction level but also wanted to ask if certain root causes were known.
3. We asked why they wanted to know the root causes instead of simply asking why the survey is six questions long.
   They did not know.

We suggested that the team simply ask how likely it was the staff member would recommend working at this healthcare organization to family, friends, and colleagues. We could later ask those who gave this question a low answer what exactly was the contributing factor if they did not volunteer to write the reason in the second question. The second question simply asked why the person rated his or her desire to recommend or not. If the person gave an answer, the group could again do a Pareto chart and focus precisely on the contributing factors that, if eliminated or reduced, would improve staff satisfaction.

Pareto analysis is a simple tool that can focus a team on the critical few issues. It can also reduce resistance by helping resistors see that often what they are resisting may not occur very often. A Pareto chart is a snapshot of a system at a point in time. What a team also needs is a chart that shows the system through time.

Statistical Process Control (SPC) Charts

An SPC chart helps you, your friends, and your relatives feel more confident that surgery will go well and that the navigation device in your GM or BMW vehicle operates correctly. SPC has been credited with helping turn Japan from a country shipping junk to one that is shipping some of the finest-quality goods ever. It is often viewed as a chart, also known as a control chart, SPC chart, run chart, and various other names. It is one of the simplest charts to use. Let me repeat, it is one of the simplest charts to use for those of you who think or hear that SPC is too complex for healthcare. What is more important, it is the correct chart to use in performance improvement (PI). PI is too complex not to consider using SPC. We will see why. And, I will teach you how to measure using a control chart even if you do not have a computer. Learning it with pencil and paper (Taylor & Francis and I make it easy again: we supply the paper) is the best way. Pencil and paper may be all you use in creating your SPC charts. The results can be all you need.

May 1924

The first SPC chart was shared in May 1924. Western Electric, a manufacturer of transmission systems, wanted to improve its reliability. Western Electric found that relying on inspecting final product to sort out defects was not reliable. Despite having a department of engineers for inspection, failures in electrical transmission systems continued to occur. Western Electric at the Hawthorne Works (yes, the same location of the Hawthorne study) relied so much on inspection, they had an engineering inspection department. This is where Dr. Shewhart worked. He wanted to improve the quality at Western Electric and find an alternative to relying on inspecting. Inspecting was not catching all the quality issues and was costly. He was looking for a method to know when a process was starting to vary, or go out of control, before defects were made. Once made, despite inspectors, defective products made it underground only to fail and cause service disruptions and costly repairs.

High-Reliability Organizations and SPC

Stop and think how many times in healthcare we hear the need to learn from high-reliability organizations (HROs). At this time, I want you to think back to Dr. Semmelweis's story and how it ended for him. He proved beyond a doubt that his change to washing hands led to the desired outcome, but his Change Leadership was weak. The system went back to its old ways, and mothers died because of the lack of sustained change. Dr. Shewhart also proved beyond a doubt how to improve reliability and reduce the waste of inspection. The end of his story, although not as grave personally as Dr. Semmelweis's, proves the need for Change Leadership because his techniques also took a while to be adopted.

Many resisted, and in healthcare I see this resistance every day. This resistance slows the increase in reliability, adds to costly inspection, and who knows how many lives have been lost for not using his technique, which we cover now. What Louis Pasteur did to convince people that Dr. Semmelweis's discovery is the right thing to do, Joseph Juran, Dr. W. Edwards Deming, and Bonnie Small did for Dr. Shewhart's discovery. You might know Juran's contribution was to engage every employee, even the shop floor employee, in learning this technique. Dr. Deming emphasized the leader's role in quality, as well as training everyone in Dr. Shewhart's technique. Bonnie Small, however, may deserve much of the credit for turning Western Electric's processes into higher reliable processes. It took twenty-five years from when Dr. Shewhart in May 1924 sent a memo to his boss with a diagram that came to be known as a control chart to more widespread use of control charts. This is the story of Bonnie Small straight from the Western Electric company Web site, a company now known as Alcatel-Lucent.[1]

> At Western Electric, this expertise on quality was communicated to the shop floor—most dramatically by Bonnie Small who joined the Hawthorne quality assurance department in 1940. Her experiences there during World War II convinced her that Shewhart's abstract ideas alone were of little help to newly hired workers, so she set out to translate the ideas of Shewhart into practical methods. After joining the Allentown Plant in 1948, Small assembled a committee of quality professionals throughout Western Electric

to write a handbook for the factory. This handbook represents the confluence of Western Electric's long-standing traditions of quality control and of education and training. Much of the material for the book was based on Western Electric training courses given to managers, engineers, and shop floor people from 1949 to 1956. The "Western Electric Statistical Quality Control Handbook" appeared in 1958, and has been the shop floor bible of quality control throughout the world ever since. It remains in print, available from the company today.[2]

Please read on and learn one of the answers to achieving high reliability. I dare say without this technique healthcare will never achieve high reliability. And, we are not talking just about using this technique in the healthcare organization. This technique is needed throughout the value stream, including suppliers of medical equipment, medicines, and distribution. This technique was used in the 3Ms to improve the reliability of perioperative processes aiding in the elimination of wrong-site surgeries. It was used to prove solutions to hand hygiene reduced healthcare-acquired infections (HAIs). Its uses are endless. It is easier than you think to apply, as I will show you.

The "Swiss Army Knife" for Process Improvement

There is not a more powerful chart in a leader's repertoire than an SPC chart. From Dr. Shewhart's first control chart in the 1920s, control charts have been used by HROs ever since, although control charts were not widely known outside Western Electric until World War II. These charts are so valuable that some customers require evidence of a controlled process before buying the first product or service from that process. This chart fits medicine like a glove. How many times have you come up against resistance by physicians because the change you wanted was not evidence based? How many times have you struggled to convince a stakeholder that what they think is improvement is only random variation, and there is no trend? Have you ever wanted some proof that what you asked for is not out of the ordinary or that your supplier should have anticipated your demand and been ready to meet your request? Most important in HROs is the ability to prevent failure. This chart can do all this and more. This same chart is so versatile and has so many benefits, I call it the "Swiss army knife" of Change Leadership.

This chart not only can show the status as it occurs, but also can be used in a measurement system analysis (MSA) to show the quality of the measurement system. SPC can tell us if a change is actually occurring or if the measure simply is from normal common cause variation. Another benefit of the SPC chart is to show capability of a service or process before and after a change is made.

See Figure 13.2 for an example of an SPC chart of hand hygiene compliance. I also include a template in Appendix 7 that you can use in your healthcare organization.

SPC charts are plots of data over time. The hand hygiene compliance for August 12 was 20%. Compliance for the next day, August 13, was 30%. A line connects the compliance for each day. The line in the center of the two horizontal lines is the average of the compliance across all six days. Therefore, the average hand hygiene compliance is immediately evident by looking at this line and reading the value, which is 26.7% (0.2667).

The other two lines are called control limits. They represent the tails of the distribution of the data. One would expect that the hand hygiene should be between these two lines most of the time. One would not expect hand hygiene compliance to fall below the lower line if there were no changes made to the process. Therefore, if the compliance went lower than the lower control limit, we have reason to conclude there might be something special happening that day. The same logic works if compliance breaks through the

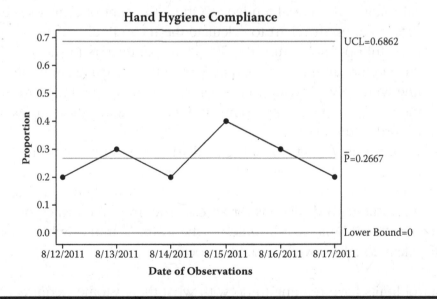

Figure 13.2   Hand hygiene compliance in a unit.

top control limit. We would not expect a day when hand hygiene exceeded 0.686 or 69%. If it did, the Change Leader is wise to practice the second M, manage to the measure. The Change Leader should immediately go out to the process and invite people to explain why the hand hygiene was so good compared with prior days.

Components of the Control Chart

SPC charts have common components, but not all SPC charts share all common components. Here are the most common:

- Data points can represent a statistic that you want to chart. In the previous case, we are charting the proportion of times healthcare professionals wash when they should have washed by day. These points could also be a single number, such as the number of defects in a surgical process; a range; or a mean of samples taken from the process at different times.
- An SPC chart is usually a time series chart. That is, the bottom scale is in order of time. Data are plotted from the earliest time period to later time periods.
  - For parameters, three lines are usually charted:
  - The mean line (center line) using the data points from the chart for a period of time that represents the period that you want to use in calculating the central tendency. Often, the control chart uses every data point on the chart to calculate the mean line.
  - A useful option is to use the SPC chart parameters to show a difference before and after a change. We do this by calculating the mean line with only the data points before the change and then recalculate the mean line with data points after the change. I show an example in further discussion.
  - Upper control limit (sometimes called a "natural process limit") that indicates the threshold at which the process output is considered statistically "unlikely" to be above this line. This line is typically at three standard deviations (or an estimate) from the centerline.
- Lower control limit, which indicates the lower bound of where points are likely to fall above in a stable process.

Control limits have nothing to do with what the customer requires. It is not your goal. Think of control limits as the "voice of the process."

Specification limits can be the "voice of the customer." Please do not confuse the two.

Specification limits could be added to the SPC chart, but we must be clear that these are not control limits. I have learned to emphasize this many times to ensure people do not confuse control limits with customer specifications. Because of this confusion, I resist adding customer specifications on an SPC chart until I am confident people understand what the control limits are.

Control and Out of Control

Statistical process control is an apt name for a control chart because the chart is able to tell us if the process, that is, a statistic from the process, is in a state of control. A process in which its control chart shows only data falling between the control limits and does not show trends or patterns is said to be a process in control. Another word for control is stable. A chart that has points falling outside the control limits, or has patterns or trends, is said to represent a process out of control, or unstable. Processes that are in control exhibit common cause variation. A process that is out of control has special cause variation. Special causes, such as when a team implements a change that really improves a process, are what makes a stable, in control chart showing only common cause variation to go out of control. Do you see the chain of events and understand the terms now? Let us take another scenario to practice understanding SPC.

Case Study: Ambulatory Surgical Center Wait Times

We start a new ambulatory surgical center, and the wait times vary tremendously as the staff and surgeons work out the kinks in scheduling. We find that on days when the surgeons who normally do not perform surgery come, the control chart of wait times goes out of control. The wait times exceed the upper control limit. We know there is a special cause because the chart went out of control. Going out of control is not necessarily bad or unfavorable. In fact, we want the chart to go out of control when we make a change. Another name for change is a special cause. A leader might find using the term *special cause* easily understood early in the change process. Later, when the team is charting the process being changed, the special cause will be seen, and celebration may be in order. Remember Bonnie Small's contribution to this wonderful tool. Make it practical.

Here is how practical it can be. Now, if you have Minitab and know SPC like the back of your hand, I want you to relax a bit here. I want others reading about SPC for the first time not to resist learning this tool, and taking a bit of liberty with statistics I find works wonders. Even Dr. Shewhart and Dr. Deming considered control charting to be more a rule of thumb, heuristic, versus a pure statistically perfect method. Estimating the control limits is done several ways, but an approximation of a variance statistic to calculate control limits is much better than not setting control limits at all. For more on this subject, read Don Wheeler and David Chamber's work *Understanding Statistical Process Control*.[3] Don was a student and worked under Dr. Deming for twenty-one years and has advanced Bonnie Small's work in making SPC practical for any industry.

Interpreting SPC Charts

The leader and team can take advantage of a special cause happening to understand the process of scheduling better. If the chart were displayed the next day, the team would have seen something special happened the day before when the chart went out of control. With this still fresh in their minds, someone might have suggested that yesterday was the day that surgeons who do not normally work at the center were working. Further investigation regarding why new surgeons performing surgery might be correlated with out-of-control wait times may have exposed that the scheduling persons in the surgeons' offices all asked the patients to arrive at the same time.

This bulge of patients arriving at the same time would have explained why the wait times were longer than on the days when the surgeons who normally perform surgery schedule their patients to arrive staggered throughout the day. The SPC chart triggered us to look for a special cause, and a solution now is self-evident: contact the surgeons or their office staff and ask them to stagger their patients throughout the day. See Figure 13.3 for examples of in control and out-of-control SPC charts. This easy-to-read chart is useful to display with SPC charts for people in the process to manage their processes.

The chart in Figure 13.4 shows how the SPC chart can alert us that the process has changed. It is clear now that we have made an improvement in hand

SPC Interpretation

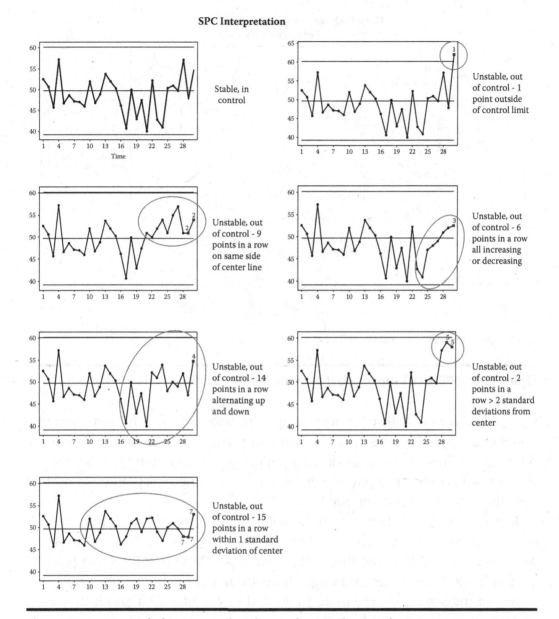

Figure 13.3   Control chart control and out-of-control examples.

hygiene because the process is out-of-control. Out-of-control is exactly what we wanted. Out-of-control means we made a change that had an effect.

We calculate the parameters (mean and control limit lines) using the baseline data. We now "lock in" these parameters knowing we have changed the process. The change we made is to train everyone in hand hygiene; we added dispensers to make it easier to sanitize, we put up posters reminding everyone of the importance of cleaning, and perhaps

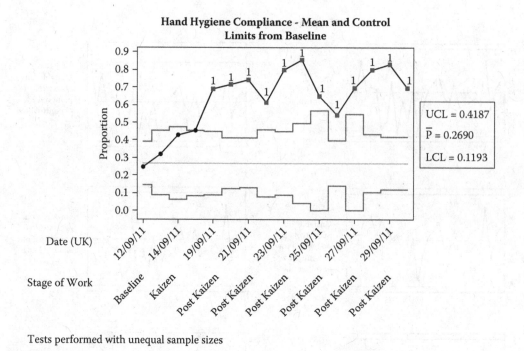

Figure 13.4   SPC chart showing out of control from baseline.

we stocked rooms with common equipment and supplies and put computers in each room so nurses do not have to waste time exiting the rooms so often to get dressings and to do their charting. We plot hand hygiene on the same chart with the parameters, not recalculating every time we add a new day, and see what happens.

In Figure 13.5, we show the three major stages of our process improvement effort and calculate the mean and control limits by each stage. This gives us a view of how the three stages compare. Note that the chart is in control in all three stages. Although there are not enough data, two points, in two of the stages, we are more interested in the later data and if they are showing improvement and stability.

Reliability and SPC

Reliability engineering benefits from some control charts that are not in time series order. For more information on these charts, please go to my Web site (http://www.rpmexec.com\reliability engineering).

The following additional features are found on some SPC charts:

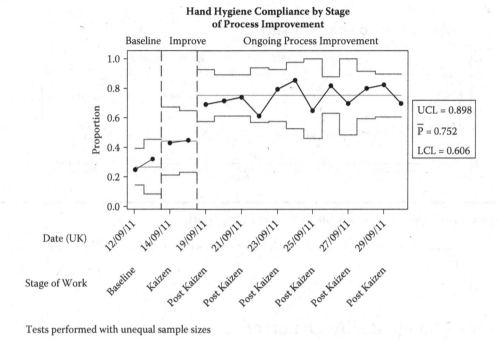

Figure 13.5   Showing stages.

- Upper and lower early warning limits, drawn as separate lines, typically two standard deviations above and below the centerline.
- Stages where special causes are known and the parameters are recalculated to show how the process has changed. (See discussion of when we recalculate the parameters to show a "before-and-after" effect.)

SPC Is Often Preferred in Managing to the Measure

The SPC chart is the preferred method of managing to the measure. Simply writing comments, questions, and suggestions on the chart demonstrates that you, the leader, are measuring and value the input of the team. This is so simple, yet so powerful. Try walking by the charts every day and making a note. On days when there was an attempt to improve the process, note the attempted special cause and stay tuned to the chart to see if the change has created an out-of-control situation. If and when it goes out of control, reinforce the team in acting. The progress principle can be seen having an effect. Make sure to reinforce progress toward the vision.

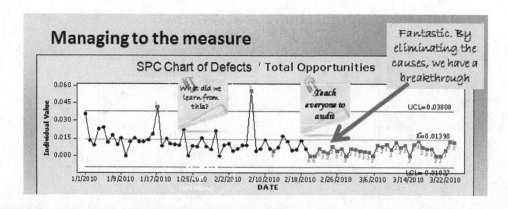

Figure 13.6　Notes made on surgical safety SPC chart.

An example of how to manage to the measure using the SPC chart is in Figure 13.6.

Prove Change Really Occurred

The Change Leader can use the SPC chart to prove change really occurred. If the team eliminated or reduced the effect that the top contributing factors had on people washing their hands, the team would know if they really improved hand hygiene when the SPC chart showed a trend of points above the upper control limit. The Pareto chart and SPC are like peanut butter and jelly. They go so well together.

Change Management without SPC?

There are some process improvement programs that do not cover charting and definitely not statistical process control. The better ones tag team with an instructor or firm that teaches Lean Six Sigma, or at least the fundamentals of quality. I do not know why any change management consultant would position his or her firm on the premise that creating consensus on a need, molding a vision, and getting teams together magically makes change and then makes change last. I do know such efforts can fail to make change happen. "If you want it, measure it" evidently is not believed by change management instructors who dismiss the value of measuring. I have heard many excuses why measurement is not taught in some change management initiatives. The worst excuse is the excuse that is most counter to the philosophy of change management: Control charting is too difficult for the people. Isn't a mantra of Change Management a belief in people development and abilities?

Frontline Workers Have Been Using SPC Since the 1920s

Dare someone to prove that SPC is too difficult for frontline workers to use. Remember that Bonnie Small and Joseph Juran successfully taught SPC to factory workers in the 1940s. I started teaching SPC in 1982 to people who did not all even have a high school diploma. I have witnessed tens of thousands of dollars spent on change management programs and thousands of hours learning change management without measuring, managing to the measure, and making it easier. After a couple of years with one of these initiatives, not one change could be attributed to the investment. This came from one of the masters herself. Not even the culture significantly changed. Reporting did not increase, there definitely was not a just culture, and no one felt safe despite all the leadership chatter on growing a safe culture. What did change were results from teams who measured, managed to the measure, and made it easier for people to do the right thing. One of the subcultures required for achieving a safety culture is a culture of reporting. SPC is a way to report. Even a line chart would be useful. Even better, SPC shows when change really is occurring. It gives evidence to a team that it is making progress, and when the team is not, it tries new ways.

I believe if you achieve the skill in using control charts, you will use SPC. Even if you approximate the control limits or use the rules of a run chart, you will do better than those who talk about change but refuse to measure the impact. SPC is a tool that is always in "your back pocket." I have not left home without it since 1980 when I first learned it.

Run Charts

One physician uses run charts, which are similar to SPC charts. Run charts and SPC charts are a leader's friend because they prove if special causes are occurring, if the process is in control, and if changes are having an effect. The difference between run charts and SPC charts is mostly that run charts do not have control limits. Therefore, run charts are not as sensitive to special causes from large variations from the norm. Some practitioners find using the same interpretation rules as SPC charts for trends and patterns gets them the information they need without calculating control limits. Run charts made more sense before computers, when control limits were an added calculation. Computers today are about everywhere, and software calculates the parameters easily and accurately.

The NHS (National Health System) in the United Kingdom makes an SPC application available to anyone with an NHS e-mail address. What a wonderful gift. The IHI (Institute for Healthcare Improvement) in America provides free training in run charts and SPC charts.[4]

There are applications that run in Excel to make control charts, and my favorite quality improvement software and the choice of many lean Six Sigma practitioners is Minitab. I challenge you to try creating an SPC chart now. Go to http://www.minitab.com, download a free 30-day trial, gather some data in time series order, and make your first SPC chart. I even include screen navigation instructions on how to make an SPC chart. For instructions and data, go to my Web site www.rpmexec.com/SPC and download the data. I include the answers, including the SPC chart, for you to compare yours to mine. The Automotive Industry Action Group book on SPC is very helpful.[5]

Even run charts are better than using a line chart in Excel. Above all, do not even think about using the Excel trend line feature unless you know how the trend line is calculated.

Measuring Common Healthcare Measures

Now that you know how powerful SPC charts are and how easy they can be created and interpreted, some of the first SPC charts I recommend are on your most critical measures for patient safety and the inputs that drive the outcomes. CMS, the Centers for Medicaid and Medicare Services, provides an extra incentive to use SPC now and where to apply this powerful tool. While writing this book, CMS was changing healthcare's world in the United States. In 2013 and 2014, the second M, manage to the measure, will take on a whole new priority. Financial incentives and disincentives will be based on the first M, measure. For hospitals, CMS is requiring minimum performance in outcome metrics and process metrics. Also included are the HCAHPS metrics on patient satisfaction. What healthcare needs to do now is to manage to the measure using SPC and PI teams and methods that will make it easier to achieve the thresholds in these metrics. The best organizations will be managing to the measure and making it easier to excel in metrics and gain the incentives of being in the top performer range. There will be more of the first M, measure, as leaders in reliability, quality, and safety discover the drivers that move these twenty-six metrics.

Now that we know SPC, we can better manage to the measure.

Key Points

■ SPC charts are the Swiss army knife for process improvement.
■ Managing to the measure is much more effective with SPC because we know if there has been a real change in a process.
■ SPC can also be an early warning of a process or function starting to vary. SPC helps prevent failures if used in a timely manner.

Notes

1. Western Electric History. http://www.porticus.org/bell/westernelectric_history. html#Western%20Electric%20-%20A%20Brief%20History.
2. Western Electric history chart. http://www.porticus.org/bell/westernelectric_ history.html.
3. Don Wheeler and David Chamber, *Understanding Statistical Process Control*, 3rd edition, SPC Press, Knoxville, TN.
4. http://www.ihi.org/offerings/VirtualPrograms/OnDemand/Run_ControlCharts/ Pages/default.aspx.
5. *Statistical Process Control (SPC) Reference Manual*, Chrysler Corporation, Ford Motor Company, General Motors Corporation, 1995.

Chapter 14

3Ms: Manage to the Measure

If you cannot measure it you cannot control it.

John Grebe

Fine, fine; don't do anything to patch it up. The way things are
going, gangrene will set in. Then we can amputate and clean up
the problem once and for all.

John Grebe

Managers taking action was more effective than their communicating about actions taken. ... Managers would be well advised
to take action—preferably substantive and intense action—in
response to frontline workers' communications about problems.

Anita L. Tucker and Sara J. Singer[1]

The Scoreboard

The 3Ms (measure, manage to the measure, make it easier) are not worth
anything if no one sees the measures. Imagine walking into a sports stadium after the event has started and hearing the crowd cheering. What is
the first thing you look for? The score. What is one of the biggest pieces
of equipment in even the largest stadiums? The scoreboard. If you want to
see what just happened on the field, what do you look at? The scoreboard.

Why do we make it so difficult in our organizations to see the score? Where is your score posted? When was it posted? Yesterday? Last month? Last quarter? Would you value seeing the score in the sports stadium three periods later than the one you are watching live? Gosh, before we get too down on how poorly our scoring systems are, realize that in our intensive care units (ICUs) we have scores showing a patient's vital signs, which everyone who needs to see the "score" can see; some such scoreboards even have alarms in case a vital sign is varying, and they are in real time. So, maybe the question is how do we scale up from our ICUs where we have been keeping score for years? I share some tips that you can use right away, especially now that you have made your first SPC (statistical process control) chart.

Visual Management

Visual management is an appropriate term for the second M. Managing to the measure is making the measure visible to the people in the process. Some healthcare organizations have gone far beyond visual management for internal use. They post their measures on their Web site and in their organizations to be completely transparent. High Reliability Organizations have a safety culture, and we know that a subculture necessary for a safety culture is a culture of reporting. A Change Leader may use public reporting to help reduce the resistance to change.

Dashboard is another term that fits the bill. Think of the dashboard in the car. In the dashboard are measures that are critical to the safe function of the vehicle. See Figure 14.1 for a dashboard example. There is a gas gauge, a speedometer, odometer, and an indicator for your headlights on virtually every car's dashboard. What would be in every ambulatory surgical center's dashboard or every skilled nursing facility's visual management board? What should be on your organization's dashboard?

Interestingly enough, our cars' dashboards never had a visual management gauge for the prime function of a car—getting to the destination. That is, until GPS systems were available. I guess we did not need one because we could look out the window to see that we reached our destination. Now, we have a visual means and a voice telling us, "You have arrived at your destination." The value of a GPS is the guidance we get along the way to our destination, our desired outcome. This is the same reason we measure the inputs that drive the outcome desired in healthcare. We measure hand

Figure 14.1   Car gauges.

hygiene to get safer care and fewer healthcare-acquired conditions. We measure the number of slips, lapses, and mistakes,[2] as James Reason lists, in our perioperative process to reduce the bad outcome of wrong-patient and wrong-site surgery. We measure the vital signs of a patient to predict the probability of poor outcomes and to treat the individual. A reporting culture is one in which people are willing to report their slips, lapses, and mistakes. The benefit is to achieve a learning culture, another subculture to a safety culture.

What to Expect Short and Long Term from Measuring

We need to understand that even SPC charts are a means to an end. Once a process has become stable and capable, the work is not over. There is a way to reduce and even eliminate the need to continue to measure. The way is to ensure stability, capability, and robustness to variation. Mistake-proofing is one way to achieve all three and thus eliminate the need to continue to measure. After all, if there was no way for the inputs to vary and the outcome was acceptable, measure has done its job and may be reduced to a level just to make sure variation does not return. An example of mistake-proofing in healthcare is the inability of hooking up the wrong gas. Unique connectors for oxygen differ from the connectors for other gases. As long as the processes that installed these connectors and maintained the connectors are mistake-proof, there is little need to measure the quality of connecting the correct gas.

For most healthcare processes, we are a long way from such control and performance. Nonetheless, as improvements occur from the third M, make it easier, and the control and capability increase, the frequency of the first M, measure, may be gradually reduced. This in turn may reduce the frequency to manage to the measure, the second M.

Instructing and Coaching

Managing to the measure requires both instructing and coaching. It is cruel to expect people to change before they have been taught what the change is, why it is occurring, and what their role is in the change. We did a stakeholder analysis as one of the first steps in process improvement. Now is a good time to "dust it off" and refresh it. Managing to the measure is both a coach's tool and an instructor's tool.

The role of the instructor is to share with others how to do a task to achieve the outcome desired. The measure is how the instructor can assess if the student learned. The measure is also how the coach knows skill and progress are gained.

Training within Industry

Learning how to instruct is a good way to learn how to manage to the measure. Training within industry (TWI) has been credited with much of the success among the Allies in winning World War II. The situation in the early 1940s was dire. Men went off to war and left a vacuum of talent in the factories to provide equipment and munitions to support the men overseas. A commission reached back to research work started in the 1920s to improve the method of instructing workers, women, to be exact, who would replace the men in the factories. The method they discovered evolved into TWI.

There are four steps in TWI:

- Job instructions (JI)
- Job methods (JM)
- Job relations (JR)
- Program development (PD)

Job Instructions

If the Worker Hasn't Learned, the Instructor Hasn't Taught.[3]

There are two steps in job instructions for the instructor.

- How to get ready to instruct
- How to instruct

TWI breaks each step into tasks. The term *standard work* is often used in Lean Six Sigma and was borrowed from the Toyota Production System. Taiichi Ohno gives TWI credit for the basis for standard work.[4]

- How to get ready to instruct:
  - Have a timetable for you to instruct and the student to learn the skill.
  - Break down the task into the right way and with key points.
  - Have everything ready to teach and do the task correctly.
  - Have the workplace properly arranged.
- How to instruct:
  - Prepare the student to receive the instruction: put the student at ease.
  - Present the task to learn: tell the student, show the student, illustrate, ask in small doses.
  - Try out the student's performance: have the student perform the task and verbalize why he or she is doing what he or she is doing. Ensure the student states key points.
- Follow up. Ensure the student knows who can help if needed, not just anyone who may give wrong instruction.

We can practice job instructions skills using the charts. Practice instructing how to use a chart to manage to the measure. Follow the instructions in Job Instructions just as they are written. You might instruct how to read the chart, how to know when it is in control or not, and what might be a useful comment to post on the chart to show you care and want the team to succeed in process improvement.

After instructing and observing the person manage to the measure, ask your pupil how you did as an instructor. If we make it easy to learn, we will utilize the 3Ms faster and better.

Job Methods

A practical plan to help you produce greater quantities of quality products in less time by making the best use of the manpower, machines, and materials is now available.

Step 1. Break down the job.
- List all the details of the job exactly as done by the present method. Be sure details include all
  1. Material handling
  2. Machine work
  3. Hand work

Step 2. Question every detail.
- Use these types of questions:
  1. Why is it necessary?
  2. What is the purpose?
  3. Where shall it be done?
  4. When should it be done?
  5. Who is best qualified to do it?
  6. What is the best way to do it?

Step 3. Develop the new method.
  1. Eliminate
  2. Combine
  3. Rearrange
  4. Simplify

Step 4. Apply the new method.
  1. Sell your proposal to your boss.
  2. Sell the new method to the operator.
  3. Get full approval of all concerned on safety, quality, quantity, cost.
  4. Put the new method to work.

One can see that the job instructions and job methods are very similar to what many call lean. That is no coincidence. Japan was taught by Americans using TWI after the war. Not all credit goes to either country. It is surprising to me how we again are reinventing these materials for their third or fourth time. TWI actually evolved from work done in World War I.

Job Relations

Job relations is the third part of TWI. It starts with, "A supervisor gets results through people."

Our change leadership principles follow closely the job relations methods, including engaging the workers who do the work, training them, and enabling them in process improvement.

Program Development

The fourth and final program is program development. According to TWI, program development is about problem solving. Its steps are:

- Spot a production problem.
- Determine a plan to study it.
- Get a plan into action.
- Check results.

This is very much why the 3Ms work. Program development is about using measures to help improve a process.

Standard Work to Manage to the Measure

The article in Figure 14.2 from one of the original TWI government brochures talks about hospitals and how TWI was valued in healthcare.

What many of you know as Standard Work started out as shown in Figure 14.3. How to make it easier to do the right work the right way is shown clearly in this layout. Note the term *key points*. It is no coincidence that I used key points to help you capture the essence of each chapter in this book. The instructor will ensure that the tasks are done correctly and ask the trainee to state the key points to ensure the student knows the importance of the work.

In Figure 14.4, I share with you an actual standard work form on the same task. We might be a little more conscious these days about hand hygiene, but the similarities are striking.

Utilization of the 3Ms has been going on for years, as evidenced by these 1940s items. Measuring is mentioned throughout the four steps, managing to the measure is in all four steps, and making it easier is what concerns program development.

HOSPITALS in various parts of the country are finding that the Training Within Industry program of the War Manpower Commission holds a great deal of value to them. This program was first described for hospitals in an article by Ellen Aird entitled "You Can Keep Employes," published in The MODERN HOSPITAL for December 1942.

Figure 14.2 TWI in hospitals.

CLEANING AN OCCUPIED ROOM

STEPS	KEY POINTS
1. Clean rug with carpet sweeper. Clean with vacuum cleaner once a week. 2. Dust floor with dry mop.	1. Do not bump bed or furniture with cleaning tools, as this annoys the patient and mars the furniture. When vacuum cleaner is used also clean the floor with it.
3. Dust all furniture.	3. Be careful to dust all hidden corners.
4. Dust windows, sills and window shields, wood work and hardware.	4. Wash when needed.
5. Clean face bowl and plumbing.	5. Dry all nickel or chrome plate.
6. Empty and clean wastebasket.	
7. If there are dirty spots on floor, wipe them up with wet cloth.	
8. Wash floor every other day, except in unusual cases, which might require washing the floor every day.	8. When rug is vacuum cleaned, also wash the floor. This makes the patient feel the room is thoroughly cleaned.

Figure 14.3 Standard work for cleaning an occupied room.

Coaching Is Key in Managing to the Measure

I wanted to share some tips on coaching. Instructing is necessary so the skills are learned, but coaching is what makes process improvement occur and sustains gains.

Teaching is the Job method. Standard work is the Toyota term. Standard work alone is not enough, though. The World Health Organization (WHO)

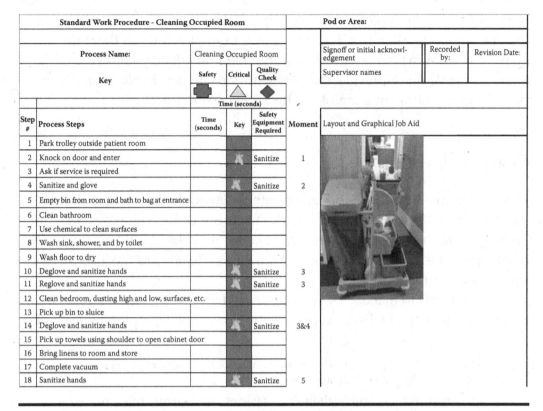

Standard Work Procedure - Cleaning Occupied Room					Pod or Area:		

Process Name:		Cleaning Occupied Room			Signoff or initial acknowledgement	Recorded by:	Revision Date:
Key		Safety	Critical	Quality Check	Supervisor names		

Step #	Process Steps	Time (seconds)	Key	Safety Equipment Required	Moment	Layout and Graphical Job Aid
1	Park trolley outside patient room					
2	Knock on door and enter			Sanitize	1	
3	Ask if service is required					
4	Sanitize and glove			Sanitize	2	
5	Empty bin from room and bath to bag at entrance					
6	Clean bathroom					
7	Use chemical to clean surfaces					
8	Wash sink, shower, and by toilet					
9	Wash floor to dry					
10	Deglove and sanitize hands			Sanitize	3	
11	Reglove and sanitize hands			Sanitize	3	
12	Clean bedroom, dusting high and low, surfaces, etc.					
13	Pick up bin to sluice					
14	Deglove and sanitize hands			Sanitize	3&4	
15	Pick up towels using shoulder to open cabinet door					
16	Bring linens to room and store					
17	Complete vacuum					
18	Sanitize hands			Sanitize	5	

Figure 14.4   Standard work in the twenty-first century.

surgical safety checklist is an example of standard work, but it does not alone guarantee performance. And instructing is not enough to change behaviors. Change leaders know that coaching is required to achieve the performance after instructing. And, "in the moment" or "just-in-time" coaching is much more successful than "a week later" coaching.

Just-in-time coaching can only occur in the process or with real-time measurement shared remotely. A Change Leader must be an instructor and a coach. One cannot coach correctly if the coach does not know the right way to do the task. Simply instructing, without following up to observe the person doing the task, will not guarantee the reliability and quality of the performance. Everyone needs a coach; even star musicians and athletes have coaches. Executives who want to improve often have coaches.

Now is a good time for a reminder of the progress principle: Of all the things that can boost inner work life, the most important is making progress in meaningful work. A coach carves out progressive goals for the person he or she is coaching. If we want people someday to accomplish the remarkable, we should instruct and coach them on the fundamentals. An example is when I instruct people in how to do the 3Ms. I teach them the three Ms with the overview slide that I shared listing examples. I teach them the key point of each M, which is included in the title immediately following each M. Next, I have them practice the 3Ms with a relatively simple example in class or, even better, an example in his or her work area.

Coach's Playbook

At Motorola, we helped each coach create a playbook. The playbook lists standard work for routine and regularly occurring tasks. The playbook can even have alternative plays based on variables that change. Interestingly, the quality program was named Quality Vital Signs. Healthcare has had a favorable impact on many industries.

A coach needs to manage by walking around and engaging the people in the process. Instead of telling people what to do, a wise coach listens, observes,

---

(1) **Knowledge of the Work** — materials, tools, processes, operations, products and how they are made and used.

(2) **Knowledge of Responsibilities** — policies, agreements, rules, regulations, schedules, interdepartmental relationships.

These two knowledge needs must be met currently and locally by each plant or company.

Such knowledge must be provided if each supervisor is to know his job and is to have a clear understanding of his authority and responsibilities as a part of management.

(3) **Skill in Instructing** — increasing production by helping supervisors to develop a well trained work force which will get into production quicker and have less scrap, rework and rejects, fewer accidents, and less tool and equipment damage.

(4) **Skill in Improving Methods** — utilizing materials, machines, and manpower more effectively by making supervisors study each operation in order to eliminate, combine, rearrange, and simplify details of the job.

(5) **Skill in Leading** — increasing production by helping supervisors to improve their understanding of individuals, their ability to size up situations, and their ways of working with people.

These three skills must be acquired individually. Practice and experience in using them enable both new and experienced supervisors to recognize and solve daily problems promptly.

Figure 14.5 Coaching in TWI.

and asks the right questions at the right time to engage the person's intellect and obtain feedback on how well the instruction given earlier has been absorbed.

The coach should lead off conversations with a question regarding how things are proceeding. The measure is what the coach is expecting to hear. By asking how things are going, the coach is looking for the person to demonstrate performance and issues using the measures. The dashboard is a wonderful method to show the coach how the process is running.

Again, TWI has the same message we teach today (see Figure 14.5).

Key Points

- Managing to the measure started with the charting skills being built.
- The SPC chapter gave us powerful and easy-to-use charts to know what we can do as managers to build on the success and to support the teams.
- TWI is clearly the parent of standard work and how we instruct workers today. TWI had extensive reach into healthcare as well.
- Coaching is vital to managing to the measure. A little common sense and the golden rule go far in helping us become better coaches.
- The key aid is the measure allowing us more confidence in how things really are.

Notes

1. Anita L. Tucker and Sara J. Singer, Going through the motions: an empirical test of management involvement in process improvement, *Harvard Business Review*, April 2009.
2. James Reason, *Human Error*, Cambridge University Press, Cambridge, UK, 1990.
3. C. R. Dooley, *Report III: Vocational Training, International Labor Organization* (Montreal, 1946).
4. Yasuhiro Monden, *The Toyota Production System*, 2nd edition, Institute of Industrial Engineers, Norcross, GA, 1993.

Chapter 15

3Ms: Make It Easier

Performance Improvement Makes It Easier to Change

The "Laws" in Change Leadership

If change were easy, you would not be reading this book. The "laws" of process improvement follow other laws, as we have witnessed with electricity and now from Sir Isaac Newton. Sir Isaac Newton is considered one of the most important scientists of all time. He studied motion and developed three laws; his first law of motion is often paraphrased in Change Leadership to explain resistance. We think it has a dual value. Besides referring to a body at rest, we think his law supports the benefits of a culture of continuous improvement.

For Newton's first law, every body persists in its state of being at rest or of moving uniformly straight forward, except insofar as it is compelled to change its state by force impressed.[1] The process improvement leader simply presents the force to help people change, whether the change is to start moving or to change direction.

Newton's second law is easier to understand if we understand his third law first. The third law is that for every action there is always an equal and opposite reaction. Let us say that you want your son and daughter to become more active. You find them too often sitting in their rooms watching TV, and you are concerned about the lack of exercise. You decide that you want to be a Change Leader and lead them to engage in a sport or to play a musical instrument. You literally have bodies at rest, in your view. You try to pull them off the floor to go outside with you. You pull, and they pull back: resistance. If they are the same size as you, the resistance is considerable. Now, let us add the second law and relate it to how a Change Leader can use these three laws of motion to lead change more easily.

The Second Law is that the acceleration of motion is ever proportional to the motive force impressed and is made in the direction of the right line in which that force is impressed.

Newton explains that the forces may be

- Equal
- and
- Opposing,

but the acceleration of change on the two bodies is dependent on the mass of the bodies. In other words, when the kids are young and small, Mom or Dad can change these bodies at rest into bodies in motion much easier than when they outgrow poor Mom and Dad.

Case Study: Nurses Spending Time with Patients

Relating this to change in the workplace, we want to change a nurse's behavior with patients. Often, administrators and nurse managers want to increase the face-to-face time nurses spend with patients. They believe this change will result in patients who are more satisfied because patients feel that the nurse and hospital care more than in those healthcare organizations that have too few nurses, who are not able to spend much time at all with patients. You, the nurse manager, find the nurses everywhere but in the patients' rooms. You find them running around getting supplies, charting at the nurses' station, and attending meetings that you set up. To make the change easier, we suggest applying process improvement to the first and third issue. Process improvement could include eliminating the reasons that the supplies are not where they are supposed to be or in insufficient quantities. The third issue could be caused by other changes going on that you want them to know. Legitimate reasons, but even legitimate reasons in and of themselves may be a force that is keeping your next change from happening. A Change Leader must often choose timing of changes so changes do not create a resistance themselves from overburden.

Once we have the first and third issue resolved and resistance to change reduced, let us focus on the second issue: charting at the nurses' station.

Job Satisfaction

Before I show how Newton's laws can help a Change Leader improve a process, realize that this book has actually given you tips throughout on making change easier. Remember the "Hawthorne effect?" Let us use it to answer if a patient's level of satisfaction improves with more attention. Even though the study measured productivity, perhaps satisfaction with the job actually improved first, resulting in improved productivity? Applying this same idea with nurses, will nurses be more satisfied and "productive,"[2] with productive meaning the amount of time spent with patients, if their manager spends more time with them? Try this in leading your next change and see if simply spending time with the stakeholders reduces the resistance and gets the change you want to occur. Now, let us go back to our example using Newton's laws in leading change.

You walk to the nurses in the station on the computers charting their notes. You start with an icebreaker to create a safer culture for reporting and chat a bit. Next, you share with them the benefits you believe occur for the patients, physicians, and the nurses if charting can be done with the patient in the patient's room. You purposely pause to let them respond and watch for nonverbal communication to understand their receptiveness to this conversation on change.

You get some remarks about how they normally chart in the rooms, but the "computers on wheels" (COWs) do not hold a charge, and they end up having to use the nurses' station computers. You promise to get someone down from information technology (IT) to help fix this issue. Even then, they share that they like to sit at the nurses' station, where they can print and file the forms, which they cannot do in the patient rooms. Voila, you are finding that this change is going to be tougher than expected because there are a number of valid issues that make this change to charting in patient rooms more difficult than charting at the nurses' station.

Realize again the benefit that Abraham Lincoln found in his principle to "circulate among followers consistently." And, as I have shared with you, "If we know what each other knows, then we'll feel like each other feels, and we will do like each other does." In Toyota, they have the saying, "Go to the Gemba." Translated, this means "go to where the work is." The value of being where the work is is invaluable in process improvement.

The change that you wanted the nurses to make—spending more time with patients—has been resisted for valid reasons. The forces acting on the nurses to chart outside the patients' rooms was greater than the force from others to chart in the rooms. In fact, it was impossible to chart in the rooms when computers were not operating. Any force that a nurse manager would apply without helping them with time and support to solve these issues would have been met with an equal and opposing force. And for this action, there would always be an equal and opposite reaction. The nurses outnumber the managers, so the mass of the nurse group being greater than the one manager would result in the acceleration of the nurse manager being greater than the bodies at rest behind the nurses' station.

Making Change Easier Is What We Need to Do

What would make it easier for the nurses to spend time with patients in this story? This entire book is about this chapter: make it easier. Let us start from the top: the Roadmap for a Change Leader and process improvement leader. This chapter walks you through the entire book of key points. We use the Roadmap to guide us. By the end of this chapter, I think you will have the knowledge to utilize the 3Ms (measure, manage to the measure, make it easier) for process improvement and more confidence from practicing it with me (see Figure 15.1).

The issue is to improve the process so nurses spend more time with patients. Let us get started at the top left of the Roadmap.

To prepare stakeholders for the change, do the following:

1. Train. Training them in the value of spending time with patients begins the preparation phase. The best way to train is to be a role model and show them the behaviors that you seek. Go to the patient rooms and

Roadmap to Performance Excellence™				
PDSA	What are we trying to accomplish?	How will we know when a change is an improvement?	PDSA Cycle - What are the possible solutions and how do we implement the best solution?	How do we maintain the gains we have achieved and standardize?
Lean Six Sigma	Define the issue What does the customer value?	Measure the current state	Measure /Analyze for	Improve and Design Achieve flow and let the customer pull	Control
Change Leadership	Prepare for change - Train, Envision, Engage, Enable and Empower	Explore Together	Explain	Experiment, Explore, Build Consensus	Train, Enable, Empower, Hold Accountable Celebrate

Figure 15.1.   PDSA Lean Six Sigma and Change Leadership Principles.

observe the nurses. If possible, do this as a team and have everyone observe and record what facilitates spending time with patients and what detracts. If the staff is trained in value stream mapping or SIPOC (supplier, input, process step, output, customer) mapping, use a mapping technique to see the issues more clearly. Regardless, use the time to train them in the behaviors that you seek.

2. Envision. Envisioning the future when nurses are able to spend time with patients due to a reduction in wastes and quality issues is key. What are those variables that prevent nurses who trained extensively, often with great hardship, from spending time with patients? We should envision nurses' extra value from spending more time with patients. Help them envision "what is in it for them," not just what is in it for the patient, the physician, and other staff who benefit from nurses spending more time with patients.

3. Engage. Engaging the nurses in the change is the only polite and effective method, but so often it is ignored. You already incorporated engage by observing with them in their environment and listening. I often wish people wanting to lead change would listen instead of talk. My father was a car salesman all my life. He was the leading salesperson for the dealership where he worked. What did he do better than others did? He listened and knew when to quit talking. It just was not from my observations of my dad that I learned to listen.

    I was in high school and went to a large party at my classmate's father's gas station. At the party, I overheard a mailman who evidently just bought a car from my dad. He said, "that [expletive deleted] Walt Morrow wasn't saying a thing, and I basically sold myself the car." Such is the power of silence. I would relearn the power of listening, which should be coupled with silence, many times over my career in leading process improvement. If I could suggest only one thing to most consultants, it would be to listen.

4. Enable. Enabling the people in improving their work delivers improvement. Teach them how to eliminate, or at least reduce, the issues that prevent nurses staying with the patient. We have shown that change can happen with very simple tools and methods. Change can be accelerated and even enhanced by using Lean and Six Sigma methods. I have taught and launched Lean Six Sigma and Change Leadership across the globe for Eaton, SKF, Motorola, United Airlines, the Joint Commission, and many healthcare organizations with Healthcare Performance Partners. All of these programs have sustained, and I am very proud of

the people, my staff, and the thousands of people who learned these performance improvement methodologies and continue to apply them to enact change. If you are interested in how these methodologies can accelerate and improve the change, contact me at my Web site (http://www.rpmexec.com) for more information on these methods.

5. Empower. This is a key differentiator in programs that sustain. Too often, management talks a good game and offers training and cheer-leading, but to make change happen, someone has to do something. It is much better to empower people in process improvement.

There is a change management practice within a large company that purposely denies people the ability to execute because its process denies the person with authority to approve to be part of the work. The teams who work in this method of change management must present their find-ings that they explored together to management for approval to execute. This is absolutely counter to empowerment and continuous improvement. I can also tell you that this was not the practice years ago at the same company that invented this particular change management program. I participated at this company in continuous improvement frequently, and the people in the room were empowered to make the decisions and execute. It worked much better inside this company than what is being taught today when they teach others. The other issue with this change management program is the almost total disregard for measurement.

6. Explore together. Now that the team is trained, the vision is shared, and the team is engaged, enabled, and empowered, we should explore the contributing factors that are the reasons we need change. Discovering the contributing factors to a problem is the better way to change than jumping to solutions. Jumping to solutions without knowing the root causes often fails because one is acting blindly by forcing counter-measures onto unseen root causes. The first M, measure, pays off in the explore together phase. Measuring the current state using value stream maps or SIPOC maps with data helps in the next phase, Explain. Exploring the process together helps the team see the issues that explain why problems occur.

I do not remember a single group who did not benefit from exploring contributing factors together. I often hear, "I had no idea that happens the way it does." This shared discovery is a wonderful team-building and Change Leadership method. It can pay dividends for the next change. Observing and listening is easier than the stress of talking over everyone, which may be caused by a Change Leader who is unsure and a bit anxious. When I coach process improvement leaders, I watch for people talking over, and I look for the root causes of this rude and wasteful practice.

Going back to our story of getting nurses to spend more time with patients, we often find no one trained, envisioned, engaged, enabled, empowered, and explored together the change. We told you the end of this story in Chapter 1. The change to COWs failed because there was insufficient to nonexistent

Training
Envisioning
Engaging
Enabling
Empowering
Exploring together and explaining the issues as the next steps

In this case study, the team needs to explain the issues of why nurses were not spending more time with patients. The good news is this hospital's staff members are getting training, envisioning a brighter future, and enabling physicians, clinicians, and staff to work on process improvement. They are engaged and empowered and exploring better ways to care for patients and improve their inner work life

And, we are measuring the effect on them and the patient. As of this time, the 3Ms are in their infancy with this change. Many organizations in healthcare, aviation, and other consumer industries have a long way to go to get the 3Ms working for them. In healthcare, the patient satisfaction measures are only required to be sampled, which leads to a nonresponse bias. Worse, the results are far from timely, with some not available until a year after the patient's experience. There are some simple fixes to this delay. One specialty clinic asks 100% of its patients at discharge the likelihood they will recommend its organization to a relative or friend.

Satisfaction and Loyalty Measurement

The question of satisfaction and loyalty comes from Fred Reichheld and Rob Markey's book, *The Ultimate Question*.[3] This system also manages to the measure every day using the responses from the prior day. The results are posted and visible not only to staff but also to the patients. Third, they practice the third M; they make it easier to help the nurse help the patient by empowering him or her to provide services to patients. Some requests may be out of the ordinary, such as providing acupuncture therapy at a patient's request at a cancer clinic. The facilities department employees at this same cancer clinic are measured on the quality and the timeliness of repairs. This information is relayed to the maintenance staff every day, by the next day.

The nurse manager in this story also made it easier to change by training the team in the 3Ms and Change Leadership. The team of nurses and the Change Leader nurse manager all shared equally. The nurse manager could have forced the change by threatening disciplinary actions if the nurses did not spend more time with patients, specifically charting in the patient rooms with the COWs. That change might have been met with an equal and opposing force. What would the effect have been on the patients? There are many studies that correlate staff satisfaction with patient satisfaction.

Explain

Explaining the reasons for the issues that hinder the change is to validate the contributing factors. In the nurse example, simple observation can confirm that the COWs do not work; that there is a lot of printing required, with the only printer located at the nurse's station; and the other issues discovered exploring together. Asking why five times is a powerful tool in explaining and validating the contributing factors.

Explaining can take a more statistical approach. When data are available, it is useful to use data to explain correlations. Simple line charts showing the variable that one thinks is an issue and a line representing the measure to change can suggest correlation visually. People who are trained in testing for correlation can speed change by speeding and improving the quality of the explain phase.

Measure, again, is the vehicle to explain the issues affecting the process and thus the reason for change. We measure the effects of the contributing factors. An example would be to measure the time away from patients caused by nurses needing to leave the room for supplies. In one study in the operating rooms (ORs) at a major hospital, the OR staff left the OR an average of seven times for at least ten minutes lost. Add these for the forty rooms and an average of three or more cases per OR per day.

The hospital's improvement champion and I did not get the chance to see if the supply issue was the same on the medical/surgical floors, but if they have issues in the OR with supplies, it is also likely supply issues hinder the nurses on the floor from staying with the patients. Use measure to help explain the issues and make the change easier to spend more time with patients. Measure the correlation of the changes the team is making with the change desired, $Y = f(Xs)$. The Y outcome of what you are leading the change to achieve is a function of the Xs, the inputs that the team needs to change to get the outcome desired.

Without measuring the baseline, how would we know now if we have improved?

Experiment, Explore, Build Consensus

Once the team has identified contributing factors, the countermeasures, solutions, and the changes to be made are self-evident. A strong process improvement leader will validate how the changes to the variables affect the change desired by experimenting and exploring the effects of the changes. Again, measure is what the Change Leader and team use in the experiments and explorations. PDSA (plan, do, study, act) is based on measuring what happens in the "do." Study is using the measure to know if the do part had an effect. The act is to implement the change. It is critical to measure the Y and the key Xs to ensure sustained change.

Choosing the Best Countermeasures

Note the word *countermeasure*: counter and measure. Counter is to change the variables in the process that are causing the issue. Measure is included in the term *countermeasure* to reinforce that measuring the change is critical to know if the countermeasure works. *Countermeasure* is sometimes synonymous with the word *improvement*. However, sometimes we are not absolutely sure we know the root causes, so countermeasure is a more conservative term.

On our Roadmap, the team sees the question to be answered in this phase.

Piloting and Choosing the Best Countermeasures

Before you pilot and after you pilot, a process to find the best set of countermeasures to achieve the goals on your charter will make it easier for you

CBE Matrix Form

Choosing the Best Countermeasures

	Rating of Importance to Customer	10	10	10	10	10	10	10	10	10	10	10	
		Criteria for Choosing the Best Solution											
	Countermeasure Ideas	Contribution to the charter goals	Ability to implement	Cost to implement	Empowerment of the process members	Relia-bility	Risk	Scalability to other areas	Technology available	Learning opportunity	Safety	Builds on Core Competency	**ImportanceTotal**
1													
2													
3													
4													
5													
6													
7													
8													
9													
10													
11													
12													
13													
	Total												

1
2
3
4
5
6

Figure 15.2 Solution decision matrix.

and your team. I include an easy-to-use decision matrix. Here is how to use it, and it is available at http://www.rpmexec.com (see Figure 15.2):

Step 1. Brainstorm for all improvement ideas and list them in the matrix in the "Countermeasure Ideas" column.

Step 2. Choose the criteria that add value in your decision. Simply zero out the row labeled "Rating of Importance to Customer" to completely eliminate a criteria from your process.

Step 3. Rate the criteria. Often, some criteria are very important to you and the team. Weight these criteria with a high value, say nine or ten. Rate the least-important criteria as a one, two, or three. Finally, rate the balance of the criteria using some number between three and nine.

Step 4. Have your team rate each improvement idea for each of the criteria. Use the following values, with a nine as high impact: 1, 3, 9.

Step 5. Sort the ideas using the "Importance Total" column.

Step 6. Choose the best countermeasures from among the highest values in the "Importance Total" column.

Now, the team has a set of countermeasures that makes piloting much easier and more productive.

Piloting to See If the Measure Moves

Measure now comes back into play for the team. It is time to measure the impact that the countermeasures have on the measures on the charter. Piloting and building consensus are much easier when measure has proven the change has been achieved. We mentioned a fact-based and data-driven methodology not only validates that the change has occurred but also validates the contributing factors and helps the Change Leader build consensus through facts. Debating without facts not only wastes time but also may increase resistance on this change and future changes that you may attempt.

Sampling practices again add value as well as ensuring our measurement system is able to measure the impact the countermeasures have accurately and precisely. Of course, statistical process control (SPC) is the right tool to use during the pilot. Basically, circle back on the roadmap to ensure that all the questions that needed to be answered are not forgotten (see Figure 15.3).

The last phase of Change Leadership separates those who think they achieved change and those who did.

Train, Enable, Empower, and Hold Accountable

This phase is to ensure the stakeholders are trained in the changes, enabled to enact the change, empowered to continuously improve, and that a control system exists that includes holding people accountable. One of the key accountabilities for people in the process is to continue the 3Ms. Only in

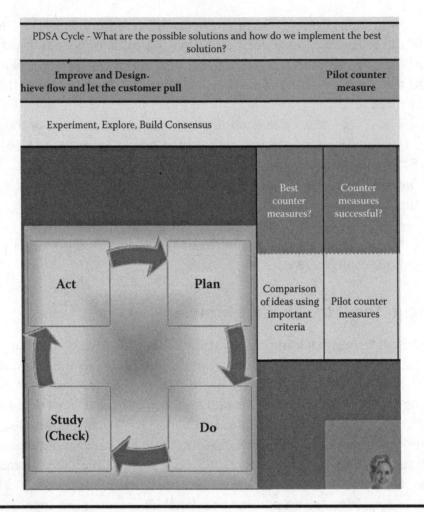

Figure 15.3   Roadmap improve and pilot.

those changes for which the process is stable, capable, and mistake-proof can the 3Ms be relaxed. People are identified to maintain control and act or report when special causes occur. I share stories in further discussion of managers who have failed to utilize the 3Ms.

Mindfulness and Control

Control comes from knowing if control is occurring. SPC gives the team in the process real-time knowledge if its process is in control. What better tool is there? Mindfulness is what high-reliability organizations (HROs) practice, and SPC and mindfulness go together well.[4] Did you wonder how HROs can be mindful all the time? Isn't that exhausting, if not impossible? To be ever mindful is a nice catch phrase, but is there a way that we can turn on or increase our mindfulness at certain times? SPC again is an answer.

SPC can help us know when to act and when not to act. Special causes are identifiable when special cause variation occurs, and the persons accountable to sustain the change have a clear signal. We also know when not to act. Tampering with a process that is stable can be like "crying wolf." Reacting and tweaking a process in a stable situation may also cause the stability to go out of control and achieve exactly what is not wanted. And soon when the time comes to act, the people in the process may disregard signals in the measurement system.

What happens when there is confusion to act? Accidents can happen. In the *Columbia* shuttle disaster, engineers were concerned about the cloud of particles visible in video of the launch. The issue was brought up during the mission. The decision was made to disregard the information despite tile damage that occurred in earlier shuttle flights. Once again, NASA disregarded information. As *Columbia* entered the atmosphere, the damage to the tiles allowed overheating, resulting in the deaths of seven more astronauts and loss of another shuttle.

Mindfulness

Preoccupation with failure is easy to suggest, but how do we "stay on our toes"? In countless hospitals, I see refrigerated medications in unstable and unpredictable systems. The system is often simply a refrigerator, thermometer, and a chart of the temperature. The thermometer is read at regular intervals, and the temperature is plotted on a chart like that in Figure 15.4.

I found a similar setup as this and noticed there was a dot plotted in the upper red zone on a refrigerator for medications on a hospital medical/surgical floor. The pencil mark was crossed out, however, and there was another dot directly below this dot, but it was in the acceptable range. I was curious after having seen this all too often. I asked the nurse to tell me about this chart. She mentioned it was important to make sure the refrigerator kept the medications from getting too cold or hot, or they could change properties and either not provide the benefit or, worse, injure the patient. I thanked her, and she was quick to walk away (yes, she was really busy and probably wondered who this "bloomin' idiot" was asking about the obvious need to

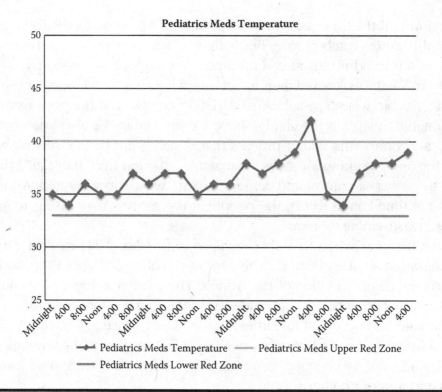

Figure 15.4 Refrigerator temperature for storing medicine.

control the temperatures of refrigerated medications). Note she did not mention the two points. I asked her if she could answer one more question. I asked her about the point in the red zone. She shared that she called maintenance as soon as she saw the temperature was too high. She went on to say maintenance checked something on the refrigerator and told her that her plot was wrong. The maintenance engineer must have corrected her point, she said, and she returned to her duties.

What happened here? Have you turned on your state of mindfulness? Maintenance came, said all is well, and remarked about the chart showing the refrigerator was in the safe zone. What would happen in an HRO? To start, maybe some would buy self-recording temperature devices for their medication refrigerator systems and have alarms if the temperature exceeded boundaries. Many hospitals have these, but not all. There is nothing wrong with manually recording data on the refrigerators, so how could we improve on what this hospital, and many others, do?

First, let us take the same data and plot it on an SPC chart (see Figure 15.5). Here is how SPC can help us heighten our mindfulness. Understand please that the control limits would have been set long ago

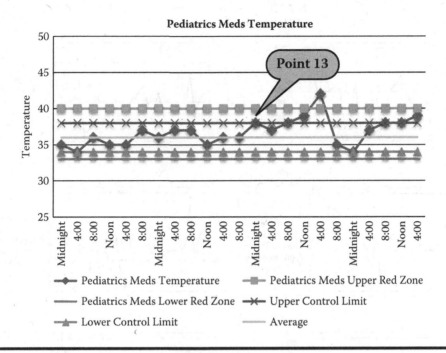

Figure 15.5 Statistical process control chart of medications refrigerator.

on this refrigerator. The first ten or twelve points starting from the left show no points out of the upper or lower control limits. Based on this test, we would say the refrigerator temperatures are stable. We can also see they are within the danger zones denoted by the uppermost line and lowermost line. There are a couple of points (points eight and nine) that might be two standard deviations consecutively above the mean. Referring to our handy SPC interpretation diagram (Figure 15.6), we now have reason to be mindful. So, going out of control helps us to heighten our mindfulness. The nurses and maintenance person were not only *not* mindful, they also failed at another element in mindfulness: They oversimplified. The maintenance person dismissed completely why the nurse had plotted a point in the red zone. When he or she came to check the temperature, there was a temperature below what the nurse had; the maintenance person evidently thought the nurse misread the thermometer. Unfortunately, both the maintenance person and nurse oversimplified the root cause, dismissed the information gained, and went on about their business.

Look at point 13, in Figure 15.5. If this hospital were in Houston, we might say, "Houston, we have a problem." The refrigerator temperature was out of control. With deference to expertise, another element in

SPC Interpretation

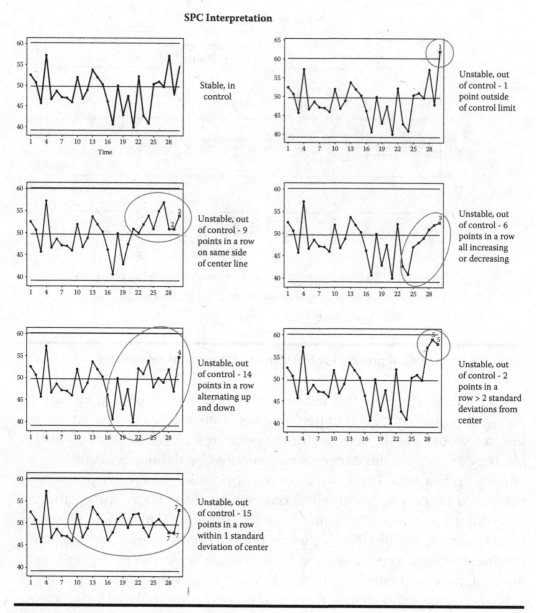

Figure 15.6   SPC interpretation.

mindfulness would have been to trust that the nurse knows how to read a thermometer, as we know nurses are well trained. Maybe the refrigerator had just finished cycling, and the temperature was simply lower by the time the maintenance person checked it. As we can see in SPC, the temperatures vary, and the control limits denote the normal operating variation in the temperatures.

Commitment to Resilience

Another element of mindfulness is commitment to resilience. The refrigerator and temperature measurement system were not very resilient to failure. There was no fail-safe system when the temperature became too high in this piece of equipment. In your refrigerator at home, you might have resilience in your fresh food section. Refrigerators with fresh and frozen food sections may have a design that allows colder air in the freezer compartment to flow into the fresh food section if the temperature is not maintained low enough.

In summary, I fear the medications reached a temperature beyond their limit and should have been removed. The nurse and maintenance person should have become mindful back around the ninth point and had a higher sensitivity to operations in monitoring the temperature. At point 13, they definitely should not have oversimplified by merely plotting a new point and carrying on. If they had acted with a commitment to resilience when the chart went out of control, they would have prevented the temperature from exceeding the allowed upper temperature by repairing the system.

Case Study: Penn Medicine Utilizing the 3Ms

At the University of Pennsylvania Health System, Dr. Dan Feinberg, chief medical officer (CMO) at Pennsylvania Hospital, said, "This chart (holding up his team's SPC chart of children who were getting immunizations) is what High Reliability Organizations use and healthcare needs to do more of it."[5] Penn Medicine's teams are utilizing the 3Ms and Statistical Process Control charts taught in their Performance Improvement in Action course. Every team is truly interdisciplinary with most teams comprised of physicians, nurses, and staff from services most relevant to the project that they are working on, such as pharmacy, radiology, finance, IT, quality, and other services and professions. They learn together as a team using a unique Lean, Six Sigma, and Change Leadership and PDSA. Healthcare Performance Partners developed the course with Kristi Pintar, corporate director of organizational development and leadership practice, and the Penn Medicine faculty. Judy Schueler, vice president of organizational development, and Pat Sullivan, vice president of patient safety and quality at UPHS, lead the initiative that has grown quickly and delivered results. What you may find most amazing is the productivity of learning and getting results. The latest class size is 120 people, in eleven projects, and all learning the entire roadmap.

What's not so amazing is that all teams measure, manage to the measure, and make it easier for the people in the process to do the right thing.

One last point should be made. SPC also prevents tampering with temperatures. How many times have you seen people adjusting the thermostat in a conference room only to end up at the other extreme of temperature? Often, the discomfort is not from an out-of-control heating system. The system simply has a wide variation in temperatures as it cycles on and off. This is especially true in forced air systems compared to hot water radiant systems. If there was an SPC chart on the room temperature, it may show the variation is in control. When someone adjusts the thermostat, it does not reduce the variation that makes us uncomfortable, but the new extreme now has increased the variation and results in an even higher or lower temperature depending on the direction in which the person turned the thermostat.

SPC Making It Easier

Using SPC in making change easier is a wise move. It gives the team early notice that the change really does make a difference and how much of a difference. It also gives the team an easier way to know if the change is starting to slip away. And, SPC provides them a tool to continuously improve—to continue to change.

The people who are targets of the change should be trained, enabled, empowered, and held accountable. Training them in SPC will be the start to leading change successfully. They must be enabled to make the change with a minimum of difficulty—making it easier. Empowerment allows the stakeholders to continuously improve to sustain the change. Complex changes are seldom without issues. Empowering the people to problem solve and improving the change is a powerful way to reduce resistance to the change. Empowerment does not mean blind abdication of authority. Empowerment has been referred to as freedom to make decisions with boundaries to keep the system and stakeholders safe.

The 3Ms are the most important tool for leadership and process improvement leaders, including Change Leaders, to sustain the gains. In the hundreds of organizations where I have worked, many have asked how to sustain the gains. I have asked a number of consultants how the organization they left has sustained the changes they were a part of before leaving the company. Many report embarrassingly that their organization has reverted to its old ways. Why? In every case that I have observed, at least one of the 3Ms was missing. Most often, all three were missing. It is surprisingly simple. We know to lead change, the 3Ms can make the difference between achieving the change and wasting time. The 3Ms are also necessary in human controlled processes to sustain the changes.

Key Points

- This chapter walked us through the entire Roadmap.
- Process improvement utilizes the 3Ms from start to finish.
- Without all 3Ms, sustaining is unlikely.
- The next chapter shares how to reduce the reliance on all 3Ms, but it is not that easy.

Notes

1. Isaac Newton, *The Principia*, translation by I.B. Cohen and A. Whitman, University of California Press, Berkeley 1999.
2. Doris C. Vahey, Linda H. Aiken, Douglas M. Sloane, Sean P. Clarke, and Delfino Vargas, Nurse burnout and patient satisfaction, *Medical Care*, 42(2 Suppl): II57–II66, 2004.
3. Fred Reichheld and Rob Markey, *The Ultimate Question*, Harvard Business School, Cambridge, MA, 2006.
4. Karl Weick and Kathleen Sutcliffe, *Managing the Unexpected*. Wiley, New York, 2007.
5. Used with permission, University of Pennsylvania, Penn Medicine, Dan Feinberg, M.D.

Chapter 16

High Reliability

Introduction

Even when we think we have done the 3Ms (measure, manage to the measure, make it easier) well, there may still be difficulty. The third M is make it *easier*, not easy. We cannot always make doing the right thing and change easy.

This is a story of a change that seemed easy to me. However, it was not so easy for a plant manager despite being in a High Reliability Organization (HRO). The plant was one of many in SKF.[1] SKF is based in Sweden and has locations around the world. SKF services healthcare, aerospace, aviation, automotive, industrial, mining, and countless other smaller companies specializing in reliable products. SKF is referenced in textbooks on reliability engineering because of its pioneering work in design and performance reliability.

Case Study: SKF

SKF is considered one of the highest quality manufacturers and service companies in the world, evolving from a bearing and seal manufacturer to one that makes products found deep in space to the deepest depths of our oceans. SKF makes products for which safety is critical, such as in the rotor connector for military aircraft that holds the entire rotor system to the helicopter. SKF also has made "brake-by-wire" systems that demand the highest reliability to protect the vehicle and passengers. These systems have a higher hurdle for reliability than conventional braking systems because of the public's demand that high technology must have higher reliability than conventional hydraulic systems that have failed in the past.

Claes Rehmberg, quality leader for the corporation, was my superior when I was vice president of total quality. Claes was also my coach and mentor who taught me much about high reliability. We later worked together in another role as we launched the 3Ms with SKF's Lean Six Sigma initiative globally. In my first meeting with Claes, he began teaching me how an HRO operates. Claes shared with me two programs that I needed to learn. Claes also shared that he thought my business unit especially needed these programs because my business was behind most of SKF's other units in quality and reliability. Here are several practices they pioneered that were instrumental in their success achieving high reliability.

High-Reliability Program Number 1

The first program was named Zero Defects. Ah, you are thinking, this is another buzz word. That is why I did not put the words in the headimg for fear that you would not even read the story. You say that even Dr. Deming said that "zero-defect" programs were ill advised? Let me explain what SKF meant by Zero Defects. Zero Defects meant zero, period. Yes, no defects reaching the customer was recognized as a zero-defects product line. SKF even had a poster clarifying it really meant zero. And, it had products that had achieved zero defects for over five consecutive years. OK, so maybe zero defects with a time attached to it is cheating? I was not a believer at first either. I found out soon that SKF had quality management systems that exemplified what is shared in this book. SKF truly had achieved zero defects. But, how does an SKF product line get to truly zero-defects quality to the customer?

High-Reliability Program Number 2

SWOC. SWOC? This is an acronym for *scrap without compromise*. It took SKF years to get to Zero Defects in some product lines. SKF also is one of the oldest manufacturing companies and has had many opportunities to learn. One thing SKF learned is that even the best production processes occasionally had a defect escape to the customer. After applying process improvement similar to what is shared in this book, SKF found a recurring, although very infrequent, root cause for a defect escaping. The defects came from a process that had stopped flowing or some variation started occurring. The process often quit flowing because SKF had designed it to stop when a process measure showed the process was varying out of control.

The Products Surrounding the Variation

Sometimes, the escaped defective product that reached the customer was traced back to one of the products taken out of the process to inspect it when a process problem occurred. The product was one that came before, during, or after a process issue. Stopping the process is what all good companies do. Toyota even has a term for stopping the line when a quality abnormality occurs. It is called *Jidoka*. In healthcare, we reinforce stopping a procedure if anyone senses something is wrong. This is Jidoka. Not stopping the process or procedure has often been cited in accident investigations. The time-out in surgical procedures is required in many countries and is a pause to reflect on the patient being the correct patient and the site of the incision and procedure being correct. Too often, we hear people wish that they had stopped instead of going on.

What SKF discovered in analyzing these escaped defects is what many miss. These products could be inserted back into the wrong sequence, be damaged in the effort to ensure they were not damaged, or put back with a defect because human inspection is not reliable enough to catch all defects.

Scrapping versus Inspecting

Once a process becomes reliable, the defects and wastes may be so miniscule that it is far less risky to throw them out than to inspect and reinsert them in the process. SKF swallowed hard but pioneered doing what many do today. They scrap the products around a process failure without question—without compromise. The risk of a defect escaping to a customer is less than the cost of the product scrapped.

Utilizing the 3Ms in Zero Defects and SWOC

Zero Defects and SWOC cannot occur without also utilizing the 3Ms. SKF measures critical parameters in its processes to know there is an issue early enough to prevent an escaping defect. The frontline people also manage to the measure. When the statistical process control (SPC) chart or other measure suggests, SKF's people manage to the measure by stopping the process until all is well. Last, they learn from earlier failures and make it easier to do the right thing. There is nothing much easier than scrapping products after a process issue with no fear of punishment. It is easier to scrap products than inspect them, especially when many of the features can only be measured using advanced test equipment in a remote location.

Program 3: Building a Safety Culture[2]

A safety culture is not discussed much at SKF. As one of its leaders, I did not have to do this. It is truly a way of life. I surely did not create it, but I benefitted from it every day. To be fair, Zero Defects and SWOC compromise would not have been achieved without SKF's safety culture. For the sake of time, let me get on with the story, but please realize SKF's leadership created a culture that promotes reporting and learning, is just, and is flexible

A Story of a Seal and Its Grease

The 3Ms were found throughout SKF. One example was in its sealing group. A seal is found in virtually every high-performance pump, whether it is for water, intravenous fluids, blood, or waste. In medical pumps, aircraft engines, faucets in your home, and countless other devices that make our life better and safer, seals protect the function of these vital products. Seals are a critical component of many systems, especially systems with bearings in them for parts that rotate or move linearly, as in many high-technology and safety products, such as medical pumps. Actually, a seal is often a system itself. The sealing system consists of a seal, an installation tool to minimize damage to the seal in assembling it into the pump, jet engine, and so on, and last, grease. I learned that what seemed like a simple piece of rubber connected to a metal casing was engineered to do some amazing things with specifications so incredibly tight that one could not see the quality level needed with the naked eye. A flaw that could only be seen with magnification could cause a failure.

In this story, the 3Ms paid off after a plant manager saw the value of measuring unstable processes. This lesson is how this plant manager struggled with a change to measure and manage to the measure but in the end did the right thing.

One purpose of the seal is to ensure that there is a barrier from contaminants such as water. Water reaching the bearing may destroy the bearing, resulting in catastrophic failure. Bearings that are damaged may allow high friction, which results in extreme heat and eventual failure of the device. In the case of surgical instruments, the failure can result in delays in surgeries and perhaps risk to the patient. In the transportation industry, "wheel-offs" have occurred when the bearing failed and the wheels flew off the tractor. Sometimes worse, the heated assembly did not fly off, creating a fire and consuming the tractor and risking injury to the driver and environment. Wheel-offs occur for a variety of reasons, including mishandling at the truck assembly plant and improper maintenance. SKF worked to ensure they did not happen because of their products.

Measuring the seal greasing process, managing to the measure, and making it easier to get grease into the seal makes sense. What do we measure? We can measure if grease is in the seal by weighing the seal after grease is installed. This is a bit late, though, requiring rework to apply grease or scrapping the seal. We would prefer to measure the key input variables that tell us how well the grease process is working. Some processes do not lend themselves to measuring what we want. But, there is always a way to measure. Let us start with the one type of process to manufacture the seal.

Grease is pushed into the seal using a pneumatic injection system. Pneumatic equipment is often unreliable for the precise control of dispensing grease. If the pneumatic pressure that pushes the grease into the seal varies, this variation could result in too little or too much grease. Insufficient grease may not provide enough of a barrier to water, especially from high-pressure washers found in some wash stations. This water, if allowed to reach the bearings, may cause early failure of the bearing and the unit in which the bearing is installed.

One cannot see inside the seal to know if grease is present, unfortunately. So, measuring the linear distance of the rod that pushes grease into the seal is one way to measure the process to ensure grease is in the seal. However, there is another variable called air gaps, which occur in the grease container. The same travel distance in the action of the rod therefore does not guarantee the correct amount of grease is applied if an air gap is pushed instead of grease. Therefore, until a system to apply a stable and capable amount of grease is in place, each seal needs to be weighed to see if the correct amount of grease was applied. SPC charts on the weight of the greased seal are a good way to know if the process is starting to vary and to check the quality of the grease process. Inspection is never completely reliable, and we did not know of a mistake-proof process. It was better to weigh and chart than not measure at all.

This is exactly what we did in one seal-making process. We used an SPC chart to track the amount of grease installed in each seal and asked the worker to stop the process if the control chart showed the process was out of control. The measurement system analysis proved the SPC would assess the amount of grease accurately and precisely enough. The chart was doing its job. We had not completely eliminated seals with insufficient grease, but we were catching them now before they "escaped." Measure was working. We were on our way to Zero Defects.

Some time later, I was in the shop and saw that the SPC chart was not being updated. I asked the worker why the chart was not being updated, and he said that his engineer said it was not needed. Managing to the measure had failed. The chart was being ignored by the front line and by management. Not managing to the SPC measure was one thing, but worse was the fact that management allowed measure to stop. They told the people in the process they did not need to measure the grease any more.

We found seals from the time that the SPC was not used and we found seals lacking grease, which was no surprise. I immediately went to the engineer and asked him if he knew the SPC had stopped. He said he allowed it to stop after hearing that it was time consuming to measure every seal and chart the results. He said, "The change to start measuring every seal and charting was difficult." The measurement was reinstated and charting reinstated after I shared the risk.

Change Is Not Always Easy, Except …

I guess change for the wrong reason can be easier in the short run, such as in the preceding story. Changing back to the old ways of not measuring and managing to the measure was easier in the short run for them, I guess. This is a story that has been told countless times because people do not utilize the 3Ms. I wish I knew how to prevent this story from reoccurring.

I do know the end of every good story. Utilizing the 3Ms may not be as beautiful a story perhaps as a kiss turning a frog into a prince, but the outcome is just as princely. Sorry about that pun; it was intended.

Stakeholder Analysis Revisited for Making It Easier

Those who ignore the stakeholders make change very difficult. Sustaining the change is impossible long term if the stakeholders resist and the 3Ms are not achieved.

Another reason that change is difficult is we did not reengage the stakeholders in the selection of changes. One proven way to make change easier is to engage the stakeholders in selecting the changes using the matrix covered previously. Part of the selection process is the discussion of the countermeasures and the rating of each. We often find that stakeholders add much value in the process because they know things outside the awareness of the Change Leader and team.

Designing an Experiment Should Start with the People Doing the Work

I do not think I will ever forget a pilot of a countermeasure in Puerto Rico. We had worked long and hard to identify the variables that were causing the problems in safety products. Defects in the plastic casing of the circuit breaker could result in failure of the circuit breaker to cut the flow of electricity and thus not stop an electrical hazard. The team of managers designed a pilot to test the variables at levels that they thought would minimize the potential for defects. When the managers went out to the shop to ask the machine attendants to set the controls to the levels desired, the attendants said they could not.

At first, I wondered if there was some insubordination or at least heavy resistance. Actually, the change was difficult not because the machine attendants were resisting. The reason that they refused to set the controls for the pilot the way that management wanted was because the levels extended beyond the capability of the machines. Management asked for levels not possible. We should have engaged the people who did the work to help us judge the best countermeasures. This would have made the change easier for all.

I would like to share another way to make it easier as to this common issue of wanting nurses to spend more time with patients. The Institute for Healthcare Improvement (IHI) and Robert Wood foundations share freely their Transforming Care at the Bedside (TCAB) initiative.[3] Check it out for ideas if the change to increase time with patients is a change that you wish to make.

Launched in 2003, TCAB is a national program of the Robert Wood Johnson Foundation (RWJF) and the IHI. One of the most exciting combinations of changes that have been developed within TCAB is the ability that has been developed to remove hassles and waste from processes on medical-surgical units so that nurses and other clinicians can spend more value-added time caring for patients. This how-to guide builds on relevant research and published literature and integrates what staff in TCAB hospitals have learned as they strive to significantly increase nursing time in direct patient care, which contributes to patient safety, better outcomes for patients, and greater staff satisfaction with the work environment to support their professional practice.

Key Points

- HROs utilize the 3Ms for process improvement.
- SKF has pioneered HRO practices such as a true zero-defects program and a culture in which it is safe to scrap products rather than try to salvage them due to inherent risks.
- A safety culture and mindfulness are key to becoming an HRO.
- HROs measure their cultures and mindfulness
- HROs use Change Leadership principles.
- Maintaining the 3Ms is critical.

Note

1. Used with permission, SKF, Claes Rohmberg.
2. James Reason, *Managing the Risks of Organizational Accidents*, Ashgate, Surrey, UK, 1997.
3. P. Rutherford, A. Bartley, D. Miller, et al. *Transforming Care at the Bedside How-to Guide: Increasing Nurses' Time in Direct Patient Care*, Institute for Healthcare Improvement, Cambridge, MA, 2008. Available at http://www.IHI.org.

Chapter 17

Summary

Utilizing the 3Ms Is the Answer

Utilizing the 3Ms is the answer to process improvement that is real and sustains. We leave you with one technique that reduces the need for the 3Ms: mistake-proofing.

Mistake-Proofing?

Mistake-proofing is any method that can help workers avoid mistakes and prevent equipment and other resources from failing. This concept recognizes that the optimal location to prevent or correct mistakes is at the point of creation of the problem. Late recognition of a mistake or defect is never as efficient, and typically has a cumulative effect. Is it better to mistake-proof or have a fail-safe device? What are the differences?

Fail safe by definition involves a failure. An example is when an electrical circuit has a short; the circuit breaker "trips" and stops the flow. The fault still occurred, but it failed safely. Mistake-proofing would prevent the failure from occurring in the first place. Shigeo Shingo[1] believed that zero defects are possible, but it takes strong stability, capability, and techniques to stop a process if variation begins to occur to abnormal levels. Even statistical process control (SPC) is often not robust enough to prevent some failures.

Shingo researched methods for mistake-proofing, and most industries are using some, if not most.

Mistake-Proofing Promotes Defect Prevention versus Detection

Mistake-proofing also should respect the intelligence of workers by taking the judgment out of repetitive tasks for which errors are likely to occur. It utilizes people working in the process to mistake-proof the work because they *own* the process.

Shigeo Shingo, expert in problem solving and creator of mistake-proofing methodologies, found:

■ SPC greatly improved quality, but sampling and SPC alone may not guarantee zero defects in unstable processes.
■ Shingo focused on detecting errors before they became escaping defects and reached the customer.

Types and Levels of Mistake-Proofing Devices

■ A *prevention* device renders the process so that it is impossible to make a mistake.
■ A *detection* device signals the user when a mistake has been made so that the user can quickly correct the problem. Detection devices typically warn the user of a problem, but they do not enforce the correction.
■ There are levels to mistake-proofing:
  – Levels range from level 1, basic visual, to level 5, bypassing the risk.
■ See Figure 17.1 regarding mistake-proofing levels.

Start with Failure Modes and Effects Analysis, Then Mistake-Proof the High Risks

Errors Cause Defects

■ Use a proactive tool to detect ways of failing and prevention.

Mistake-Proofing Types and Levels

Level 1 Type: Detection Minimal protection	Level 2 Detection Low-level Single sensory alert	Level 3 Detection Mid-level Dual sensory	Level 4 Prevention Mid-level Dual + Barrier	Level 5 Prevention High-level Bypass fail-safe
100% Inspection required.	100% Inspection required.	Redundant inspection suggested.	Minimal inspection.	No inspection.
Real-time measurement required of fail-safe operation. (Knowledge of train approaching.)	Real-time measurement.	Real time measurement. Calibration testing of alert required periodically.	Minimal measurement required. Calibration testing of barrier periodically.	No measurement required. Inspection of structure infrequently.

Figure 17.1   Mistake-proofing levels.

- Design the process so that errors are eliminated—or at least easily detected and corrected.
- Suppliers should be required to do failure modes and effects analysis (FMEA) before they are awarded business.

Human Error Drives the Need for Mistake-Proofing

Errors are slips, lapses, or mistakes or purposeful mistakes according to James Reason.[2] It is difficult, if not impossible, to eliminate these incidents entirely. Therefore, utilizing the 3Ms continuously is critical until the system can ensure any slip, lapse, or mistake will not result in a failure.

Examples of mistake-proofing in healthcare are seen in Figure 17.2.

Mistake-Proof Approaches

1. Facilitate: make the task easier
2. Detect/magnify the sensing
   a. Install sensors to detect the problem or the preventive measure.

Mistake Proofing in Healthcare

Dialysis and IV pumps – Air detector – prevents air from entering the patient's bloodstream

Smart pumps: in an area where decimal-point medication errors can be fatal, smart infusion pumps are adding a line of defense

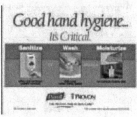

Hand hygiene

Childproof medicine bottles

Figure 17.2   Mistake-proofing in healthcare.

    b. Redundancy: failure requires two or more things to go wrong simultaneously.
3. Provide a fail-safe device such that the staff understands its operation. Fail-safe devices have actually caused catastrophic failures, such as when a pilot overrode his stick, bypassing the fail-safe device that would have probably saved the flight.

Train, Engage, Enable, and Empower the People Doing the Work

Dr. Deming and HROs practice the following:

1. Process owners check themselves at the source, not the final audit.
2. They use fail-safing for nonrobust processes.
3. They take immediate action versus inspecting and sorting out defects.

    Physical mistake-proofing may include both parties pointing to the control. This is in addition to verbal attention to the control. Pointing and touching the surgical site is a mistake-proofing technique used by some organizations to reduce the risk of wrong-site surgery.

Mistake-proofing relies on plans to maintain control of the variation or make the system robust to variation.

Control Plans

- Anything and everything required to sustain the gains is used.
- Often, the measurement system is critical to sustain the gains because the variation is not completely fail safe.
- Make charting in real time and posted in the area.
- The sampling may be reduced once stability is achieved and capability well within customer needs.

Last and Definitely Not Least: Reinforcing Continuous Process Improvement

If you read the first few lines in this book and these last few lines, you are vastly more knowledgeable than all those who have failed to improve processes and sustain the gains. These last paragraphs may be some of the most important lessons in sustaining your process improvement and thus your real desired outcome: performance excellence. I utilize the 3Ms (measure, manage to the measure, make it easier) to share with you the only proven way to reinforce people to improve their processes.

In some cultures, the desire to work for the good of the many is perhaps more pronounced than in others. It is well known that Toyota measures its managers on the number of ideas implemented. Note that this is ideas implemented, not ideas placed in a suggestion box.

In America, few organizations have begun counting and managing to that measure. I think it is a shame and an easy way to measure, manage to the measure, and make it easier to reinforce process improvement. I implemented it while at Motorola, and our Asian vice president, Lee King Tan, found strong results by simply counting the ideas implemented monthly.

Maybe individual certification is one answer? We have had clients ask for programs that result in an opportunity to certify the individual is trained *and* has improved processes and designs. I invite you to try one or both of these methods, which is utilizing the 3Ms.

Thank you for reading, and I look forward to hearing of your successes at http://www.rpmexec.com.

Key Points

In utilizing the the 3Ms for process improvement,

- *Measure* accurately and frequently
  - Keep score—the more real time the better
  - Use SPC to validate changes
  - Ensure everyone can see the score—"the entire game"
  - *Manage to the measure*: just in time
  - Do not pass up a chance to coach
  - Reinforce to the charts
  - Share the control charts daily—and reference them
  - Be a role model
  - *Make it easier* to measure and to improve performance
  - Make it easier to do the right things:
    - Hand hygiene
    - Operate on the correct knee, for example
    - Do standard work
  - Reinforce process improvement continuously to achieve performance excellence
- Practice the skills of the Change Leaders and remember:

The best fertilizer for a piece of land is the footprints of its owner.

Lyndon B. Johnson

Notes

1. Shigeo Shingo's works as cited in Yasuhiro Monden, *Toyota Production System, An Integrated Approach to Just-In-Time*, 2nd edition, Industrial Engineering and Management Press, Norcross, GA, 1993.
2. James Reason, *Managing the Risks of Organizational Accidents*, Ashgate, Surrey, OK, 1997.

Appendix 1: Roadmap for Performance Excellence

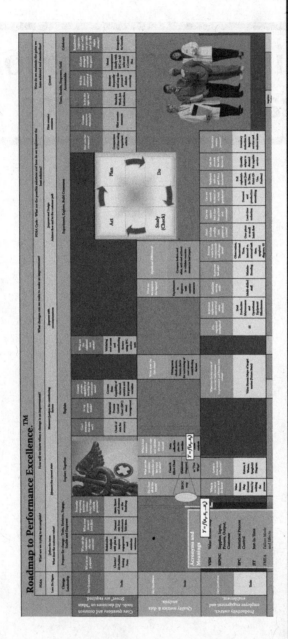

Figure A1.1 Roadmap to Performance Excellence.

Appendix 2: Process Improvement Foundational Tools

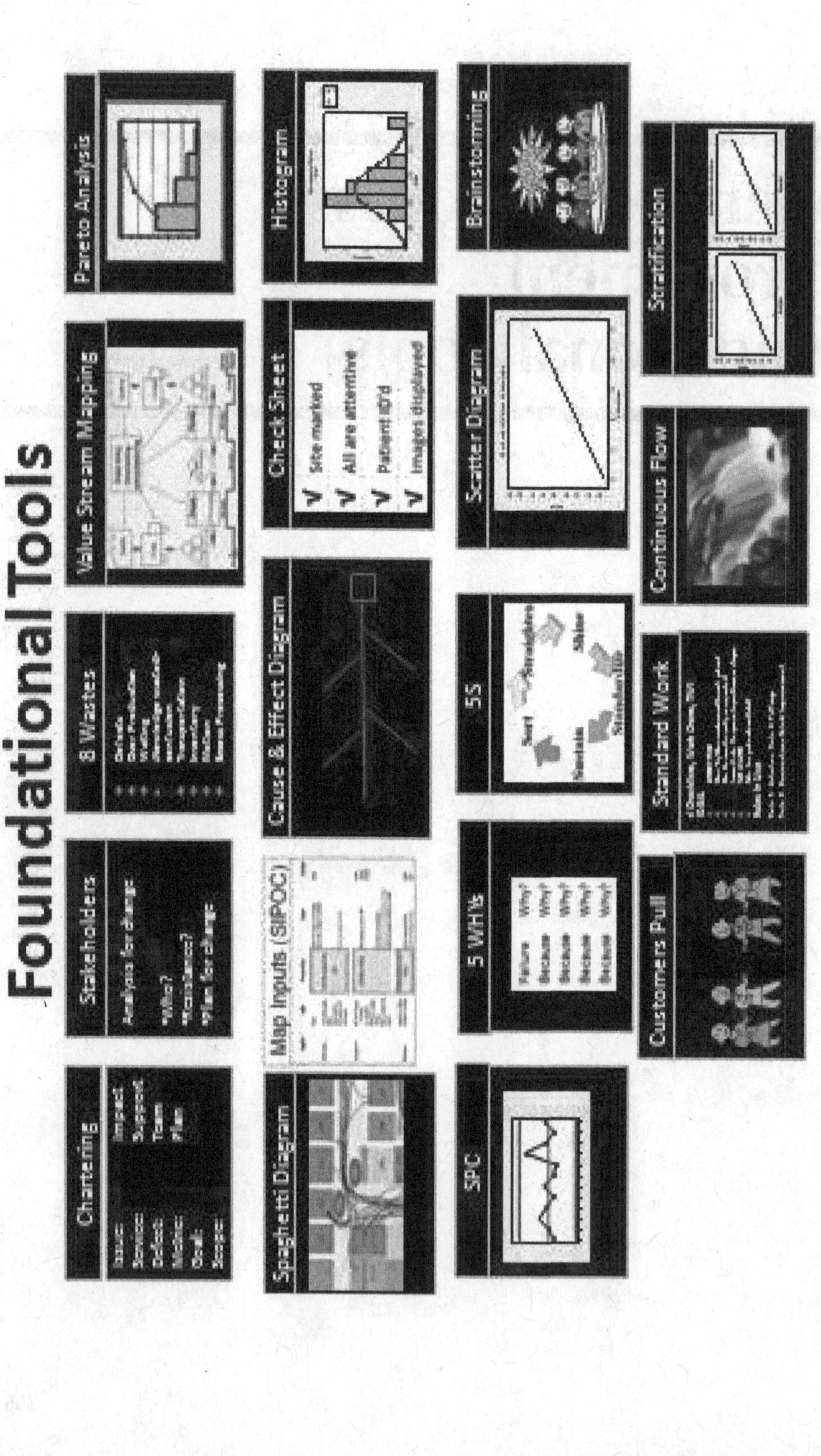
Foundational Tools
Chartering
Stakeholders
8 Wastes
Value Stream Mapping
Pareto Analysis
Spaghetti Diagram
Map Inputs (SIPOC)
Cause & Effect Diagram
Check Sheet
Site marked
All are attentive
Patient ID'd
Images displayed
Histogram
SPC
5 WH's
5S
Scatter Diagram
Brainstorming
Customers Pull
Standard Work
Continuous Flow
Stratification

Figure A2.1

Appendix 3: The Emancipation Proclamation

January 1, 1863
A Transcription
By the President of the United States of America
A Proclamation.

Whereas, on the twenty-second day of September, in the year of our Lord one thousand eight hundred and sixty-two, a proclamation was issued by the President of the United States, containing, among other things, the following, to wit:

> That on the first day of January, in the year of our Lord one thousand eight hundred and sixty-three, all persons held as slaves within any State or designated part of a State, the people whereof shall then be in rebellion against the United States, shall be then, thenceforward, and forever free; and the Executive Government of the United States, including the military and naval authority thereof, will recognize and maintain the freedom of such persons, and will do no act or acts to repress such persons, or any of them, in any efforts they may make for their actual freedom.
>
> That the Executive will, on the first day of January aforesaid, by proclamation, designate the States and parts of States, if any, in which the people thereof, respectively, shall then be in rebellion against the United States; and the fact that any State, or the people thereof, shall on that day be, in good faith, represented in the

Congress of the United States by members chosen thereto at elections wherein a majority of the qualified voters of such State shall have participated, shall, in the absence of strong countervailing testimony, be deemed conclusive evidence that such State, and the people thereof, are not then in rebellion against the United States.

Now, therefore I, Abraham Lincoln, President of the United States, by virtue of the power in me vested as Commander-in-Chief, of the Army and Navy of the United States in time of actual armed rebellion against the authority and government of the United States, and as a fit and necessary war measure for suppressing said rebellion, do, on this first day of January, in the year of our Lord one thousand eight hundred and sixty-three, and in accordance with my purpose so to do publicly proclaimed for the full period of one hundred days, from the day first above mentioned, order and designate as the States and parts of States wherein the people thereof respectively, are this day in rebellion against the United States, the following, to wit:

Arkansas, Texas, Louisiana, (except the Parishes of St. Bernard, Plaquemines, Jefferson, St. John, St. Charles, St. James Ascension, Assumption, Terrebonne, Lafourche, St. Mary, St. Martin, and Orleans, including the City of New Orleans) Mississippi, Alabama, Florida, Georgia, South Carolina, North Carolina, and Virginia, (except the forty-eight counties designated as West Virginia, and also the counties of Berkley, Accomac, Northampton, Elizabeth City, York, Princess Ann, and Norfolk, including the cities of Norfolk and Portsmouth), and which excepted parts, are for the present, left precisely as if this proclamation were not issued.

And by virtue of the power, and for the purpose aforesaid, I do order and declare that all persons held as slaves within said designated States, and parts of States, are, and henceforward shall be free; and that the Executive government of the United States, including the military and naval authorities thereof, will recognize and maintain the freedom of said persons.

And I hereby enjoin upon the people so declared to be free to abstain from all violence, unless in necessary self-defense; and I recommend to them that, in all cases when allowed, they labor faithfully for reasonable wages.

And I further declare and make known, that such persons of suitable condition, will be received into the armed service of the

United States to garrison forts, positions, stations, and other places, and to man vessels of all sorts in said service.

And upon this act, sincerely believed to be an act of justice, warranted by the Constitution, upon military necessity, I invoke the considerate judgment of mankind, and the gracious favor of Almighty God.

In witness whereof, I have hereunto set my hand and caused the seal of the United States to be affixed.

Done at the City of Washington, this first day of January, in the year of our Lord one thousand eight hundred and sixty three, and of the Independence of the United States of America the eighty-seventh.

By the President: Abraham Lincoln
William H. Seward, Secretary of State

Appendix 4: Charter Template

Charter Title:				Role	Responsibility
1. Issue Statement Elements **a. Customer name:**		Business Case:		**Executive Sponsor:**	Senior level manager who selects Work. Has authority to solve cross-functional issues.
b. Characteristic to improve:				*Signature*	
c. Process name(s):				**Champion:**	Leader who owns the process and manages staff. Prime responsibility with Project Leader for success.
2. Product/Unit: *Name of what is produced in the process*				*Signature*	
				Clinical Leader	Decision-maker for clinical issues
				Signature	
3. Defect: *How we sense a failure in the product or service*				**Process Owner(s):**	Responsible for the design, continuous improvement, and sustaining the process.
4. Metric(s) to Improve	Current Baseline	Goal (S.M.A.R.T.)	Date to Achieve	*Signature(s)*	
				Project Leader:	Leads the team and execution of the methodology. Shares prime responsibility with Champion for success.
				Signature	
5. Financial Impact Metrics:	Type of Impact	Traceable	Non-Traceable	**Mentor/Coach**	Coaches and mentors sponsor, champion, and project leader in their roles
	$ Annualized Amount			*Signature*	
6. Scope: Process Begins and Ends when....	**7. Scope: What must be included or excluded is...**			**Team Members**	Key contributor to Work. Participates with Project Leader in methodology and responsible for success.
				Core Member	
				Core Member	
				Core Member	
				Core Member	
				Core Member	
				Core Member	
High Level Project Plan: Rick Morrow				Core Member	
Phase	Planned Start Date	Planned End Date	Actual Start Date	Actual End Date	
Define/Charter signed					
Measure/Baseline obtained				Subject Matter Expert	
Analyze/Root Cause validated				Subject Matter Expert	
Improve/Improvement piloted				Subject Matter Expert	

Figure A4.1

Appendix 5: Stakeholder Analysis Template

Stakeholder Analysis												
Project			Stakeholder role							Contributor names:		
Date												
Organization/ Location/ Area	Name (or group name)	Role or Title	Customer of the process	Process owner	Decision-maker/ Approver	Target of the change	Interested party	Supplier to the process	Current level of buy-in to change. Rate 0 - 10 with 0 being no buy-in - heavy resistance	Needed level of buy-in to change. Rate 0 - 10 with 0 no buy-in needed	Gap	Strategy to close the gap

Figure A5.1

Appendix 6: Hand Hygiene Data Collection Sheet

Hand Hygiene Observation and Contributing Factor Form

Date of observations: _____   Collected by: _____

Possible Contributing Factors to Washing

Observable | Observable by asking person

Observation Number	Unit name (2 South, ITU, etc.)	Circle time of observation (AM is 0801-1700, PM is 1701-0800)	Circle role of health care professional observed (RN=Nurse, T=Therapy, RSW=Housekeeping, CATR=Catering, Phil=Phlebotomist, ThStf=Theatre Staff, ThPor=Theatre Porter, ODP=ODP, Con=Consultant) all others please identify in the comments section)	Did person perform hand hygiene?	Comments 24
1		AM PM	RN T MD Diet Rx PHL HSK / CATR ThSstf ThPor ODP Con	1 2 3 4 5 / Yes No	
2		AM PM	RN T MD Diet Rx PHL HSK / CATR ThSstf ThPor ODP Con	1 2 3 4 5 / Yes No	
3		AM PM	RN T MD Diet Rx PHL HSK / CATR ThSstf ThPor ODP Con	1 2 3 4 5 / Yes No	
4		AM PM	RN T MD Diet Rx PHL HSK / CATR ThSstf ThPor ODP Con	1 2 3 4 5 / Yes No	
5		AM PM	RN T MD Diet Rx PHL HSK / CATR ThSstf ThPor ODP Con	1 2 3 4 5 / Yes No	
6		AM PM	RN T MD Diet Rx PHL HSK / CATR ThSstf ThPor ODP Con	1 2 3 4 5 / Yes No	
7		AM PM	RN T MD Diet Rx PHL HSK / CATR ThSstf ThPor ODP Con	1 2 3 4 5 / Yes No	
8		AM PM	RN T MD Diet Rx PHL HSK / CATR ThSstf ThPor ODP Con	1 2 3 4 5 / Yes No	
9		AM PM	RN T MD Diet Rx PHL HSK / CATR ThSstf ThPor ODP Con	1 2 3 4 5 / Yes No	
10		AM PM	RN T MD Diet Rx PHL HSK / CATR ThSstf ThPor ODP Con	1 2 3 4 5 / Yes No	

Column headers (1–5, before/after patient contact, etc.):
1 Before patient contact
2 Before aseptic task
3 After fluid risk
4 After patient contact
5 After contact with person's surroundings

Contributing factors column headings:
- Dispenser location not in path of person; hand hygiene?
- Dispenser empty
- Leaves patient room; in path of person or obstructed/hidden
- Hands full; Supplies/Equipment (e.g. food trays, lab supplies)
- Hands full; Meds
- Gloves – Did not wash before or after gloving
- Urgency to act for patient safety/ safety concern
- Person entering/exiting room followed someone who did not wash
- Admission or discharge process
- Frequent entry and exit
- Isolation area (gown + gloves when required)
- Lack of immediate feedback to person
- Distractions (forgot, lack of knowledge that hand hygiene is required)
- Perception (thought leaving or wash rituation or dislike of alcohol based cleanser)
- Perception (Chose not to wash)
- Perception (thought the patient care area hand hygiene is not necessary)

Instructions:
1. Use a separate row for each entry or exit.
2. When known, check any contributing factor for each observation.
3. Emergency situations are EXCLUDED from the data collection process.

	Count of "Yes"	Count of observations (rows used)	
Calculate compliance for this sheet		=	=

Figure A6.1

Appendix 7: Hand Hygiene Compliance Chart for Posting

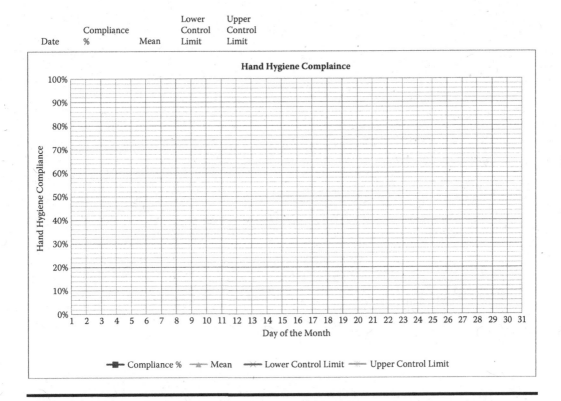

Figure A7.1

Appendix 8: Measure Data Collection Tool

Visitor (Remember Patient Confidentiality Rules, So Use Something Like a Number or Destination)	Outcome Metric: Number of Wrong Turns in Getting to the Destination	Errors in Giving Direction (Count the Times that You Change Your Instruction, Regardless of Reason)	Signage: Missing, Wrong, Confusing, Too Many Signs, Blocked	Visitor Taking a Wrong Turn (Turning Differently than the Directions that You Gave or the Signage Directs)
1				
2				
3				
4				
5				
6				
7				
8				
9				
10				
11				
12				

Appendix 9: FMEA Severity, Occurrence, Detection Tables

The team defines the rating scale (1–10) for the severity, occurrence, and detection ratings. You and your team choose the levels and numbers (as long as they are on a scale of 1–10).

How Severe Is It?
Not severe = 1
Somewhat = 3
Moderately = 5
Very severe = 10 (VERY BAD)
How Often Does It Occur?
Never/Rarely = 1
Sometimes = 3
Half the time = 5
Always = 10 (VERY BAD)
How Well Can You Detect It?
Always = 1
Sometimes = 3
Half the time = 5
Never = 10 (VERY BAD)

Rating	Severity of Effect	Likelihood of Occurrence	Ability to Detect
10	Hazardous without warning	Very high; Failure is almost inevitable	Cannot detect
9	Hazardous with warning		Very remote chance of detection
8	Loss of primary function	High; Repeated failures	Remote chance of detection
7	Reduced primary function performance		Very low chance of detection
6	Loss of secondary function	Moderate; Occasional failures	Low chance of detection
5	Reduced secondary function performance		Moderate chance of detection
4	Minor defect noticed by most customers		Moderately high chance of detection
3	Minor defect noticed by some customers	Low; Relatively few failures	High chance of detection
2	Minor defect noticed by discriminating customers		Very high chance of detection
1	No effect	Remote; Failure is unlikely	Almost certain detection.

Appendix 10: The Soda Drink Challenge to Learn Attribute Agreement Analysis

- Run the tasting in the order of the randomized worksheet.
- It is okay to have each taster drinking simultaneously as long as the taster drinks in the order on the data collection worksheet.
- It helps to dedicate a "runner" to each taster.
- Someone direct the runners by saying which taster and holding up fingers noting which of four cups.
- Record the decisions as the tasters taste.

Data Collection Template for The Soda Drink Challenge to Learn
Attribute Agreement Analysis

Taster	Cup	Decision. Brand A or Brand B.	Truth if Brand A or Brand B.
2	2		
2	4		
2	1		
3	1		
2	3		
1	2		
2	3		
3	1		
3	3		
3	3		
1	1		
1	1		
3	2		
3	2		
2	4		
1	4		
1	2		
2	1		
1	4		
2	2		
3	4		
3	4		
1	3		
1	3		

Figure A10.1

Set-Up for the Challenge

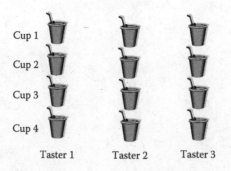

Cup 1
Cup 2
Cup 3
Cup 4

Taster 1   Taster 2   Taster 3

Figure A10.2

Data Collection Plan and Tests

Collect two samples from each cup from each Taster

Discrimination –

Able to differentiate one product from another

Stability –

Same decision through time

Accuracy –

Correct decision

Repeatability –

Same cup from same Taster should get the same decision

Reproducibility –

Same cup (1,2,3,or 4) with same product by different Taster gets
the same decision

Figure A10.3

Index

A

B

C